# New Perspectives
# on the Public–Private Divide

## Legal Dimensions Series

The Legal Dimensions Series stems from an annual legal and socio-legal research initiative sponsored by the Canadian Association of Law Teachers, the Canadian Law and Society Association, the Canadian Council of Law Deans, and the Law Commission of Canada. Volumes in this series will examine various issues of law reform from a multidisciplinary perspective. The series seeks to advance our knowledge about law and society through the analysis of fundamental aspects of law.

The essays in this volume were selected by representatives from each partner association: Frederick Zemans (Canadian Law and Society Association); John McEvoy (Canadian Association of Law Teachers); Jacques Desmarais (Canadian Council of Law Deans); and Susan Zimmerman, Dennis Cooley, and Nathalie Des Rosiers (Law Commission of Canada).

1 *Personal Relationships of Dependence and Interdependence in Law*
2 *New Perspectives on the Public–Private Divide*

LAW COMMISSION OF CANADA
COMMISSION DU DROIT DU CANADA

*Edited by the Law Commission of Canada*

# New Perspectives
# on the Public–Private Divide

**UBC**Press · Vancouver · Toronto

09 08 07 06 05 04 03     5 4 3 2 1

Printed in Canada on acid-free paper

**National Library of Canada Cataloguing in Publication Data**

Main entry under title:
New perspectives on the public-private divide / edited by the Law Commission of Canada.

(Legal dimensions series 1701-2317)
Includes bibliographical references and index.
ISBN 0-7748-1042-4 (bound); ISBN 0-7748-1043-2 (pbk.)

1. Public law – Canada.  2. Civil rights – Canada.  I. Law Commission of Canada.
II. Series.

| KE4120.N48 2003 | 342.71 | C2003-910540-7 |
|---|---|---|
| KF380.N48 2003 | | |

## Canadä

UBC Press gratefully acknowledges the financial support for our publishing program of the Government of Canada through the Book Publishing Industry Development Program (BPIDP), and of the Canada Council for the Arts, and the British Columbia Arts Council.

UBC Press
The University of British Columbia
2029 West Mall
Vancouver, BC V6T 1Z2
604-822-5959 / Fax: 604-822-6083
www.ubcpress.ca

# Contents

# Introduction

*Nathalie Des Rosiers*

Knowledge requires categorizations. In order to better understand the world around us, we arrange it in boxes that serve to highlight similarities and differences. The public–private distinction is one of those categorizations that has been used in almost all disciplines. It can be found in geography, history, sociology, psychology, ethics, political science, religious studies, public health, tourism, and information sciences.[1] The distinction between private and public also structures legal analysis. Both civil and common law are organized around the notions of public and private law. Public law is often understood as law that structures the interactions between the state and its citizens (administrative, constitutional, and criminal law), while private law regulates relations between private actors, persons, or corporations. In civil law, private law also includes the law of obligations and of persons; and in common law, one speaks of contracts, torts, and property. Indeed, the application of the *Canadian Charter of Rights and Freedoms* is premised on the existence of a distinction between private (in the sense of non-governmental) and public (governmental).[2]

Like many characterizations, the public–private distinction reveals certain aspects of reality while masking others at the same time. This series of essays is about reflecting on the questions that are both highlighted and hidden when we use the private-public distinction, in particular in the circulation of legal knowledge. The private-public divide is indeed rich terrain for an inquiry about the complex and malleable uses of legal characterizations because it conjures so many different meanings and images.

First, in its most common understanding, the public–private distinction opposes state and non-state actors in the sense of the *Charter* and the traditional legal regulation of public and private law. This state/non-state distinction may have symbolic appeal for governance, but it often masks the way in which non-governmental private actors require state intervention to enforce their contracts, torts, and private obligations. This state/non-state dichotomy is the framework typically associated with an analysis of the disengagement of the state through privatization, contracting out, or simple abandonment, all of which have characterized Western neoliberal economies. For example, the provision of security for citizens has traditionally been associated with the state through its near-monopoly on the use of force and the array of police agents, army personnel, and other security forces under its command. Now that we are witnessing an enlarged role for private security firms in such areas as border control, the investigation of white collar crimes, and the patrolling of many large urban spaces, our understanding of what should be public and what should be private is being questioned. The state/non-state legal distinction is called into question when state and non-state actors are exposed to the same risks or when they are asked to perform similar tasks. Indeed, there is now a growing body of "governmentality" literature premised on the notions of the permeability of the public and private spheres and that governance is not monopolized by the state.[3]

The distinction between state and non-state also invites an opposition between public good and private property. In this understanding of the public–private divide, the public represents the collective, the commons, and the interests of all combined, whereas the private represents the individual, the owner of private property who acts in a self-interested way. We often associate the public good with the state, assuming that the state allows for the expression of collective interests, and we relegate the private in order to protect private property and individualistic pursuits. This simplistic dichotomy is constantly challenged in a world where the state can no longer meet the aspirations of its citizens for the public good, and where private and semi-private entities may be asked to perform selfless acts. For example, the private sector may be asked more and more to contribute to literacy programs or support schools. Although these actions may, in the long-term, benefit a private employer in ensuring access to qualified workers, the short-term gains for the private sector may not appear to be as certain.

We also use the public–private distinction in another sense, referring to what can broadly be thought of as "the home" and "the street." Feminists, in particular, have shown how much the legal protection of the "private" has hurt women who have been abused in the privacy of their homes – the private thus becoming a place that has contributed to victimization. As a legal characterization, it was immune to scrutiny. Susan B. Boyd, in her book on the public–private divide,[4] indicates that this insight may lead to other types of victimization: the private lives of Aboriginal women, for example, are "publicized" more than others since the way in which they raise their children is more often policed by the state through child protection services. The "private," it would seem, is more private for some groups than for others. Again, the public–private distinction in the sense of "place for private activity" versus "location for public activity" highlights important differences in the expectations of privacy, but it also masks realities of abuse of power within the home and within society.

In the many images that it evokes, the private-public distinction assumes difference and gives meaning. Like many organizational concepts in our law, it has served both to protect certain interests and to ignore others. It has worked to organize our views about appropriate governance of different activities, different actors, and different places. It has not only regrouped obligations and contracts between individuals and contracts between individuals and corporations (private law), but it has also contrasted them to the interaction between the individual and the State (public law). Traditionally, administrative law, which is a part of public law, has integrated questions of access to social benefits with immigration status or labour protection, to name a few. The experience of a citizen dealing with a bank manager may not be different from his or her experience dealing with a tax auditor or a clerk in a local welfare office, but law has put these relationships into different boxes. Political scientists and philosophers may think that the "contract" model applies equally to the relationship between the state and its citizenry, but for some reason, up until now, law has preferred to distinguish between administrative law and the law of obligation or law of contracts. Law reform often requires that we question these traditional categorizations. Do they still make sense? Do they help us understand reality or do they impair our ability to respond to our aspirations for justice?

The goal of this series of essays is to illustrate various meanings and dimensions of the public–private divide through different case studies. What does the public–private distinction mean in a particular context? Who is empowered by it? Who is using it? What does it highlight and what does it hide? The seven authors have been asked to illustrate some of the changing ways in which the public–private divide is understood. All of them describe a complex reality behind the public–private articulation and reflect on the role of law in supporting, structuring, or challenging the distinction. The aim of this book is to stimulate a debate on the nature of the public–private distinction – not so much to propose a better understanding of it but rather to elicit new questions about law and its role in our society.

In the remainder of this introduction, I will begin by reflecting on the role of the public–private divide in structuring the legal environment for the personal, social, economic, and governance relationships that citizens have. This relationship approach is a way of reframing questions about law in society. I will reflect on how the seven authors have questioned the legal organization of relationships in their analyses. Finally, I will explore the lessons for law reform that emerge from an analysis of the private-public divide in relationships.

## Relationships and the Public–Private Divide

When it was created in 1997,[5] the Law Commission of Canada was mandated to develop a multidisciplinary approach informed by an analysis of the context in which law is lived and applied.[6] The commission has developed analytical tools that encompass not only the static description of the law in the statute books and casebooks but also the dynamic forces that shape its day-to-day practice and reframing. Since law is experienced in the context of relationships between human beings, and not only as an aspect of an isolated legal personality, it is often enlightening to look at the impact of legal concepts on the different relationships that citizens have, including personal, social, economic, and governance relationships. I have chosen to use this approach in order to illustrate how a distinction that is as central to law as that of the private-public influences the way in which relationships are shaped and experienced.

The six essays that follow all identify ways in which relationships are structured by the public–private distinction. I will highlight briefly some of the findings of the different authors.

### Personal Relationships

Much of Canadian law is based on assumptions about how people organize their private lives and how they relate to their partners, parents, children, and others that are close to them. These assumptions may not adequately or accurately reflect the reality of current relationships, and they often serve to maintain relationships of power and dependence as opposed to creating opportunities for change and the redefinition of relationships on a more equal basis. A stimulating example of this idea is given by **Lisa Philipps** in her essay "There's Only One Worker: Toward the Legal Integration of Paid Employment and Unpaid Caregiving." She studies the way in which personal relationships are shaped by the fact that they are deemed "private" in the sense of being "unpaid." Philipps shows how this private, at home, unpaid work supports a private interest that is exercised publicly, namely "paid" work. The essay forcefully argues that the productivity of workers is enhanced by the "private" support that they get at home. It goes on to suggest changes to laws to reduce gender inequality, to eliminate the divide between paid and unpaid work, to promote men's greater responsibility and involvement in unpaid work, to promote more choice in work, and to facilitate entry and exit from the market. The idea that private, unpaid work subsidizes public, paid work forces a rethinking of many legal assumptions about tax law, workers protection, and pension law.

### Social Relationships

The public–private divide also affects communities in their relationships with one another. Vibrant and healthy communities are often associated with healthier and happier citizens. Is there a role for law in supporting communities, helping to rebuild fragile ones, or inspiring people to build communities founded on principles of justice? At times, legal structures can actually undermine the development of communities or skew their priorities and evolution. In this context, we may witness, for example, how some communities are marginalized by the private-public divide: the homeless are excluded from public spaces because their appearance, behaviour, and the challenge they represent is unwelcome to the middle class. In their chapter, "Private Needs and Public Space: Politics, Poverty, and Anti-Panhandling By-Laws in Canadian Cities," **Damian Collins** and **Nicholas Blomley** examine the emergence of anti-panhandling bylaws in several Canadian cities. The authors argue that "liberal-legal categories are not autonomous, but can be crosscut by other understandings, ethics, and practices." In the case of panhandling, they demonstrate that bylaws are imbued with moral anxieties over poor people's money (that they spend it on alcohol, tobacco, and illegal drugs), notions about the appropriate use of public spaces, and historically rooted beliefs that have excluded homeless people and other marginalized groups from participating in public spaces.

In this regard, the authors argue that anti-panhandling bylaws intertwine notions of public and private, essentially informing the regulation of the seemingly private activity of panhandling with broader public values over the legitimate use of space. The relationships between the very poor and the rest of society are marked with claims of ownership of space: public space is middle class and should remain so, and thus, the homeless, who by definition have no private space, are left in limbo.

The scientific community is also subject to pressures from the structures of private and public legal ownership rules. In "Private Life: Biotechnology and the Public–Private Divide," **Nathan Brett** argues that the move toward the privatization of scientific inquiry is fundamentally opposed to core liberal democratic values of freedom of expression. He analyzes the bid by Harvard University to patent the "Onco mouse" and argues that this attempt is a "further step in the direction of a form of partiality that is fundamentally at odds with the spirit of free inquiry upon which liberal democracy depends." In this context, privatization means that something that was once held in common is now exclusive and partial. His chapter challenges the way in which the legal regime of intellectual property privatizes "life" in this context and makes it a profit-making commodity disconnected from the common good.

Finally, the Internet community can also be analyzed through the public–private lens. Is the Internet public or private space? Is it a place for an enhanced and enlarged public discourse or is it a place to shop and be bombarded by advertising? Will it lead to better public participation or better consumerism? Will it enhance community linkages or screen out messages from other individuals? **Darin Barney** is dubious of the community-enhancing value of what is increasingly privatized Internet space. In his essay, "Invasions of Publicity: Digital Networks and the Privatization of the Public Sphere," he draws upon two accounts of the public sphere and its fate under modern conditions – Hannah Arendt's theorization of the ancient Greek *polis*[7] and Jürgen Habermas's account of the bourgeois public sphere[8] – in order to isolate some critical questions regarding the status of the democratic public sphere under the new regime of digital technology. He argues that contrary to popular imaginings about its inherently democratic character, the Internet is currently deployed in a context in which "politics has been eclipsed by economic activity in markets, rational-critical debate has been supplanted by consumer choice, and the public sphere understood as a site of citizenship remains conspicuous by its relative absence."

### Economic Relationships

The private-public distinction can be seen to be at the core of our understanding of economic relationships. Indeed, one could argue that traditionally we have envisaged the roles of the private and the public in terms of the opposition between the economic and political worlds: the private sector generated the wealth and the public sector redistributed it (through taxation) or corrected its errors (through regulation). This equation, though, was obviously never that straightforward.

First, the intervention of the public sector in regulation always coexists with private sector efforts of self-regulation. Indeed, in "Green Revolution or Greenwash? Voluntary Environmental Standards, Public Law, and Private Authority in Canada," **Stepan Wood** speaks about the eclipse of the private-public distinction in governance of the environment. For him, the example of environmental management strategies demonstrates that environmental regulation is accomplished by an array of public and private authorities and institutions (for example, standardization bodies, environmental management systems (EMS) auditors and certifiers, corporate managers, customers, courts, and regulatory agencies). As he says, "distinctions between public and private, state and non-state, mandatory and voluntary, are not particularly helpful in understanding the significance of EMS standards. Rather, EMS standards demonstrate that the practices of government traverse the categories on which our understandings of law and politics are typically based."

However, there is no doubt that the public–private distinction continues to protect economic power. Indeed, economic advantages are often framed by the public–private divide. For example, the inability to receive a pay cheque for housework done in private has had a tremendous impact on the ability of women to feel economically secure. Generally, privatization means huge profits. This is certainly the case with respect to the categorization of the Onco mouse as a private, "patentable" object, and, in his essay, Brett shows how the attempts by pharmaceutical companies to obtain biological patents on life forms (which would result in economic gain) are examples of how an object can move from the public to the private domain. Privatization is the key to capitalization and profit-making.

It is also interesting to note how the institutions that aim at ensuring economic security for the weakest – for example, unions – have been structured by the private-public divide. The union is a place that often speaks with one public voice in order to fulfill its mandate to adequately represent its members. Any dissenting voices are expressed in private. In "The Emergence of Parallel Identity-Based Associations in Collective Bargaining Relations," **Christian Brunelle** explores how the recent emergence of identity associations are "public" expressions of the dissenters' voices and how their very existence challenges the monopoly of union representation and its role in society.

In his essay, Brunelle describes the relationships that exist between workers with respect to age conflicts. He refers to a particular development in Québec labour practices that shocked many. Recently, concessions made by unions were seen to prejudice younger workers and have led to the emergence of new associations that advocate for younger workers. The author argues that this intergenerational conflict challenges unions to better reflect diversity within their ranks because younger workers are moving outside the unions to fight for equality. They are leaving the "private" world of the union to move into a "public" space to challenge the power dynamic. Brunelle also identifies certain legal shifts, namely the identity associations that have emerged because of unsatisfactory aspects of the private space (for example, the silencing of dissent within unions). These associations now constitute new actors that play the legal game – they sue the traditional unions in front of the Human Rights Commission, seeking to effect change from the outside.

Again, the legal divide between private and public is sometimes unclear and confused. Unions, once "private entities" in the sense of being sheltered from public scrutiny, now have to remodel themselves in a more publicly acceptable way. It is no longer adequate to simply advocate for the position of the majority of their members (a private ordering). They must also develop an agenda that is seen to be fair publicly and accepting of a social responsibility to ensure justice between generations (a public-interest position).

Finally, there is no doubt that the space for economic transactions is controlled by the public–private divide. Collins and Blomley suggest that there is "considerable irony in the contemporary criminalization of panhandling." On the one hand, we live in a neoliberal state that emphasizes minimal state interference in private financial transactions. Yet, on the other hand, cities increasingly regulate the act of begging for money, which "closely resembles an economic or 'market' activity of the sort that has occupied the heart of the private realm within much liberal thought."

## Governance Relationships

Two governance issues emerge from the essays. First, there is a concern that "private" or privatized space is synonymous with depoliticized space. It is a place where political issues are submerged. The market is devoid of concerns over justice; decisions are rational only in the context of maximizing profit. Essentially, the market is arguably non-equal and non-just. It is also a space that is for the most part devoid of political content, where issues are presented in the absence of social context. Such ideas are "technicalized" as Wood suggests; environmental protection is only a matter of consumer preference and is no longer a societal issue.[9] Barney also suggests that private space depoliticizes exchanges: opposition is screened and one is sitting in front of a computer, not having to interact with differing or opposing points of view.[10] Brunelle raises this issue as well when he recounts that young workers had to go outside, into public space, in order to make the point of their unfair treatment. To a certain extent, Brett makes a similar point. He explains that private space is partial, it accepts that like cases can be treated differently, for example, that nepotism can exist in recruiting employees or that children in the same family can receive different levels of help.

Politicized spaces ("public spaces," as these authors call them), on the other hand, are about managing claims of unfairness and entitlement. To be in the public domain requires a recognition of the other as well as a discussion regarding the allocation of power and the making of choices. Collins and Blomley bring an important nuance: several contradictory social forces confront each other in the public, politicized place. Some "others" are excluded, namely the marginal and the poor whose participation is unwanted and therefore removed from public viewing. They are the "too disturbing" others, which can be screened out.

The second point that emerges from these essays is that governance is no longer the monopoly of public actors. Wood's essay is particularly significant in this respect. He notes how the role of government is no longer simply as the law maker, but that its influence is marked by "steering; self-discipline; knowledge production; reward; command; benchmarking; challenge; and borrowing." Governance occurs both inside and outside of public space. The corporation is the locus of environmental governance, in Wood's view. For Philipps, it is the locus of labour transformation, and she suggests that "in seeking solutions to social inequalities and problems through law reform, one must look at the responsibilities of market actors and their relationships with the public and the state, not just the relationships between the public and the state. We need to broaden the sense of social responsibility and the range of solutions to corporations/the market/private actors." Unions are also a locus of governance. How they manage the challenge of minorities within their ranks cannot be organized by governments. It must come from within. This is the challenge that Brunelle sees for unions.

Ultimately, though, it is the citizenry who must change, since changes in governance occur through people thinking differently about an issue. All seven contributors invite the public to reflect critically on categorizations in our society. Barney warns against the myth of the Internet as a place for community expression, Brett cautions us against accepting the privatization of scientific endeavours, Wood wants greater public involvement in the discussion of environmental issues, Brunelle advocates new thinking within the workforce about intergenerational justice issues, Collins and Blomley challenge society into rethinking its approach toward the act of begging, and Philipps suggests that we must integrate unpaid work with paid work in people's attitudes and in their perceptions of the workday. Each of these seven authors present a complex and enriching view of how law and society manage the public–private divide. How can law reform respond to such a challenge?

### Lessons for Law Reform

If the public–private distinction often obscures meaningful issues, is it necessary to organize our legal thinking in these terms? What does it mean for our understandings of governance and for the very enterprise of law reform? What are the lessons that one can draw from these essays in terms of law reform?

Three conclusions come to mind. First, any law reform initiative must question the claim that the private-public distinction has universal appeal. Reference to public and private as unambiguous notions is certainly not appropriate, and we must reflect on the role that this construction has played and continues to play in highlighting certain interests and obscuring others. We must speak about the functions of the distinction, its purpose and its use, as opposed to assuming its undeniable existence. This could lead to a review of the way in which the terms are used in case law, statutes, and legal education. It is not that the conceptualization *per se* is unhelpful but, rather, that it can prevent a realistic assessment of the role that it plays in reinforcing imbalances of power. It is often too easy to hide behind conceptualizations such as private and public, which are presented as being self-evident. A distinction is a means to better understand the world, and it should not become an end in itself. Law reform must therefore go beyond the classifications of private and public. The public–private divide may be blurring, but this does not make it irrelevant. The fact that the divide and, indeed, the very meaning of the terms are being redrawn, accentuated, distorted, or reformulated in almost all policy fields signifies that there are shifts in power structures. Effective law reform requires an examination of these emerging fault lines.

Second, it must be remembered that, like all socio-legal constructs, the public–private divide is a concept that can be manipulated and that it does influence the power dynamics between people. The seven authors illustrate well how the labelling of a space as "private" serves to protect the power of certain groups. The private protects the generational advantage of older workers (Brunelle), excludes certain people from participating in activities (Collins and Blomley), commercializes public space such as the Internet (Barney), science (Brett), or the environment (Wood), and, to a certain extent, ensures the gendered structure of work (Philipps).

Third, law reform must speak to more than governments, and it must engage the public. Governance has different modes and different sites,[11] and recognizing this fact must influence the way in which law reform is carried out. Law reform was once primarily about legislative changes and the role of public administration. In that context, law reform certainly raises issues and contributes to the politicization of certain injustices. Even in its most traditional form, law reform is about "publicizing" (in its best sense) the inadequacies of law. To borrow from Wood's terms, the role of law reform should become one of creating space to "re-politicize" issues, to create space for those who want to resist, challenge, or redefine private standards, and to allow public issues to be framed in a manner that works toward greater justice, equality, human health, and ecological integrity. In other words, law reform should allow a multiplicity of sites to debate the appropriate values that ought to support human conduct.

However, this role of raising and politicizing issues and engaging the state in amending statutes is not sufficient. Law reform must also speak to a multitude of actors and to a plurality of normative orders, including unions, the scientific community, the enlightened corporation that supports the entire contribution of the worker, the corporation that has adopted environmental management standards, and the community of Internet users. It must move beyond governments and provoke other sectors to ask questions about justice.

These lessons create challenges for law reform. It must diversify its modes of intervention. The commonly used report to Parliament or legislature may no longer be sufficient, and, in the future, such reports will have to be accompanied by a strategy of speaking in the language of other actors. Consultations about the scope of the problem and the range of solutions, as well as about the means to speak to different actors, will now become an integral part of the work. Innovative strategies to engage and understand a wider range of institutional players will have to be devised.

Such innovation is necessary because changes, and particulary law reform advocating change, have to occur in the private, the public, and the in-between areas where governance is exercised. This is not to denigrate the role that the public sector can assume. In the words of Philipps, "law, alone, cannot make fundamental changes to society's values, but it has the capacity to shape background assumptions, expectations, and values that influence voluntary behaviour." Law, the symbolic power of legislation and of commitment of public resources, is an important tool, but it is simply not sufficient.

In reaching out to different constituencies, law reform must also be wary of creating new classes of "experts" within the different normative orders. It must reflect on its tendency to consult primarily with the power brokers within institutions (both private and public) and with the most vocal voices on issues, and remain aware of its resulting loss of ability to reach sufficiently far into the general public. Ultimately, law reform does not occur if the citizens are indifferent or opposed to it. Law reform must engage the general public. Law reform should also seek to empower citizens to question concepts and power structures in whichever space they are in: the private, the public, and the in-between. Ultimately, law reform must contribute to the creation of a questioning and self-reflecting legal culture – one that moves beyond the law as icon and toward the law as a living and self-questioning entity.

**Notes**

1 The following references indicate the proliferation of the discourse on public–private in the most recent years (2000-1):

**Geography:** N. Blomley and G. Pratt, "Canada and the Political Geographies of Rights" (2001) 45 Canadian Geographer/Géographe Canadien 151-66.

**History:** M. Archangeli, "Negotiating the Public Sphere through Private Correspondence: A Woman's Letters of Liberty in Eighteenth-Century Germany" (2000) 53 German Life and Letters 435-49.

**Sociology:** J. Bailey, "Some Meanings of 'the Private' in Sociological Thought" (2000) 34 Sociology 381-401.

**Psychology:** J.M. Monteil and N. Michinov, "Effects of Context and Performance Feedback on Social Comparison Strategies among Low-Achievement Students: Experimental Studies" (2000) 19 Cahiers de Psychologie Cognitive 513-31; and J. Harden, "There's No Place Like Home: The Public/Private Distinction in Children's Theorizing of Risk and Safety" (2000) 7 Childhood 43-59.

**Ethics:** J. Fisher, S. Gunz, and J. McCutcheon, "Private/Public Interest and the Enforcement of a Code of Professional Conduct" (2001) 31 Journal of Business Ethics 191-207.

**Political science:** Barbara Arneil, "Women as Wives, Servants and Slaves: Rethinking the Public/Private Divide" (2001) 34 Canadian Journal of Political Science 29-54 at 29; and L.A. Crooms, "The Mythical, Magical 'Underclass': Constructing Poverty in Race and Gender, Making the Public Private and the Private Public" (2001) 5 Journal of Gender Race and Justice 87-130.

**Religious studies:** M.E. Henneau, "Private and Public Prayer: The Prayer Life of Nuns in Early Modern Liege" (2000) 217 Revue de l'Histoire des Religions 327-44 (translation).

**Public health:** D.S. Brennan, A. Gaughwin, and A.J. Spencer. "Differences in Dimensions of Satisfaction with Private and Public Dental Care among Children" (2000) 51(2) International Dental Journal 77-82.

**Tourism:** A. Marino, "The Tourist Sector: Public versus Private – The Italian and Spanish Experience" (2001) 22 Tourism Management 43-48.

Information sciences: S.J. Lukasik, "Protecting the Global Information Commons" (2000) 24 Telecommunications Policy 519-31.

2  Section 32(1) of the *Canadian Charter of Rights and Freedoms,* Part 1 of the *Constitution Act, 1982,* being Schedule B to the *Canada Act 1982* (U.K.), 1982, c. 11 [hereinafter *Charter*], makes it specifically applicable only to the Parliament and government of Canada and to the legislature and government of each province "in respect of all matters within the authority" of the respective legislative body. In *RWDSU* v. *Dolphin Delivery Ltd,* [1986] 2 S.C.R. 573 [hereinafter *Dolphin Delivery*], the Supreme Court of Canada decided that the *Charter* did not apply to a private action unconnected to "government." (See also *McKinney* v. *U. of Guelph,* [1990] 3 S.C.R. 229; *Stoffman* v. *Vancouver General Hospital,* [1990] 3 S.C.R. 483.) However, the Court considered that the common law should evolve in light of *Charter* values. Over time, courts have tested common law principles against the fundamental values expressed in the *Charter* (*Canadian Broadcasting Corp.* v. *Dagenais,* [1994] 3 S.C.R. 835, 120 D.L.R. (4th) 12, *Hill* v. *Church of Scientology of Toronto,* [1995] 2 S.C.R. 1130) and have also focused on the functions of government (*Eldridge* v. *British Columbia (A.G.),* [1997] 3 S.C.R. 624). They have also challenged governmental inactions to deal with private wrongs (*Vriend* v. *Alberta,* [1998] 1 S.C.R. 493). While the private-public distinction is often said to be misleading in this context (see P. Hogg, *Constitutional Law of Canada,* 3rd edition (Carswell, 1992) at 849-50), it may be just as fluid as the notion of state or governments. For a discussion of the applicability of the distinction established in *Dolphin Delivery* in Québec civil law, see Danielle Pinard, *Les dix ans de la Charte canadienne des droits et libertés et le droit civil québécois: quelques réflexions* (1992) 24 Ottawa L. Rev. 193. For a discussion of the application of the notions in the healthcare field, see Martha Jackman, *The Application of the Canadian Charter in the Health Care Context* (2000) 9 Health L. Rev. 22, and in the education sector, see, among others, René Pépin, *La Charte canadienne des droits et libertés s'applique-t-elle à l'Université de Sherbrooke?* (1990) 20 R.D.U.S. Revue de droit de l'Université de Sherbrooke 433.

3  Nikolas Rose, "The Death of the Social? Re-Figuring the Territory of the Government" (1996) 25 Economy and Society 327-56; Mariana Valverde, Ron Levi, Clifford Shearing, Mary Condon, Pat O'Malley, *Democracy in Governance: A Socio-Legal Framework,* report prepared for the Law Commission of Canada (Ottawa: Law Commission of Canada, 1999); Pat O'Malley, "Risk and Responsibility," in A. Barry, T. Osborne, and N. Rose, eds., *Foucault and Political Reason* (London: UCL Press, 1996); Rose, Nikolas, and Mariana Valverde, "Governed by law?" (1998) 7(4) Social and Legal Studies 541-552; Nikolas Rose, *Powers of Freedom: Reframing Political Thought* (Cambridge: Cambridge University Press, 1999); David Garland, "Governmentality and Crime Control: Foucault, Criminology, Sociology" (1997) 1(3) Theoretical Criminology 454.

4  Susan B. Boyd, *Challenging the Public/Private Divide: Feminism, Law, and Public Policy* (Toronto: University of Toronto Press, 1997).

5  *Act Respecting the Law Commission of Canada,* R.S.C., c. L-6.7.

6  Preamble to the *Act Respecting the Law Commission of Canada, supra* note 5.

7  Hannah Arendt, *The Human Condition* (Chicago: University of Chicago Press, 1958).

8  Jürgen Habermas, *The Structural Transformation of the Public Sphere: An Inquiry into a Category of Bourgeois Society,* translated by Thomas Burger (Cambridge, MA: MIT Press, 1991).

9  Wood is concerned about the depolitization of the environmental discourse. For a similar argument on the role of expert management as a cause of depolitization in the context of world trade issues, see Kantola A. Leaving, "Public Places: Antipolitical and Antipublic Forces of the Transnational Economy" (2001) 8(1) Javnost – The Public 59-74.

10  For a similar discussion of the impact of the Internet on democratic society, see also Y. Baruch, "The Autistic Society" (2001) 38(3) Information Management 129-36.

11  The Law Commission of Canada has used this expression to describe its research on governance. It wanted to convey the idea of the multiplicity of ways in which governance occurs (regulation, taxation, ethics, etc.) and the multiplicity of places where it is experienced (in corporate structures, non-governmental organizations, schools, and churches). For a description of these ideas, see Roderick Macdonald, *Grotius, Gandhi and Governance,* which is available on the Law Commission of Canada's website: <http://www.lcc.gc.ca/en/pc/speeches/s290698> (accessed 30 November 2002).

# 1

# There's Only One Worker: Toward the Legal Integration of Paid Employment and Unpaid Caregiving

*Lisa Philipps*

The object of this essay is to imagine how law might look if it took seriously the idea that unpaid caregiving is an economic activity, a work process that generates human capacities without which markets could not function. Instead of warm, fuzzy statements about how much we value our caregivers, this essay calls for cold, hard accounting and a recognition that the market sector of our economy is dependent upon the production and maintenance of healthy, socialized, skilled labour power in the household sector. This recognition is not meant to deny the ethical and emotional dimensions of caregiving. However, it is meant to react against the notion that care work can be reduced to these things. The question is how law might help to dismantle the conceptual architecture that treats caregiving as a private matter of love and duty, which is marked off from the realm of economic relations. Just as law has helped to construct this market/family opposition and the gendered roles of breadwinner and caregiver,[1] it must now play a part in exploding them. Law needs to be restructured around the idea that there is only one worker and that she is plum exhausted from trying to fill two jobs.

The goals of such a law reform agenda, I suggest, should be: (1) to ensure that more powerful market actors internalize the costs of caregiving work from which they benefit, and (2) to integrate market work and family work more fully for both women and men. A project of integrating paid and unpaid work is needed both to improve the efficiency and sustainability of our economy and to address gender, race, and class inequalities, which have persisted despite women's greater involvement in paid labour. These claims are developed in the second part of this essay where I draw on the work of feminist political economists to explain how the contribution of household labour to market productivity has been obscured and why the tension between paid and unpaid work has intensified in recent times. This analysis exposes the heavy costs to society and to women, especially of treating unpaid caregiving as an economically valueless activity. It also offers a model for reconceiving the household and the market as interdependent sectors of the economy, which are both required for the production of wealth and the reproduction of society. This theoretical enlargement of the economy has promise, I argue, as a model for law.

In the third section, I propose that an agenda for law reform could be constructed around two principles derived from a feminist political economic understanding of unpaid work. The first, which I call the "anti-free ride" principle, is that market actors should internalize the costs of caregiving work that never appear on a balance sheet but which are, in fact, a valuable input to the production process.[2] Essentially, this is about removing the economic gains that employers and some market workers currently obtain from the unpaid and low-paid caregiving work of others. Such unearned gains should be redistributed to compensate and support caregiving work. The second principle, referred to in this chapter as the "integration" principle, is that work practices must be restructured around the expectation that all individuals, male and female, will normally combine paid duties with substantial unpaid duties in a total working day. The objective in this case is to improve overall living standards for all workers, and especially to enhance women's equality, by "dismantling the gendered opposition between breadwinning and caregiving."[3] I anticipate a number of objections to these principles, including concerns about the erosion of family values, the commodification of caregiving relationships, the possible reinforcement of gender roles if caregiving is explicitly valued, and the dubious power of law to effect social change. After responding to these objections, I outline the general nature and possible strategies of a law reform program based upon the anti-free ride and integration principles.

In the fourth section, I discuss how this model of law reform might be operationalized in key areas such as employment standards and labour law, partnership and corporate law, taxation law, and family law. I consider how each of these areas would need to be redesigned to implement the anti-free ride and integration principles. The purpose of this exercise is not to propose minor changes that could be easily achieved but rather to outline a fundamental program of law reform. Other policy analyses of caregiving have focused specifically on the improvement of social welfare programs delivered by the state.[4] My proposals seek to complement this work by focusing more heavily on the legal regulation of market activity, in keeping with the overall theme of this essay that caregiving is an issue of economic policy and not only one of social policy. The law reform proposals are not detailed or comprehensive given the limited scope of the chapter. Instead, I highlight major legal issues and suggest possible approaches to reform, pointing out areas where further research and refinement is needed. The fifth section concludes the discussion.

**Love's Labours Located:**
**Feminist Political Economy Perspectives on Caregiving**

Economic theory did not always discount the value of household labour. However, the rise of wage labour markets in the late eighteenth and nineteenth centuries was accompanied by a clear shift in economic thought in which housework was deemed unproductive on the grounds that it did not produce commodities for sale.[5] As subsistence production was replaced by a division of labour in which some household members went out to work for wages, production and reproduction were severed. Those people who retained a heavier role in household maintenance and caregiving, primarily women, were reconstructed as dependents who relied on others for their living.[6] The economy became synonymous with markets and the flow of cash income, and the household and state sectors were portrayed merely as the consumers of income that was generated through market production.[7]

It was not until the early twentieth century that some economists began to attempt the valuation of goods and services produced in the household and to call for their inclusion in government statistics and economic analysis.[8] More recently, in the 1990s, a new branch of feminist political economy literature has developed rapidly to challenge the narrow focus on markets as the exclusive site of production. This literature has detailed the failure of both neoclassical and Keynesian macroeconomic theories to account for how labour power is socially reproduced on a daily and generational basis and made useful for market activities through the development of physical, intellectual, and social capacities.[9] The implicit assumption of mainstream economics is that "no work or investment is required to maintain these resources."[10] Their continuous replacement is taken for granted as though obtained from some free and unlimited natural resource. As it is still women primarily who nurture and replenish human capacities, at the expense of their own market opportunities, the definition of unpaid caregiving as not being work but rather something more akin to leisure or consumption neatly justifies women's economic marginalization.

The devaluation of women's care work is often framed too narrowly as a problem of looking after certain classes of designated dependents, such as the young, the old, the ill, and the disabled. For example, policy discussions of home care sometimes imply that caregiving burdens are a new issue arising from a specific demographic trend – the aging of the population. Other policy discussions of caregiving focus almost exclusively on the difficulties of combining motherhood with employment. Certainly, these are major components of unpaid work that need to be addressed in their own right. However, singling out only some people as dependents or caregivers obscures the fact that all people need care on a daily basis to replenish themselves physically, to nurture their self-confidence, and to prepare their bodies and minds for the next day's demands.[11] As Martha Fineman has written, "no one is self-sufficient, either economically or socially. We all live subsidized lives."[12] While some of our needs are met through self-care, a great deal are met by relying on a flow of family and community support. A large part of the unpaid work done by women is still done for healthy, non-disabled adult men. Thus, it is misleading to say, for example, that "women may be approaching equality, but mothers are still far behind,"[13] because it wrongly implies that childless women face no gender-based expectations to provide care and that they therefore enjoy market opportunities similar to men.

Defining the problem only in terms of children or others who are singled out as dependents also tends to generate limited policy recommendations, which often focus on public benefits for parents who remain home with children, or subsidies for replacement care of children, seniors, or others constructed as dependents. While these may be important parts of a solution, they do not touch on the deeper dynamics of an economic system that exploits unpaid work. By contrast, the larger concept of social reproduction within feminist political economy emphasizes the importance of unpaid care in producing all human capacities and supporting all market activity. It therefore demands a more far reaching revision of economic, as well as social, policy. This approach also has the advantage of revealing connections among the experiences of different groups of women in the economy, all of whom are affected, albeit in different ways and degrees, by the gendered and devalued status of caregiving work.

Diane Elson has addressed the failings of mainstream macroeconomics by formulating an alternative conception of the total economy that comprises three interdependent sectors: the domestic sector (households and communities), the public sector (governments), and the market sector (firms).[14] All three sectors are understood to be producers of wealth in this model. In particular, the domestic sector is seen as providing a stream of physical and intangible social assets that enable wealth creation in the market sector, including the cultivation of ethical values such as trust and honesty, citizenship norms, and communication and learning abilities. Elson underlines this point as follows:

> Brute economic and political power can get deals done; but without an underpinning of ethical norms and the participation of people with some sense of ethics and some willingness to trust, no well functioning market is possible. The primary site of production of these key social assets is the process of bringing up children in the home and the neighbourhood, a process which rests upon unpaid domestic labour.[15]

Likewise, the success of investments in training and education by governments and firms is contingent upon the quantity and quality of unpaid work done in the domestic sector (for example, to teach basic learning skills to children, help with homework, provide encouragement, or liberate a family member to attend night school).[16] Indeed domestic support for workers may be more critical than ever before "in a productive world which requires self-confident personalities to be used in flexible jobs with great geographical mobility and a high degree of insecurity."[17]

The late-twentieth-century decline of secure full-time jobs and welfare state supports has introduced new stresses and risks to be absorbed by households. In the face of these pressures, households have basically two ways of trying to maintain living standards. One is to take on more hours of paid work, often by having more members of the household employed. The popularity of this strategy is reflected in the rapid decline of the one-earner couple and women's increasing presence in the labour market. The other strategy is to reduce the need for market income by relying more heavily on goods and services produced at home or in the community.[18] For many women, the combination of these two strategies amounts to heavier paid and unpaid workloads simultaneously and a worsening time squeeze.[19] The restructuring of welfare states and labour markets has been carried out precisely on the assumptions, which have been attacked by feminist political economists, that the supply of unpaid domestic services is unlimited and provides an infinitely expandable safety net for those left behind in the new economy.[20] The fallout from these developments, which could be characterized as an emerging crisis of social reproduction, is troubling from the point of view of both economic sustainability and equality.

Overstressing the social reproductive capacities of households and communities threatens the sustainability of market growth over the long term. Market production depends on the reproduction of workers and, eventually, will be compromised by a decline in the quality and quantity of care work available to support these workers. It is very unclear whether cost cutting measures by governments and employers add to efficiency or simply shift the costs off the books and into the domestic realm where they cannot as easily be measured. The fallacy lies in thinking that such costs can be contained in the domestic sector and that they will not spill over to affect the functioning of markets on both the supply (production) and demand (consumption) sides.[21] In Elson's words, "if the care economy is overburdened, there will be negative feedbacks to the commodity and public service economies which will reduce their productivity and increase their costs, because of inadequate maintenance of human resources and of the social framework."[22] These negative feedbacks may include, for example, higher absenteeism and lower productivity in employment, poor results in training and education programs, and higher costs in the criminal justice system.

The inequalities associated with this rising pressure on household resources are also problematic in their own right. The restructuring of labour markets has involved two trends: (1) the increase in temporary, part-time, or other non-standard jobs, held more often by women, but increasingly by men as well, which is often referred to as a feminization of employment;[23] and (2) the intensification of the masculine "ideal-worker norm"[24] in more highly paid occupations, in which employees are expected to work long hours of overtime, for which they are sometimes paid but often unpaid. Together with the sharp retraction of welfare state supports, these trends have helped to produce a pattern of growing economic polarization.[25] This pattern of rising inequality is both gendered and racialized. Although women have made gains in terms of paid labour force participation, they have fewer opportunities to take up the most lucrative market opportunities, even when they are highly qualified, due to their disproportionate responsibilities for care work as well as employers' presumptions that women are secondary workers and less committed to career progress. Likewise, recent immigrants and people of colour are often excluded from the better jobs regardless of their formal qualifications due to biases about cultural difference or de-mands for "Canadian experience" as well as presumptions that they will accept the worst forms of work more willingly.[26] In addition, even when some women and men are able to break through to the highest tiers of the employment market, it is very often by hiring poorly paid women, often immigrant women of colour, to perform childcare and other domestic work. Ironically, then, the liberation of some white, middle class women is achieved by exploiting the caregiving work of less privileged women. Moreover, those who work for low pay, including nannies and other domestic servants, of-ten have no choice but to leave their own children in poor quality replace-ment care settings so that they can do waged work that may be far less rewarding and empowering to them than taking care of their own fami-lies.[27] As discussed in later sections in this essay, these dynamics suggest that any strategy for improving the treatment of caregiving needs to ad-dress both the unpaid and low-paid forms of this work.

As a partial result of these disheartening trends, the issue of women's caregiving work has received a surge of attention internationally over the last decade from feminist researchers and activists and also, to some extent, from governments and policy-makers. A great deal of energy has gone into lobbying for, and then producing, better statistics on the amount of unpaid work being performed, its distribution between the sexes, and its economic value.[28] The Canadian data are typical of other industrialized countries in showing that unpaid work comprises a huge share of economic activity, with fully half of Canadians' total work hours being spent on unpaid activi-ties.[29] A starkly gendered division of labour has been confirmed up to the most recent data from 1998, which show that women's share of unpaid work has remained fairly constant since the 1960s (at about two-thirds) despite the dramatic increase in their paid labour market participation.[30]

There is an almost perfectly inverse pattern of time use between men and women. Women spend just over 60 percent of their working hours on unpaid activities and just under 40 percent on paid work, while men do the opposite, spending over 60 percent of their work time in paid activities versus under 40 percent on unpaid work.[31] Comparisons of total workloads differ depending on the study, with one study showing total working days of about equal length for men and women (7.2 hours averaged over seven days),[32] and another concluding that women work about fifteen minutes longer per day, or two weeks per year.[33] Notably, these studies reveal nothing about the intensity or quality of the work performed during these hours – for example, the extent to which parents must complete laundry, cooking, or other domestic tasks while simultaneously caring for children. Women retain the greater share of household work in married couples even when both partners are employed full-time, and women report higher levels of severe time stress than men when they are married with children and employed full-time.[34] Notably, the presence of children does not increase men's likelihood of reporting severe time stress, whereas it almost doubles the rate of severe time stress among women. The recent progress in measuring unpaid work has increased its visibility, but, with a few minor exceptions, it has not yet led to economic or social policy changes to support this work or demarginalize those who do the bulk of it.[35] The next section of the essay explores how these policy issues might be broached in the legal context.

## Constructing a New Worker: Toward a Model of Law Reform

Law is deeply grounded in assumptions about the family as a private sphere of altruism and love, which exists to offer shelter from the self-interested competition of the market – the caring home versus the counting house. Hence, a new map of the economy, which encompasses not only the market but also households, communities, and states, issues a powerful challenge to law. This section explores how the reconstruction of care work as productive by feminist political economists could be translated into a vision for law reform. I develop two guiding principles – the anti-free ride principle and the integration principle – that could be applied to analyze what changes are needed in different fields of law. I then respond to four possible objections to these principles. Finally, drawing on the helpful work of other legal and social policy scholars, I outline the general features and strategies of a reform agenda.

### Anti-Free Ride Principle

This principle holds that law should seek ways of preventing relatively powerful market actors from retaining the material benefits of unpaid or low-paid caregiving work performed by others. A free rider can be defined quite simply as someone "who does not pay for the goods or services he/she consumes."[36] Care work provides essential inputs for market production that do not have to be paid for directly. Thus, the wages and profits derived from market activity have embedded within them a quantity of uncompensated reproductive labour.[37] In effect, women's caregiving labour is subsidizing those individuals who engage successfully in market work.[38] Nancy Folbre explains that the care of children and others produces positive spillovers or "externalities" for employers, fellow citizens, and others from whom the care provider has no power to extract direct compensation through a higher price for her services.[39] Since market transactions cannot capture this value, state intervention is required to ensure that the beneficiaries of caregiving internalize its costs. A portion of their gains must in some manner be redirected to support the caregiving activities that enable market work. This redirection could be achieved, for example, through taxation measures that would redistribute more of the income and wealth of the relatively prosperous market actors to caregivers or by requiring employers to improve wages, benefits, and other supports to ensure that those doing paid care work earn a reasonable wage and that all employees can engage in substantial unpaid caregiving activities without suffering a loss of income or opportunity.

The aim of the anti-free ride principle is not to penalize market actors for their individual success but to make earnings and profits more reflective of the actual costs of producing, maintaining, and nurturing labour power. As discussed earlier in this essay, a strategy of reinvesting market gains in the work of the domestic sector could improve both the equity and the efficiency of our economic system. A central feature of this principle is its focus on the responsibilities of market actors. It demands that support for caregiving be provided not only by the state, as a social security measure, but also by employers and others who benefit from the maintenance and socialization of the paid workforce. It is crucial that the value of these services be made visible to those people who previously have been encouraged to see their market success as independently achieved. Instead of economically marginalizing those who do care work, on the expectation that individual breadwinners or governments will provide safety nets, the various beneficiaries of this work must become more directly involved in covering its costs.

### Integration Principle

This principle states that law should encourage a restructuring of work around the assumption that both men and women combine paid and unpaid duties over their working lives, that each component of the total workload has essential productive value and entitles people to reasonable income security, and that both must be accommodated within a total working day that is not unduly onerous. The roles of breadwinner and caregiver, which implicitly inform so many legal regimes, need to be jettisoned in favour of a new unified conception of a worker as anyone engaged in household and/

or market labour. This principle not only aims to enhance women's economic equality and freedom of choice about caregiving but also to persuade men to participate more actively in caregiving, to raise the living standards of all workers, and to enhance long-term economic growth by strongly supporting the development of human capacities. Though individual experiences and choices about work and family would, of course, continue to range across a full spectrum, the image of the fully integrated worker would serve as the norm or standard underpinning the legal system. Individuals who deviated from this norm to pursue market work more exclusively would be subject to the anti-free ride principle detailed earlier.[40]

The idea that paid and unpaid work should be better integrated is accepted more easily in policy, academic, and business circles than is its more threatening anti-free ride counterpart. However, measures to implement the integration principle are likely to remain relatively superficial and toothless unless they are backed by the anti-free ride principle, which demands that market actors bear the costs of caregiving that subsidize market production. Many employers and governments are already striving to present themselves as family friendly. Yet the extent to which such policies actually reflect higher corporate or state spending on family benefits, as opposed to public relations efforts, is unclear. "Family benefits" sometimes amount to nothing more than a relabelling of pre-existing health or income replacement plans, or they may be designed to minimize costs to firms or governments (such as allowing time off without pay or providing referral services to help people identify replacement care options, without actually subsidizing the cost of such services).[41] More ambitious steps to integrate paid employment with unpaid caregiving will entail significant costs to private actors and to the state. The anti-free ride principle justifies these costs by highlighting the unfairness of imposing them alternatively on individual caregivers. Treating care as a valuable input to production is a means of exploding the dichotomy between social programs and economic policy and building consensus around the collective interest in supporting care work. These supports must be "seen as essential social infrastructure for the household economy rather than as 'welfare handouts,'"[42] if they are to gain political currency.

**Four Objections to the Anti-Free Ride and Integration Principles**
At least four objections are likely to be heard against these two law reform principles.

*Erosion of Family Values*
Some conservatives would likely object to the idea of promoting better paid work options for those people with heavy caregiving responsibilities because it requires some use of replacement care services in place of full-time

unpaid care. Groups organized under the banner of protecting family values have long accused feminists of representing only those women who wish to take on traditionally masculine roles in the paid work force and of denigrating those who work exclusively in the home. My proposal would likely be considered guilty of a similar pro-market bias. Conservatives have instead advocated that caregiving be valued by giving tax concessions to breadwinners who support a stay-at-home parent or by ensuring that full-time caregivers have access to old age pensions.[43] They often invoke the rhetoric of choice, arguing that many women would prefer a traditional gender role if possible and that their individual choices should be supported rather than discouraged.

The major downfalling of this argument is its failure to offer any remedies for women's economic inequality except for a blind faith in male breadwinners to provide for their wives. The rise of divorce and the decline of any semblance of a family wage for most men makes this model even less reliable than it always has been as a guarantee of women's security. Even if a breadwinner's wage is adequate to support a wife, this arrangement denies women any right to control consumption decisions and leaves them extremely vulnerable to poverty upon separation. The assertion that many women would choose to do more unpaid caregiving if they could afford to ignores the factors that frame and constrain women's choices, including ideologies of domesticity and selfless motherhood and a labour market that makes juggling paid work with family an extremely difficult and stressful task. The following exchange quoted by Joan Williams exemplifies this point:

> "I decided to quit my job and stay home. But it was my choice; I have no regrets ..."

> "Wouldn't you really rather be able to continue in your career, earning at your current salary rate, while being able to give your children the time you feel they need?"

> "Well of course, that's what I really want."[44]

Despite its basic weakness, the family values argument does carry a useful reminder that a significant number of women are still full-time unpaid caregivers – a fact that is easy to forget with the blurring of gender roles and the massive increases in female employment. In 1999, women in all age ranges were more likely to be outside of the paid labour force than men, and, among twenty-five to forty-four year olds, women were almost 2.5 times as likely as men to be outside of the paid labour force entirely. Likewise, the number of two-adult families with a stay-at-home parent has declined dramatically from the 1976 figure of 52 percent, but it was still significant at 22 percent in 1997 (more than one in five two-parent families).[45] It is likely wrong to imagine that all of these women would (or should) enter paid labour even if it was much better integrated with caregiving work. An integration strategy that assumes that all caregiving can be facilitated through enlightened labour markets and better replacement care services would therefore fail to address the contributions and needs of those who are full-time caregivers for a period of time. Also needed are systems to provide full-time unpaid caregivers with independent access to private and public sources of income, as well as programs to facilitate market entry and to eliminate market penalties following periods outside the paid labour force. Such strategies are needed both to recognize the economic contribution of women and to make the choice of unpaid caregiving an economically rational one for more men.

### Commodification of Care

The commodification of care is the concern that valuing unpaid work in monetary terms and emphasizing its link to market production will commodify caregiving relationships and undermine them as a place where emotional bonds and ethical values can flourish.[46] The caring home, in other words, should not be converted to a counting house. This objection is sometimes linked to the first one – the erosion of family values – but it is also made by some feminists who argue that women's cultural identity as caring people is a difference that should be cherished and fostered more widely.

One problem with this type of argument is that it may romanticize care work as purely altruistic and inherently fulfilling. While activities such as reading to a child may be personally fulfilling, others, such as doing several loads of laundry per day, likely are not. Moreover, as Lourdes Beneria points out, "it is not difficult to find exceptions ... i.e. market-based care providing selfless emotional support beyond the exchange contract, and family care based on selfish expectations or on some form of coercion."[47] Nor does accounting for the economic contribution of care work mean erasing its moral importance. Economists who advocate valuing unpaid work are careful to acknowledge the ethical dimensions of care, and they tend to agree that it is not qualitatively identical to waged labour.[48]

While the commodification objection remains too attached to the idea of the family as a haven from market competition, it does serve to warn us away from solutions that simply assimilate caregiving with the orthodox economic concept of work. As Antonella Picchio argues, "the challenge is not to ... consider human development simply as human capital to be used for profit production ... Rather it is to show the dialectical relationship between production and reproduction in order to practice new civilizing mediations."[49] The agenda should focus on exploding the false dichotomy between productive relations and caring relations and better integrating the two in both the household and the market. The aim is to enable and encourage time spent on these tasks as a universal responsibility and as an essential contribution to living standards (defined broadly to include incomes, other material comforts, and social relationships) rather than exploiting women's unpaid labour as though it was a free, unlimited natural resource. Indeed, this agenda may reduce the commodification of care in another way if more workers have the time and support to perform more care work personally rather than purchasing replacement services to free them for long hours of waged labour.

### Reinforcing Gender Roles

Some feminists have been wary that efforts to value unpaid work may glorify the domestic role and be used to curtail women's access to paid work. For example, Barbara Bergmann in the United States has argued against the provision of subsidies for stay-at-home parenting, even including paid parental leaves of more than one or two months because such policies may undermine the improvement in women's economic and social status that has accompanied their mass entry into paid labour.[50] She writes: "Workplace policies that simply allow the resumption by the wife of ... [caregiving] duties, or facilitate her doing them, can be viewed as a partial return to ... traditional arrangements."[51] Bergmann observes that the costs of withdrawing from paid labour cannot easily be limited to those people who freely choose such a life path (whatever free choice may be). Paying mothers to look after their own children even for a period of time reduces the job opportunities of all women, she argues, because employers come to presume that all women are temporary workers. Bergmann also worries about increased social pressure for women to stay at home if financial need is removed as an "excuse" for returning quickly to paid work. This social pressure is more likely to be visited on women, she asserts, even if subsidies are gender neutral and permit either a father or a mother to take leave.

Bergmann is clearly right that the idea of valuing care work is open to a range of political interpretations. In Canada, it has been alarming to watch certain groups appropriate feminist discourses about the value of caregiving work in order to promote a social conservative vision of family values.[52] However, I agree with Beneria that such regressive appropriations cannot be allowed to deter feminist research and should be challenged with alternative policy prescriptions.[53] Even more importantly, the type of objection voiced by Bergmann does not address the fundamental problem that women's increased labour market access has not delivered gender equality and never will do so without a corresponding reorganization of unpaid care work. Far from attaining full equality in the market, women now have a choice (if they are lucky) between male-pattern careers that may preclude family life, and lower class status in a slightly less demanding job on the so-called "mommy track" of the paid economy. Many less privileged women experience the worst of both worlds: long hours in low-paid domestic jobs. The tension between women's roles in the market and in the household is producing severe time stress as well as a racialized pattern of offloading care work from more privileged to more marginalized women.

Yet the objection about reinforcing gender roles does provide a useful reminder that measures to value caregiving must be developed in tandem with (not in competition with) better supports for women to access market labour. The political divisions between employed women and full-time caregivers can be defused by highlighting the connections between women's marginalization in both production and social reproduction and by pursuing policies that facilitate both kinds of work simultaneously or over the life cycle. Hence, this objection mitigates against policies that would support only exclusive, full-time forms of unpaid care work, without also supporting market access for caregivers. In addition, it calls for policies to be designed creatively to overcome social and economic pressures for women to take on domestic roles by creating more incentives for men to participate in caregiving.

### The Limited Power of Law

Any project that focuses on the law reform implications of a problem is vulnerable to the criticism that legal mandates are powerless to overcome dominant political, economic, and ideological pressures. A central theme of socio-legal scholarship has been to show how and why "the 'fit' between the 'law in the books' and the 'law in action' is not usually a complete or smooth one."[54] Feminist legal theorists, in particular, have remarked upon the frustrating intransigence of social and economic inequality for women despite decades of reform in family law and other areas.[55] And many scholars have criticized the way legal debates tend to distract from the broad-based political action needed to support social change.

Certainly, it would be absurd to suppose that enacting new legal measures could, by itself, transform the way work is understood and practised. The political struggles that would be needed to develop support for, and implement, such a fundamental change must not be minimized. This essay does not attempt to address this challenge. However, it does attempt to avoid narrow legalism by looking at the political economic context in which law operates, at the combined effects of multiple areas of legal regulation, and at the responsibilities of market actors in addition to the state.

Law reform is not a simple recipe for a better world, yet analysis of the legal system is an important part of any campaign for social change. The relationship between law and society is not unidirectional, with law acting simply as a mirror that reflects pre-determined societal structures or norms. Law is better understood as one of the forces at play in constructing the social formation. The legal system cannot claim any neutral ground, in other words. If it is not contributing actively to a solution, then it is some part of the problem. Law has a particular instrumental and symbolic capacity because it is backed by the explicit coercive powers of the liberal state. This is what distinguishes a piece of legislation from a corporate human resources policy, an election platform, or, for that matter, an academic paper. Though there are obvious limits to the state's willingness and ability to exercise its coercive power effectively in the face of political resistance, it cannot be entirely ignored. It is partly because law formally authorizes the use of force that it has a discursive or symbolic capacity to shape the background assumptions, expectations, and values that influence voluntary behaviour. Law reform agendas should be understood not as self-contained solutions to a problem, then, but as components of larger political struggles. On some occasions, they may provide a focal point for mobilizing political resources. Finally, crafting law reform proposals is useful as a means of focusing the mind on how one might build from critique to reconstruction. With these objectives in mind, the fourth part of this essay canvasses several areas of law in which reforms would be needed to reflect the anti-free ride and integration principles articulated earlier.

## Reform Issues in Key Areas of Law

This section of the chapter considers what kinds of measures would be needed to operationalize the anti-free ride and integration principles in several legal fields that are critical to the relationship between paid work and unpaid caregiving. A comprehensive, fine-grained review of the legal system is far beyond the scope of this essay. This discussion aims merely to highlight the key areas where more detailed analysis is needed and to provide examples of particular issues that law reformers would need to tackle. Since a major argument of this essay is that the market sector should be held accountable for its dependence on caregiving work, I focus most heavily on the legal regulation of labour markets and business enterprises. The discussion canvasses issues in employment standards law, labour law, partnership law, corporate law, and taxation law. Finally, I revisit family law – an area that has undergone significant reform with a view to improving the lot of primary caregivers, but which remains rooted in a model of post-divorce sharing of unequal financial resources.

### Legal Regulation of Labour Markets and Business Enterprises

*Employment Standards and Labour Law*
Reforming employment standards and labour laws would be essential if market actors are to internalize more of the costs of producing labour power and other human capacities. A serious reform program could not simply rely on public social security programs to compensate for inefficient and

inequitable labour markets. It would have to tackle these problems directly. Again, this comes back to the earlier-mentioned necessity of treating unpaid work as a core issue of economic policy rather than as a matter of remedial social policy only.

An obvious problem with employment standards law is the limited scope of its coverage with respect to many of those people who do caregiving work for pay. Nannies, independent home care providers, and other domestic workers are often excluded in whole or in part from the protections of employment standards legislation. Lack of employment standards protection is only one factor contributing to the tremendous vulnerability of domestic workers, in addition to immigration restrictions, racial discrimination, inadequate public assistance for low income women, and other problems. Together, these factors facilitate the mass exploitation of domestic workers as a convenient means of reducing the tension between paid work and caregiving for the more privileged economic actors. Though not a complete solution, extending employment standards protections to all such workers would be essential if the anti-free ride and integration principles are to be effective universally and not only for those with better jobs.

Another major deficit of employment standards and labour laws is their failure to grapple with the rise of part-time, contractual, and other forms of non-standard employment. Such jobs are sometimes presented as being more flexible and therefore advantageous to employees with family responsibilities. Certainly, overburdened workers may leap at options such as compressed work weeks, job sharing, telecommuting, flex-time, or part-time jobs, which allow them to juggle their paid and unpaid work more easily. No Canadian employer is currently required by law to offer such non-standard arrangements. However, both private and public sector organizations have developed many examples through collective bargaining, discretionary human resources policies, or agreements with individual employees.[56]

Employers who provide such options are often viewed as enlightened and open to diversity in the workplace, particularly the presence of women, and, to some degree, they are in fact challenging the conventional assumptions about employment. However, the proliferation of non-standard employment is far from a solution to the gendered inequalities of work. To the contrary, it has been widely criticized for contributing to a polarization of the labour market between good jobs and bad jobs (the latter referring to precarious, low wage employment).[57] As Judy Fudge and Leah Vosko observe, "the problem is that employment flexibility does not simply provide a broad menu of employment options for workers, it allows firms to shift the costs of adjusting to changes in the economy onto workers."[58] The pattern of polarization is both gendered and racialized. In particular, non-standard employment has been criticized for sidelining women onto a "mommy track" within the job market, where they are paid less, have lower status, and enjoy fewer opportunities for challenging work or advancement.

These inequities are easily illustrated in the context of part-time employment. Despite its attractions as a way of easing job–family conflict at an individual level, part-time employment has developed in a manner that reinscribes gender inequality in the labour market.[59] Women are still far more likely to work part-time than men. Since the mid-1970s, about 70 percent of part-time workers have been women, and about 20 percent of these women indicate they work part-time because of family or personal responsibilities – a reason that is cited by only 2 percent of male part-time workers.[60] Part-time employees are easily marginalized for several reasons. Perhaps the most important reason is that there is no right under employment standards law to work reduced hours, so that employers have complete discretion to determine when and under what conditions part-time work is available.[61] Nor do part-time employees have rights in most jurisdictions to equal (that is, proportionate) pay and benefits. This fact means that part-time jobs are often designed primarily to serve the employer's interests in reducing labour costs rather than serving the employee's needs. It also means that part-time work tends not to be available in the best paid, most prestigious forms of employment. In addition, because it is voluntary on the part of the employer, employees who successfully request part-time arrangements often feel they have received a favour. This leaves the employee vulnerable to pressure from employers or co-workers to accept lower pay, work beyond their agreed hours, or acquiesce in other unfair or illegal practices.

Not surprisingly, then, part-time workers are unlikely to be paid at the same hourly rates as their full-time colleagues or to receive private benefits such as retirement pensions, disability insurance, or dental coverage. Their entitlement to public benefits, such as pensions and employment insurance, is also jeopardized. They are often excluded from training and career development activities and not considered for promotion to higher positions. Within families, married women who work part-time face a self-reinforcing pattern of economic inequality –since she earns less, it seems most rational to sacrifice her job prospects in order to maximize his – in decision-making about who will take unpaid family leave, whether to move to another job location, and so on. Workplace norms still dictate heavily against men seeking part-time or other alternate work arrangements, either because they are not offered by employers in male-dominated occupations or because it is openly or subtly frowned upon as a sign of inadequate commitment to the workplace.

Recent changes to Ontario's *Employment Standards Act* (*ESA*) provide another good example of the superficial and even illusory nature of many "family-friendly" employment initiatives.[62] The legislation extends job protection for unpaid parental leaves to match the new fifty-two-week duration of employment insurance benefits and creates a right to take up to ten days of unpaid leave for personal or family emergencies.[63] Yet these reforms are less beneficial to employees than they appear. The ten-day crisis leave is unpaid and therefore does not really shift caregiving costs to employers apart from the costs of reorganizing production around an absent worker. In addition, it applies only to those companies who regularly employ fifty or more employees, meaning that those in the fast-growing micro-business sector will be excluded – a sector on which women rely more heavily for jobs than men. Fudge explains that as a result,

> the emergency-leave provision is least likely to be available to those workers who need it most: female workers in small firms who do not have the benefit of a collective agreement. While the government has justified the 50-employee requirement as necessary to protect small business, it is unlikely that many small businesses would be made uncompetitive simply because they were not allowed to fire employees who took off a few days for personal illness or a family emergency.[64]

The benefits of having more family leave are also undercut by the simultaneous move toward longer and more variable work weeks. The *ESA* will allow employers and employees to agree to a maximum work week of sixty hours, instead of the long-time provincial standard of forty-eight hours, and to agree that the maximum hours can be exceeded in a particular week provided they are averaged down to the maximum over a period of weeks. For workers, this raises the spectre of adjusting family time and replacement care arrangements around a longer and more unpredictable weekly schedule. Though employees theoretically can refuse to agree, the balance of power in employment relationships means that most will not do so. It is difficult to see how these changes could do anything but worsen the stresses faced by those people with caregiving responsibilities.

Despite its current weaknesses, employment standards law could play a critical role in implementing the anti-free ride and integration principles. The general thrust of reform should be to reduce the length of the standard full-time work week (without reducing pay) and to mandate a right to work part-time with proportionate pay and benefits. In other words, the current problems of part-time employment should be addressed by normalizing it. Waiting for employers to create such options on their own terms will inevitably leave out many workers and will ensure that part-time employees are vulnerable to marginalization. The integration principle is meant to define a new norm of work for society, not simply the benefits enjoyed by a few.

Though such an approach is far from the current Canadian norm, it is not entirely novel. For example, Quebec already prohibits employers from paying part-time employees a lower hourly wage than their full-time counterparts (unless their pay is more than twice the minimum wage).[65] Saskatchewan has mandated that part-time employees who work at least fifteen hours per week on average are entitled to certain employment benefits received by full-time employees in comparable positions.[66] The International Labour Organization has adopted the *Part-Time Work Convention*, which calls for a wide range of comparable benefits and protections relating to collective bargaining, health and safety, discrimination, social security benefits, and maternity, sickness, and vacation leave as well as requiring various measures to facilitate access to part-time work.[67] And in July 2000, the Netherlands enacted legislation that entitles workers in firms with ten or more employees to reduce their work hours for any reason.[68] New legal rights such as these would have to contend with workplace cultures that frown upon part-time work, especially for men. They should be backed up with active monitoring to determine the numbers of people who actually exercise their legal right to reduced work hours and perhaps also with incentives and subsidies for employers with high take-up rates. It is also worth considering whether family leave times should be designed so that a portion is available only to men in order to counter the financial and cultural biases toward women taking leave while men continue in full-time employment.[69]

Finally, the reform of employment standards law should proceed alongside labour law reforms designed to broaden access to collective bargaining. Union representation is sometimes needed just for employees to obtain the full benefits of employment standards law, and it also creates the possibility of exceeding the bare minimums and reaching agreements that accommodate employees' caregiving responsibilities in innovative ways.[70]

*Legal Regulation of Sole Proprietorships, Partnerships, and Corporations*
Business enterprises cover an enormous spectrum from the single entrepreneur who carries on business from her home to the transnational, publicly owned corporation. Thus, the business law issues that are raised in attempting to integrate paid work with unpaid caregiving are numerous and disparate, depending on the specific market actors or activity being discussed. This section first considers the challenges facing individuals who combine self-employment or small business ownership with major caregiving responsibilities. It then considers questions of corporate responsibility and how the rules of corporate, partnership, and taxation law might encourage or require more proactive efforts by business entities to share the costs of social reproduction.

*Small Business Owners as Caregivers*   A striking feature of labour market change in the 1980s and 1990s was the rise of self-employment, which increased as a proportion of total employment from 12.3 percent in 1976 to 17.8 percent in 1997.[71] Most of this growth (and all the growth in the 1990s) is attributable to own-account self-employment, which includes individuals who sell goods or services to make a living without any assistance from paid employees.[72] The extent to which this trend has been driven by workers' voluntary choices or by involuntary labour market restructuring is unclear.[73] Certainly, governments have actively promoted small business and the "enterprise culture" as a response to unemployment and a means of fostering values of initiative and self-reliance.[74] However, they have done little to address the specific needs of this new class of business owners, including the needs of those people who combine business activities with significant caregiving responsibilities.

The recent trend toward self-employment is distinctly gendered.[75] Although both sexes have increased their rates of self-employment, women's has grown much faster, nearly quadrupling between 1976 and 1997, whereas male self-employment did not quite double in this same period.[76] Visible minority women, in general, are less likely to be self-employed than non-visible minority women, although the reverse is true for specific ethnic groups.[77] The rapid entry of women into the small business sector is often celebrated as a sign of economic empowerment. Yet, there are strong indications that gender inequality is reproducing itself within the new entrepreneurial class. Women are significantly less likely than men to be assisted by paid employees or to own businesses that are incorporated.[78] They are also far more likely to work part-time. Most dramatically, among own-account self-employed workers (those without employees), 45.7 percent of women worked part-time versus only 17.4 percent of men.[79] Only 2 percent of men cited the ability to work from home as a reason for entering self-employment, compared to 12.6 percent of women, and a full 20 percent of women aged twenty-five to thirty-four years.[80] Interview data from an earlier study concluded that women small business owners are not relieved of their heavy family responsibilities when they start their businesses, nor do they benefit from the unpaid assistance that many male entrepreneurs receive from their wives in areas such as bookkeeping, management, and administration. Women's partners and children may be willing to help out but not at the expense of their own careers.[81]

A large proportion of small business owners have very modest incomes with 45.1 percent making under $20,000 in 1995, compared to 25.5 percent of employees at this income level.[82] As noted earlier, women are heavily concentrated among the own-account self-employed, and more than half (55.7 percent) of this group earn less than $20,000.[83] Moreover, the gap in average earnings between men and women is greater for the self-employed than for employees.[84] Earnings differentials may be related to the discrimination that women entrepreneurs have reported facing from financial institutions, suppliers, customers, and employees. This discrimination includes having to provide more collateral or having to provide co-signers for loans more often than men, being perceived as less reliable because they have children, and, for racialized women, experiencing racial as well as gender discrimination especially when they pursue business opportunities outside their own ethnic communities.[85]

Despite the apparent attractiveness of self-employment as a means of juggling paid and unpaid responsibilities, the statistics suggest that the two spheres of work are no more well integrated than in the employment context. The data raise concerns that those people who attempt to combine business ownership with caregiving tend to be inadequately compensated or supported by other market actors with whom they transact, by family members, and by governments and that they pay a price in terms of financial security and living standards.

Identifying legal strategies to remedy the marginalization of self-employed caregivers is more complex than in the case of employment, which is already subject to more comprehensive forms of regulation. However, the starting point for reform should be to reconsider the legal definition of employment versus independent contracting or self-employment. With the restructuring of so much work to accommodate the demands of employers for a flexible labour supply, the common law distinction among these forms of work has become both outdated and incoherent.[86] Many of the newly self-employed simply work on contract for firms that previously employed them or for a small group of firms in the same sector. Yet this status is still used to determine entitlement to many of the statutory benefits and legal protections that are most critical to those with heavy unpaid workloads.

Those individuals whose work falls outside the legal definition of an employment relationship are generally excluded from employment insurance, which presently is the only public source of maternity and parental leave benefits. Nor do they accrue rights to retirement pensions or benefits for illness or disability, either public or private, unless they can finance the purchase of their own registered retirement saving plans or insurance coverage, which are largely inaccessible to those at the low end of the earnings scale. They are excluded from employment standards law and unprotected by employment equity and pay-equity legislation. And they are not included in any benefits negotiated by unions under collective bargaining regimes. Ironically, then, an individual who chooses self-employment because it allows some flexibility to juggle paid work and caregiving loses access to even the most modest programs that now exist to address this very conflict.

Serious consideration should be given to eliminating the common law distinction between employment and self-employment in favour of a single category of contracts for the performance of work, all of which would be covered *prima facie* by employment standards legislation and employment-based benefit programs.[87] Alternatively, the self-employed worker could be

covered separately under contribution schemes that would require employers and governments to fund comparable benefit packages or additional
cash compensation in lieu thereof.[88] In addition, there is a need to rethink
prevailing structures of worker representation and collective bargaining in
order to accommodate those who work under "independent" contractual
relationships, often for multiple firms. This would involve moving away
from an exclusively worksite-based model of union representation toward
the development of forms of worker representation based on sectoral, occupational, geographical, or other understandings of common interest.[89]

Further research is also needed to identify law reforms to reduce the extra
obstacles reportedly faced by women-owned small businesses, including a
relative lack of assistance from male spouses, heavier caregiving responsibilities than male entrepreneurs, a lack of access to management and other
training opportunities, and discrimination in commercial dealings. One
component of this research should involve a review of the income tax treatment of self-employed individuals and small owner-operated corporations.
For example, the restrictions on deducting expenses associated with a work
space in the home need to be reconsidered from the perspective of a self-
employed person who is also a primary caregiver. The *Income Tax Act* prohibits the deduction of home work space expenses unless the space is either
"the individual's principal place of business" or is "used exclusively for ...
the business and used on a regular and continuous basis for meeting clients,
customers, or patients."[90] Neither of these tests would be met, for example,
by a self-employed consultant or retailer who deals with clients at a commercial office while children are at school but does preparatory and administrative work from home in the evenings and on weekends. By contrast, a worker
who is free to spend long hours away from home at a commercial office
space generally can deduct all the expenses of maintaining that office.

The restrictions on home office deductions were introduced because of
the difficulty of monitoring whether such work spaces are really used for
any substantial business purpose or whether a taxpayer is attempting to
deduct the purely personal expenses of maintaining a residence. While the
policy objective of reducing tax avoidance is entirely legitimate, the un-
intended effect may be to disadvantage some small business owners who
also have significant caregiving roles. Policy makers should consider how
this provision could be redesigned to accommodate dual roles, for example,
by relaxing the "principal place of business" test to permit deduction of home
office expenses by someone who spends at least 25-30 percent of their business hours each week working at home. This adjustment would weed out
those people who work at home occasionally as a convenience and should
involve no greater monitoring costs or risk of untruthful reporting than
the current "principal place of business" test. Further, the requirement for

exclusive use of the work space is unrealistic for many low-income self-employed people and should be eliminated, perhaps in favour of a requirement that particular items of equipment be used "primarily" for business purposes, unless the nature of the business requires use of equipment that is primarily for personal use (such as using the home kitchen for a restaurant or catering business). Likewise, the requirement to meet clients, customers, or patients at the home office on a regular and continuous basis assumes that the residence is large enough to have a separate, dedicated office space to which the worker is free to retreat without fear of neglecting or being interrupted by children or other family members.[91] The current statutory tests presume a degree of segregation of personal and business activities even within the home that misses the very reason why some people engage in home-based work, namely to allow for the close integration of paid and unpaid work during certain hours of the day and night. The integration principle may require a shift in tax policy away from the traditional obsession with distinguishing business from personal expenses toward a more nuanced approach that recognizes the difficulty for many workers of compartmentalizing these activities.

There is a danger that home-based work will be seen as a substitute for providing access to affordable, high-quality replacement care services. In reality, home-based employees or business owners need replacement care that is not dissimilar to those who take jobs outside the home. Once again, the income tax system disadvantages many self-employed people. The child care expense deduction currently is the primary means by which the federal government assists parents to cover the costs of replacement child care.[92] A deduction from income can be justified on tax policy grounds as being necessary to recognize the costs of earning income, like any other overhead expense.[93] However, as a means of subsidizing access to child care services, it is highly inequitable.[94] For the many self-employed workers with low earnings or, indeed, with business losses, the child care expense deduction is of little or no value.[95] In two parent families, the deduction generally must be claimed by the lower income parent. This fact means that if one partner leaves employment to start a small business that initially loses money or produces minimal net returns, the family may actually lose access to the child care expense deduction, even though the self-employed spouse is putting in long hours in the business and the family continues to require replacement care. Reforms to the child care expense deduction should take into account the specific circumstances of self-employed parents. Converting the deduction to a refundable credit, as some individuals have recommended, would depart from the traditional tax policy understanding of child care expenses being a form of business or employment overhead that should not be part of the tax base at all. It would, however, increase support to lower-income parents. Yet individualized tax concessions, whether refundable or not, are unlikely by themselves to cure the inadequate supply of low-cost, quality services. There is a need not only to improve existing legal regimes but to make significant direct investments in child care services.

Reports of commercial discrimination against women small business owners also raise law reform questions. A review should be made of human rights legislation and enforcement mechanisms to analyze whether they are effective in dealing with instances of discrimination by financial institutions or suppliers against the self-employed, particularly those with caregiving responsibilities. More proactive forms of regulation may be called for, especially in relation to large lending institutions.

The anti-free ride and integration principles are not satisfied by improving wages and supports for more privileged workers only. By definition, they must be extended to the more vulnerable groups in the labour force. Improving the treatment of small business owners is necessary to ensure that the legal construction of more and more workers as "self-employed" is not simply used by firms and governments as a means to evade the real costs of social reproduction.

*Corporate Responsibility for the Costs of Caregiving*    There is also a need to review partnership and corporate laws governing the ownership and management of business firms to see whether they facilitate free riding on the unpaid work of family members or employees. In this section, I will canvass some issues relating to private family businesses as well as the governance of larger, widely held corporations.

In the context of family-run businesses, there is a need for further research to determine whether the legal rights of ownership, control, and management are distributed fairly to reflect the contributions of different family members. Many privately owned businesses rely upon the unpaid work of family members, often female spouses, in order to function and succeed. This includes the provision of services that are obviously related to the business operations, such as the physical maintenance of business premises, or assistance with administrative, clerical, purchasing, sales, or bookkeeping work. However, the anti-free ride principle would insist upon recognizing that the assumption of the primary responsibility for caregiving by one family member is also an essential economic input to the business.

There is a case to be made that business law should grant the rights of property ownership and, in some circumstances, the right to vote or participate in management to unpaid family members, including primary caregivers. The classic scenario is the business that is legally owned and controlled by a man but operated with the direct or indirect help of a female spouse and, perhaps, the children or extended family members as well. The law's primary response to the possible inequities of this common arrangement has been to mandate transfers of income or property following marriage breakdown under federal and provincial family laws. The need for further reform of family laws is discussed later in this essay. However, consideration should also be given to revising the doctrines of corporate and partnership law so that unpaid family members acquire legal interests in a business enterprise not just upon marriage breakdown, as a remedial measure, but also as a *quid pro quo* while the relationship and the business subsist.

Provincial partnership statutes generally define a partnership to exist among two or more persons (individual or corporate) who are carrying on business in common with a view to profit. A finding of partnership means that unless the partners contract otherwise, they are entitled to share equally in the income, assets, and management of the firm and are equally responsible for its debts and liabilities. In the case of non-family businesses, the courts have tended to apply these principles substantively, looking at the actual relationships among the parties and not just at the legal forms or express agreements. Any form of sharing of profits and losses and any contribution of property or services to the business can result in a finding of partnership. However, in the case of family businesses, the courts have been reluctant to characterize husband-wife operations as legal partnerships without an express partnership agreement.[96] Where the man holds legal title to the business property, the court has tended to view the wife as a mere employee or as providing help gratuitously in her capacity as spouse. Verbal references to the business being "ours" or "working together to get ahead" or the use of business profits to cover joint living expenses have not been interpreted as evidence of an intention to share equally as partners. In addition, judges have generally been skeptical about women's claims that they have contributed to the family business. They seem to presume that women spend most of their time on household chores and child care and assume further that such work does not count as a contribution to the business. In order to overcome these presumptions, the wife typically has had to prove that she has done an extraordinary amount of business-type labour in addition to her domestic chores.[97] These decisions reflect precisely the traditional economic understanding discussed in the second section of this essay – that market activity produces wealth independently of households, which are characterized as unproductive sites in which wealth is merely consumed. It is time to consider whether partnership law can be reformed to reflect an updated view of the family as a joint enterprise and of wealth production as a joint outcome of market and household sector activities.

Similar issues arise in the case of incorporated family businesses, though the legal context is quite different. Family members often have some formal rights of ownership or management in an incorporated business in the form of shares or appointments as directors or officers, whether or not they are actively involved in running the business. This is because tax law provides incentives to split corporate profits among a group of shareholders, while corporate law ensures that a dominant family member can nonetheless retain legal control through the creation of multiple classes of shares with different voting rights and through controlling appointments to the board of directors. *De facto* control is also ensured in many cases by the informal power dynamics of family life. Women have had some success invoking the shareholder remedies provided under corporate law statutes in order to protect their economic interests in the corporation against attempts by controlling male shareholders to limit their financial returns or their participation in management.[98] However, as in the partnership cases, their success seems to depend on showing a history of significant, direct contributions to the business operations, in addition to whatever domestic support they provided.[99]

Redesigning corporate and partnership laws to recognize the value of unpaid caregiving labour to a family business would present significant challenges. A case can be made to compensate this work by granting co-ownership or other rights to share in the financial returns of the business and, possibly, to participate in certain key decisions affecting its future. However, exposing such family members to all the financial risks associated with the business would be unfair in many cases if they have not participated equally in management decisions. The formal rights that wives may acquire as shareholders or directors often go unexercised in any substantive sense due to familial roles that are gendered and hierarchical. Yet, it is also problematic to assume that women are always subordinated within families. If the law attempts to protect women from the liabilities of family businesses, it may also limit their access to credit and their ability to assert legal rights and deal independently with their interests.[100] Law reform efforts in this area must be sensitive to, but also challenge, familial norms about who controls business assets.

Imposing shared ownership of family businesses would also have tax implications. It would permit income-splitting between spouses, which would reduce the tax burden of the family member who exercises *de facto* control over the business and would shift it to the other spouse. Indeed, the principle controller of a business often has shares issued to a spouse or otherwise asserts co-ownership precisely for this reason. The overall effect of allowing more income-splitting is to reduce the progressivity of the personal income tax and to impose tax liability on spouses for income over which they may not exercise real control. These would be troublesome side effects. However, it should be noted that spousal income-splitting is already quite freely available to taxpayers who own private corporations following the Supreme Court of Canada's ruling in *Neuman* v. *The Queen*[101] and the federal government's subsequent decision to counteract such income-splitting schemes legislatively only in relation to minor children and not spouses.[102] I am skeptical of the argument that allowing for unrestricted income-splitting for tax purposes will induce greater inter-spousal sharing of property in any *de facto* sense, as opposed to the transfer of formal title for purposes that are understood within the family to relate to tax planning only. However, permitting more income-splitting may be a tolerable side effect of redistributing property rights to caregiver spouses.

It is also important to think about what business law reforms might encourage large, widely held corporations to take more responsibility for fostering a new norm of work in which unpaid caregiving is valued and integrated with paid employment. Again, while stiffer employment standards are needed, there is also a need to review the law of corporate management. The role of corporate directors is still defined by the archaic mandate to act in the best interests of the corporation, almost always interpreted to mean the interests of shareholders in maximizing profits. There are many good reasons to expand the discretion of corporate managers, or perhaps even require them, to also take into account the interests of other constituencies, such as employees, as well as the longer-term interests of the corporation in securing a productive labour force, even at the expense of short-term shareholder interests. Certainly, corporate managers would still have to contend with the political power of shareholders and their ability to vote directors off the board. This political pressure could be diminished if a requirement for broader managerial vision was imposed on all directors by statute, rather than being left to the discretion of individual boards. By contrast, if the current regime of corporate governance is left in place, directors and officers can be counted upon to resist the improvement and implementation of employment standards and to provide little more than the minimum benefits of such legislation to employees. The scope for workers to participate in corporate management decisions could also be dramatically expanded. For example, there might be a requirement for employee representation on corporate boards or the right to ask questions or propose motions at shareholders' meetings. Reforming governance structures in this manner might be a means of overriding or at least controlling the shareholder bias of corporate managers. A final suggestion is to expand the potential for personal liability of directors, officers, and shareholders for breaches of employment standards or human rights laws.

### Personal Income Tax Law

Several tax issues have been raised earlier in the context of business deductions and the division of ownership rights in business assets. The tax system also has more general relevance as an instrument for the redistribution of income and wealth and as a mechanism for directing public support to particular groups or activities, including caregiving. Two provisions stand out in this regard: (1) the marital credit, for taxpayers who support a spouse or common law partner;[103] and (2) the caregiver credit, for taxpayers who reside with an elderly or infirm adult relative with a modest income.[104]

I have written elsewhere about the problems with the caregiver credit as a means of valuing women's unpaid labour.[105] Perhaps most seriously, the caregiver credit is non-refundable, so that a caregiver cannot claim the credit directly unless she or he has enough tax liability to absorb it. Where the primary caregiver does not work for pay, the credit can generally be claimed only by a breadwinner spouse on the assumption that the tax savings will somehow be used to improve the welfare of the caregiver. Similarly, the marital credit can be claimed only by the supporting spouse or partner, with no legal requirement to transfer the resulting tax savings to the low-income spouse or partner.

A restructuring of tax law to recognize caregiving as productive work would start by eliminating tax relief to breadwinners for supporting dependent partners. This change would help to increase taxation for those who have more substantial involvement in paid work, in keeping with the anti-free ride principle. This principle would also demand that public programs to support caregiving be financed by more progressive income taxes and wealth taxes on those who enjoy relatively higher levels of market success. The additional tax revenues raised through these initiatives could be used to finance income support for caregivers, through either refundable tax credits or direct transfers.[106] At a minimum, tax recognition for unpaid caregiving work will not advance equality interests unless it gives caregivers access to independent resources. For instance, the marital and caregiver credits could be replaced with refundable credits paid directly to individuals with little or no market income.[107] In addition, any tax relief for caregiving should not be restricted to those people who forego paid labour entirely. It should be available at some level to all those whose market opportunities are affected by unpaid caregiving responsibilities, to be used either for income support or to purchase replacement care services. This notion is consistent with the view that support for unpaid caregiving should be developed together with (but not placed in opposition to) better child care, training, and other employment-enabling measures. One other tax measure to consider is an income-averaging provision for those individuals re-entering, or increasing, paid work after a period of full- or part-time caregiving in order to ease the tax cost of wide fluctuations in income from year to year and especially the tax cost of re-entering paid labour.

**Family Law**
The flow of unpaid domestic services within families, predominantly from women (even when they are also engaged in paid labour), is one of the most obvious examples of how individuals and society as a whole free ride

on the work of caregivers. Yet family law is still reticent about recognizing the value of this subsidy to primary earners or entitling primary caregivers to share in the (indirect) market returns of their work. Williams explains that, as in Canada, the logic of US family law remains rooted in individual ownership.[108] The legal title to income or property earned through employment or other relations outside the family also determines its ownership inside the family. Thus, the major earner in a marriage, which is usually a man, initially obtains sole legal control over all, or at least the bulk, of the family resources that were in reality produced through the joint efforts of both spouses.[109] In Canada, it is then up to the non-owning spouse to make a claim for income support or property division under provincial or federal statutes dealing with marriage breakdown or sometimes under the common law of trusts.[110]

Williams argues that the effect of this modern system of family law is not dissimilar to the one-sided distribution of property rights that prevailed under the law of coverture, except that, in present times, the family's chief asset is generally human capital in the form of access to wage income. She develops a proposal for equalization of post-divorce incomes, based not any demonstrated need but rather on an automatic granting of joint property rights over the income stream available to the primary earner. This approach shifts the underlying justification for family sharing from one of altruism, duty, or need to one of entitlement, based on the economic value of unpaid care work. However, Williams's law reform recommendations are less transformative than her entitlement theory might suggest because they would grant a right to share the family wage only upon marriage breakdown and not while the marriage is ongoing.[111] This is not radically different from the rights currently created under provincial and federal family law statutes, although it might, in some cases, increase the amount and duration of income support payable on separation or divorce.

It is not clear why Williams declines to follow the principle of entitlement, which she articulates so powerfully, to its logical conclusion. It is difficult to see how family law can avoid the need to redistribute property rights during the life of a relationship and not just upon its breakdown. Giving a primary caregiver immediate legal control over a share of the income or property accumulated by a spouse would avoid the false view of families as realms of pure altruism and would better reflect the mixture of emotive and economic relationships that comprise family life. It might also reduce the incentives for many men to focus on market work to the exclusion of caregiving, thereby encouraging a less starkly gendered division of labour within families.

It must be remembered that family law cannot by itself provide adequate solutions to the exploitation of care work because it cannot increase the total amount of a family's income or wealth but only alter its distribution among the various members. The Achilles heel of family law has always been that it can do little or nothing for the large number of families who have inadequate incomes and little or no wealth or for the single adults with no spouse or former spouse against whom to make family law claims. This is the reason why Margrit Eichler, for example, insists that family law reforms must be combined with state-provided financial support for all low-income families and all lone parents.[112] It also underlines the need to regulate employment and other market relations and institutions to ensure they are bearing an appropriate share of the costs of social reproduction.

## Conclusion

As the issue of job–family conflict has become more pressing in the daily lives of Canadians, governments and firms have begun experimenting with a wide mixture of programs and reforms intended to help balance the competing demands on people's time and energy. These initiatives have proliferated across the diverse areas of law, policy, and corporate practice, often with little attempt to coordinate or rationalize their precise objectives and design features and with little follow up to determine their effectiveness. At the same time, policy makers continue to adopt a narrowly market-based view of economic relations, contributing further to the escalating tension between paid employment and unpaid caregiving.

   This essay has attempted to step back from the barrage of rhetoric about "family-friendly" policies to examine the underlying dynamics that produce job/family conflict. Recent theoretical advances in feminist political economy offer a way to reconceptualize paid and unpaid work as mutually interdependent rather than as fundamentally conflicted, and I have suggested that this revised model of economic relations could inform the development of legal and policy reforms. Drawing on this model, the essay suggests a principled approach to reform that could be applied across different substantive areas of law. The anti-free ride and integration principles are aimed to replace the gendered identities of caregiver and breadwinner with a unified image of the worker, as someone who crosses the market, household, and state sectors, undertaking both paid and unpaid responsibilities. Applying these principles in some key legal fields reveals the need for fundamental reforms if caregiving is to be taken seriously as a valued activity as well as the need for more detailed analysis of specific legal regimes. While the breadth and depth of this agenda should not discourage policy-makers from embarking on modest reforms in specific areas, it will hopefully show that recent family-friendly policy innovations are merely a beginning and do not yet approach a full solution to the tensions between employment and caregiving.

## Notes

1 F.E. Olsen, "The Family and the Market: A Study of Ideology and Legal Reform" (1983) 96 Harv. L. Rev. 1497.
2 See A. Picchio, "Wages as a Reflection of Socially Embedded Production and Reproduction Processes," in L. Clarke, P. de Gijsel, and J. Janssen, eds., *The Dynamics of Wage Relations in the New Europe* (London: Kluwer Academic Publishers, 1999), 195 at 198.
3 N. Fraser, *Justice Interruptus: Critical Reflections on the "Postsocialist" Condition* (New York and London: Routledge, 1997) at 61.
4 See, for example, R. Beaujot, *Earning and Caring in Canadian Families* (Toronto: Broadview Press, 2000) at 323-56; M. Eichler, *Family Shifts: Families, Policies, and Gender Equality* (Toronto, New York, and Oxford: Oxford University Press, 1997) at 147-64; N. Iyer, "Some Mothers Are Better Than Others: A Re-examination of Maternity Benefits," in S. Boyd, ed., *Challenging the Public/Private Divide: Feminism, Law and Public Policy* (Toronto: University of Toronto Press, 1997), 168.
5 N. Folbre, "The Unproductive Housewife: Her Evolution in Nineteenth-Century Economic Thought" (1991) 16(3) Signs 463.
6 A. Picchio, *Social Reproduction: The Political Economy of the Labour Market* (Cambridge: Cambridge University Press, 1992), ch. 1.
7 I. Bakker and D. Elson, "Towards Engendering Budgets," in *Alternative Federal Budget Papers 1998* (Ottawa: Canadian Centre for Policy Alternatives and CHO!CES: A Coalition for Social Justice, 1998), 297 at 310.
8 Manitoba-born economist Margaret Gilpin Reid is generally acknowledged as the pioneer. On the centenary of her birth, the journal *Feminist Economics* published a special issue on unpaid work. See N. Folbre, "Introduction" (1996) 2(3) Feminist Economics ix.
9 See D. Elson, "The Economic, the Political and the Domestic: Businesses, States and Households in the Organisation of Production" (1998) 3(2) New Political Economy 189.
10 *Ibid.* at 200.
11 United Nations Development Program, *Human Development Report 1999* (New York: Oxford University Press, 1999) at 79.
12 M.A. Fineman, "Cracking the Foundational Myths: Independence, Autonomy, and Self-Sufficiency" (2000) 8 Am. U. J. Gender & L. 13 at 23-24.
13 A. Crittenden, *The Price of Motherhood: Why the Most Important Job in the World is Still the Least Valued* (New York: Henry Holt and Company, 2001) at 7. Crittenden states in a footnote that she uses "mother" to mean "anyone who is the primary caregiver of another person" (at 275, note 1). Although the book is well researched and compelling in many respects, her analysis is weakened by the suggestion that caregiving expectations compromise market access only for a subset of women who have family responsibilities as obvious and consuming as motherhood.
14 Elson, *supra* note 9. See also Bakker and Elson, *supra* note 7. For a discussion of other attempts to remodel the economy to include household production, see M. Waring, *If Women Counted: A New Feminist Economics* (New York: Harper Collins, 1988) at 299-304.
15 Elson, *supra* note 9 at 195.
16 *Ibid.* at 203.
17 Picchio, *supra* note 2 at 210.
18 For example, one study found a pattern of counter-cyclical increases in household food preparation versus restaurant meals during times of economic recession when market incomes dropped: R. Colman, *The Economic Value of Unpaid Housework and Child Care in Nova Scotia* (Halifax: GPI Atlantic, 1998) at 54-57.
19 R. Colman's data, for example, reveal an increase in the total workload of women and an absolute decline in leisure time, with corresponding high levels of stress. *Ibid.* at 6; and R. Colman, *The Economic Value of Civic and Voluntary Work in Nova Scotia* (Halifax: GPI Atlantic, 1998) at 25 and 26.
20 I. Bakker, "Deconstructing Macro-economics through a Feminist Lens," in J. Brodie, ed., *Women and Canadian Public Policy* (Toronto: Harcourt Brace, 1996), 31.
21 See J. Fudge, "Flexibility and Feminization: The New Ontario Employment Standards Act" (2001) 16 Journal of Law and Social Policy 1 at 7-9.

22  D. Elson, *Gender Budget Initiative: Background Papers* (London: Commonwealth Secretariat, 1999) at 8.

23  See L.F. Vosko, *Temporary Work: The Gendered Rise of a Precarious Employment Relationship* (Toronto: University of Toronto Press, 2000) at 159-63.

24  J. Williams, "Market Work and Family Work in the Twenty-First Century" (1999) 44 Vill. L. Rev. 305 at 311.

25  The recent growth of both poverty and income inequality in Canada is analyzed in A. Heisz, A. Jackson, and G. Picot, "Distributional Outcomes in Canada in the 1990s," in K. Banting, A. Sharpe, and F. St-Hilaire, eds., *The Review of Economic Performance and Social Progress: The Longest Decade: Canada in the 1990s* (Montreal and Ottawa: Institute for Research on Public Policy and Centre for the Study of Living Standards, 2001), 247.

26  See Vosko, *supra* note 23 at 190-96.

27  See J. Williams, *Unbending Gender: Why Work and Family Conflict and What to Do about It* (New York: Oxford University Press, 2000) at 162-68.

28  See L. Beneria, "The Enduring Debate over Unpaid Labour" (1999) International Labour Review 287; M. Luxton, "The UN, Women, and Household Labour: Measuring and Valuing Unpaid Work" (1997) 20(3) Women's Studies International Forum 431; and M. Luxton and L.F. Vosko, "Where Women's Efforts Count: The 1996 Census Campaign and 'Family Politics' in Canada" (1998) 56 Studies in Political Economy 49.

29  Statistics Canada, *Women in Canada 2000* (Ottawa: Minister of Industry, 2000) at 97. Colman breaks the data down by province and finds that the ratio of unpaid-to-paid work is higher in provinces with lower rates of employment. Colman, *supra* note 18 at 48-49.

30  Statistics Canada, *supra* note 29.

31  *Ibid.* Explanations for the persistence of this gendered division of labour despite changes in women's legal and social status tend to include a mix of social, attitudinal, economic, psychological, and biological factors. See Beaujot, *supra* note 4 at 54-81.

32  Statistics Canada, *supra* note 29.

33  W. Clark, *Economic Gender Equality Indicators 2000* (Status of Women Canada, 2000) at 4-5, available at <http://www.swc-cfc.gc.ca/pubs/egei2000/egei2000_e.pdf> (accessed February 2002). This study showed that the gender disparity in total working hours per day varied significantly by age, with younger women aged fifteen to twenty-four and senior women experiencing the greatest inequality, and women ages forty-five to fifty-four experiencing near equality.

34  Statistics Canada, *supra* note 29 at 111-12.

35  See I. Bakker, *Unpaid Work and Macroeconomics: New Discussions, New Tools for Action* (Ottawa: Status of Women Canada, 1998).

36  D. Rutherford, *Routledge Dictionary of Economics* (London and New York: Routledge, 1995) at 181.

37  Picchio, *supra* note 2 at 211.

38  Bakker, *supra* note 35 at 16.

39  N. Folbre, *The Invisible Heart: Economics and Family Values* (New York: New Press, 2001) at 50-51.

40  The integration principle echoes the general approach of some other scholars, although concrete policy prescriptions often diverge. See, for example, Beaujot, *supra* note 4 at 351-56; Eichler, *supra* note 4 at 147-49 (Eichler's social responsibility model of the family); Fraser, *supra* note 3 at 60-62 (Fraser's "universal caregiver" model of social and economic policy); and Joan Williams, "Toward a Reconstructive Feminism: Reconstructing the Relationship of Market Work and Family Work" (1998) 19 N. Ill. U. L. Rev. 89 at 95 (Joan Williams's proposal for a "'reconstructive feminism' which calls for the elimination of the ideal-worker norm in market work and in family entitlements").

41  See O.S. Mitchell, "Work and Family Benefits," in F.D. Blau and R.G. Ehrenberg, eds., *Gender and Family Issues in the Workplace* (New York: Russell Sage Foundation, 1997), 269.

42  Colman, *supra* note 18 at 30.

43  See L. Philipps, "Tax Law and Social Reproduction: The Gender of Fiscal Policy in an Age of Privatization," in B. Cossman and J. Fudge, eds., *Privatization, Law and the Challenge to Feminism* (Toronto: University of Toronto Press, forthcoming).

44   Williams, "Toward a Reconstructive Feminism," *supra* note 40 at 89.

45   Statistics Canada, *supra* note 29 at 110.

46   See, for example, S. Himmelweit, "The Discovery of Unpaid Work: The Social Consequences of the Expansion of Work" (1995) 1(2) Feminist Economics 1, cited in Beneria, *supra* note 28 at 302.

47   *Ibid.* at 303.

48   See, for example, N. Folbre, "'Holding Hands at Midnight': The Paradox of Caring Labor" (1995) 1(1) Feminist Economics 73 at 85-87.

49   Picchio, *supra* note 2 at 210.

50   B.R. Bergmann, "Subsidizing Child Care by Mothers at Home" (2000) 6(1) Feminist Economics 77 at 81-82.

51   Bergmann, "Work-Family Policies and Equality between Women and Men," in Blau and Ehrenberg, eds., *supra* note 41 at 278.

52   See Philipps, *supra* note 43.

53   Beneria, *supra* note 28 at 301-2. Bergmann herself seems to accept that family-friendly policies could be redesigned to promote, rather than to undermine, gender equality (see her proposals for reforming parental leave in work-family policies, Bergmann, "Work-Family Policies," *supra* note 51 at 278-79).

54   M. Condon, "Limited by Law? Gender, Corporate Law, and the Family Firm," in D. Chunn and D. Lacombe, eds., *Law as a Gendering Practice* (Don Mills, ON: Oxford University Press Canada, 2000), 181 at 189.

55   See, for example, M.J. Mossman, "'Running Hard to Stand Still': The Paradox of Family Law Reform" (1994) 17(1) Dalhousie L.J. 5; and M.J. Mossman and M. Maclean, "Family Law and Social Assistance Programs: Rethinking Equality," in P.M. Evans and G.R. Wekerle, eds., *Women and the Canadian Welfare State: Challenges and Change* (Toronto: University of Toronto Press, 1997), 117.

56   See Berna J. Skrypnek and Janet E. Fast, "Work and Family Policy in Canada: Family Needs, Collective Solutions" (1996) 17(6) Journal of Family Issues 793 at 808. For a discussion of the reasons why employers may voluntarily institute policies to accommodate employees' caregiving roles, see M.B. Neal et. al., *Balancing Work and Caregiving for Children, Adults, and Elders* (Newbury Park, London, New Delhi: Sage Publications, 1993) at 7-11. For a detailed study of family-friendly provisions in collective agreements, see C.P. Rochon, ed., *Work and Family Provisions in Canadian Collective Agreements* (Hull, QC: Human Resources Development Canada, Labour Program, 2000), available at <http://labour-travail.hrdc-drhc.gc.ca/worklife/collective_agreement1/presentation_en.html> (accessed 9 February 2003).

57   See, for example, J. Fudge, "Fragmentation and Feminization: The Challenge of Equity for Labour-Relations Policy," in J. Brodie, ed., *Women and Canadian Public Policy* (Toronto: Harcourt Brace and Company, 1996), 57 at 63-65; and Vosko, *supra* note 23 at ch. 5.

58   J. Fudge and L. Vosko, "By Whose Standards? Reregulating the Canadian Labour Market" (2001) 22 Economic and Industrial Democracy 327 at 331.

59   See B.R. Bergmann, *The Economic Emergence of Women* (New York: Basic Books, 1986) at 306-7; A. Duffy, N. Mandell, and N. Pupo, *Few Choices: Women, Work and Family* (Toronto: Garamond Press, 1989), ch. 4; A. Duffy and N. Pupo, "Family-Friendly Organizations and Beyond: Proposals for Policy Directions with Women in Mind," in *Family Security in Insecure Times: National Forum on Family Security* (Ottawa: Canadian Council on Social Development, 1996) at 4-6; and J. Jenson, "Part-Time Employment and Women: A Range of Strategies," in I. Bakker, ed., *Rethinking Restructuring: Gender and Change in Canada* (Toronto: University of Toronto Press, 1996), 92.

60   Statistics Canada, *supra* note 29 at 103 and 104.

61   A few collective agreements contain provisions allowing employees to apply for reduced hours of work for a period of time (for example, two years), but these are generally subject to employer approval. See Rochon, *supra* note 56 at 30.

62   *Employment Standards Act*, 2000, S.O. 2000, c. 41 [hereinafter *ESA*]. See Fudge, *supra* note 21.

63   *ESA*, *supra* note 62 at ss. 48-50.

64 Fudge, *supra* note 62 at 19.
65 *An Act Respecting Labour Standards,* R.S.Q. 2000, c. N-1.1 at s. 41.1.
66 Saskatchewan Labour Standards Branch, "Toward a Reconstructive Feminism," *Rights and Responsibilities: A Guide to Labour Standards in Saskatchewan* (Saskatoon: Saskatchewan Labour Standards Branch, undated) at 17-19.
67 International Labour Organization, Convention no. C175, 1994 (in force as of 28 February 1998).
68 Amy Willard Cross, "Dutch Treat," *Chatelaine* (November 2001), 135 at 138.
69 See Beaujot, *supra* note 4 at 353.
70 See Fudge and Vosko, *supra* note 58 at 342; C.P. Rochon, *supra* note 56 at xix.
71 K.D. Hughes, *Gender and Self-Employment in Canada: Assessing Trends and Policy Implications* (Ottawa: Canadian Policy Research Networks, 1999) at 13. Hughes's study draws on labour force data from Statistics Canada, which defines "self-employment" to include working owners of both incorporated and unincorporated businesses, whether or not they employ paid help, as well as unpaid family members who work in a family business (at 9-10).
72 *Ibid.*
73 *Ibid.* at 4.
74 *Ibid.* at 6.
75 *Ibid.*
76 *Ibid.* at 14-16. See also Statistics Canada, *supra* note 29 at 104.
77 Statistics Canada, *supra* note 29 at 228.
78 In 1997, only one-quarter of self-employed women had employees or were incorporated, compared to the 41 percent of men who had employees and the 39.4 percent of men who were incorporated. See Hughes, *supra* note 71 at 16. Reasons for the gap in incorporation rates are unclear but could include differences in the size of enterprises or their profitability (money-losing small businesses may prefer to remain unincorporated for tax reasons), the amount of personal assets vulnerable to creditors, business, or administrative experience, access to professional advice, or time to attend to organizational matters.
79 *Ibid.* at 22-23.
80 *Ibid.* at 4 (based on 1995 data). The desire for flexible schedules was also cited more often by women (9.2 percent) than by men (4.4 percent).
81 M. Belcourt, R.J. Burke, and H. Lee-Gosselin, *The Glass Box: Women Business Owners in Canada* (Ottawa: Canadian Advisory Council on the Status of Women, 1991) at 39.
82 Hughes, *supra* note 71 at 24. Significantly, even these figures are understated because they do not include those individuals with negative incomes due to business losses (at 28).
83 *Ibid.*
84 *Ibid.* at 24 and 25.
85 See Belcourt et. al., *supra* note 81.
86 Fudge and Vosko, *supra* note 58 at 334-36.
87 *Ibid.* at 335.
88 *Ibid.* at 337-38.
89 *Ibid.* at 342-47.
90 *Income Tax Act,* R.S.C. 1985 (5th Supp.), c. 1, as am., s. 18(12)(a) [hereinafter *ITA*]. Such expenses could include a portion of rent, mortgage interest, utilities, insurance, fax or phone lines, renovations, repairs, and furnishings. A parallel rule applies to employees who maintain a home work space (s. 8(13)).
91 It is also horizontally inequitable in that it arbitrarily distinguishes among businesses that involve regular personal meetings or consultations with those purchasing the good or service rather than simply providing a deliverable or communicating over the telephone or electronically.
92 Section 63 of the *ITA, supra* note 90, generally allows a taxpayer to deduct up to $7,000 annually for child care expenses incurred to enable the taxpayer to perform employment duties, carry on a business, or engage in certain educational or research activities, provided that the amount deducted cannot exceed two-thirds of the taxpayer's income for the year. The *ITA* also allows certain deductions and credits for the cost of nursing or full-time

attendant care for people who are infirm or have a disability. See s. 64 and s. 118.2 of the *ITA*, and the discussion and critique in D.G. Duff, "Disability and the Income Tax" (2000) 4 McGill L.J. 797, esp. at 809-23 and 858.

93   See Duff, *supra* note 92 at 855.

94   See C.F.L. Young, *Women, Tax and Social Programs: The Gendered Impact of Funding Social Programs through the Tax System* (Ottawa: Status of Women Canada, 2000) at 19-32.

95   A recent study reported that of all those families with child care expenses in 1996, less than one-third claimed the child care expense deduction. C. Freiler, F. Stairs, and B. Kitchen with J. Cerny, *Mothers as Earners, Mothers as Carers: Responsibility for Children, Social Policy and the Tax System* (Ottawa: Status of Women Canada, 2001) at 51.

96   See J. Cassels and L. Philipps, "Why Lawyers Need Statistics on Unpaid Work," in Statistics Canada, *International Conference on the Measurement and Valuation of Unpaid Work: Proceedings* (Ottawa: Minister of Industry, Science and Technology, 1994), 41 at 54-55.

97   See, for example, *Beaudoin-Daigneault* v. *Richard*, [1984] 1 S.C.R. 2; *Berg* v. *Berg*, 82 D.T.C. 1571 (T.R.B.); and *Romas* v. *Romas*, [1949] 4 D.L.R. 423 (Man. C.A.), which are all discussed in Cassels and Philipps, *supra* note 96.

98   For an analysis of these cases, see M. Condon, *supra* note 54 at 192-96.

99   See, for example, *Godinek* v. *Godinek* (1992), 40 R.F.L. (3d) 78 (O.C.J.), discussed in Cassels and Philipps, *supra* note 96.

100  See Condon, *supra* note 54, at 191-92.

101  *Neuman* v. *The Queen*, 98 D.T.C. 6297 (S.C.C.).

102  Following *Neuman*, *supra* note 101, the government introduced the so-called "kiddie tax," which imposes tax at the highest marginal rate on minors who receive certain private corporation dividends or income from business via a partnership or trust. See *ITA*, *supra* note 90 at s. 120.4, as am. by S.C. 2000, c. 19. s. 30; and A. Macnaughton and T. Matthews, "Is the Income-Splitting Tax Needed? Some Empirical Evidence" (1999) 47(5) Canadian Tax Journal 1164.

103  *ITA*, *supra* note 90 at s. 118(1)(a). The marital credit reduces federal tax payable by a maximum of 16 percent x $6,294 in 2001, if the spouse or common law partner's income does not exceed $629.

104  *Ibid.* at s. 118(1) (c.1). The caregiver credit was introduced in 1998 and its value increased in the October 2000 mini-budget. It reduces federal tax payable by a maximum of 16 percent x $3,500, where the adult relative's income does not exceed $11,953.

105  See Philipps, *supra* note 43; and L. Philipps, "Taxing the Market Citizen: Fiscal Policy and Inequality in an Age of Privatization" (2000) 63(4) Law and Contemporary Problems 111 at 127-31.

106  For a discussion and comparison of refundable tax credits and direct transfers, see L. Philipps, "Disability, Poverty and the Income Tax: The Case for Refundable Credits" (2001) 16 J.L. & Social Pol'y 77 at 80-96.

107  See Eichler, *supra* note 4 at 161-62.

108  See Williams, *Unbending Gender*, *supra* note 27 at 114-41; and J. Williams, "Is Coverture Dead? Beyond a New Theory of Alimony" (1994) 82(4) Geo. L.J. 2227.

109  Williams, *Unbending Gender*, *supra* note 27 at 114-16; and "Is Coverture Dead?," *supra* note 108 at 2248-53.

110  Rights under statutory family law vary depending on the jurisdiction concerned as well as the status of the former couple as legally married, opposite-sex common law partners, or same-sex common law partners.

111  Williams, "Is Coverture Dead?," *supra* note 108 at 2263.

112  Eichler, *supra* note 4 at 155-56.

## Bibliography

### Jurisprudence
*Beaudoin-Daigneault* v. *Richard*, [1984] 1 S.C.R. 2.
*Berg* v. *Berg*, 82 D.T.C. 1571 (T.R.B.).
*Godinek* v. *Godinek* (1992), 40 R.F.L. (3d) 78 (O.C.J.).

*Neuman v. The Queen*, [1998] 1 S.C.R. 770, 98 D.T.C. 6297 (S.C.C.).
*Romas v. Romas*, [1949] 4 D.L.R. 423 (Man. C.A.).

## Legislation
*An Act Respecting Labour Standards*, R.S.Q. 2000, c. N-1.1.
*Employment Standards Act*, S.O. 2000, c. 41.
*Income Tax Act*, R.S.C. 1985 (5th Supp.), c. 1, as am.
*Part-Time Work Convention*, 1994, ILO Convention no. C175 (entered into force 28 February 1998).

## Books and Articles
Bakker, I., "Deconstructing Macro-Economics through a Feminist Lens," in J. Brodie, ed., *Women and Canadian Public Policy* (Toronto: Harcourt Brace, 1996).
—, *Unpaid Work and Macroeconomics: New Discussions, New Tools for Action* (Ottawa: Status of Women Canada, 1998).
—, and D. Elson, "Towards Engendering Budgets," in *Alternative Federal Budget Papers* (Ottawa: Canadian Centre for Policy Alternatives, 1998).
Beaujot, R., *Earning and Caring in Canadian Families* (Toronto: Broadview Press, 2000).
Belcourt, M., R.J. Burke, and H. Lee-Gosselin, *The Glass Box: Women Business Owners in Canada* (Ottawa: Canadian Advisory Council on the Status of Women, 1991).
Beneria, L., "The Enduring Debate over Unpaid Labour" (1999) International Labour Review 287.
Bergmann, B.R., *The Economic Emergence of Women* (New York: Basic Books, 1986).
—, "Subsidizing Child Care by Mothers at Home" (2000) 6(1) Feminist Economics 77.
Cassels, J., and L. Philipps, "Why Lawyers Need Statistics on Unpaid Work," in Statistics Canada, *International Conference on the Measurement and Valuation of Unpaid Work* (Ottawa: Minister of Industry, Science and Technology, 1994).
Clark, W., *Economic Gender Equality Indicators 2000* (Canada: Status of Women Canada, 2000).
Colman, R., *The Economic Value of Civic and Voluntary Work in Nova Scotia* (Halifax: GPI Atlantic, 1998).
—, *The Economic Value of Unpaid Housework and Child Care in Nova Scotia* (Halifax: GPI Atlantic, 1998).
Condon, M., "Limited by Law? Gender, Corporate Law, and the Family Firm," in D. Chunn and D. Lacombe, eds., *Law as a Gendering Practice* (Don Mills, ON: Oxford University Press Canada, 2000), 181.
Crittenden, A., *The Price of Motherhood: Why the Most Important Job in the World Is Still the Least Valued* (New York: Henry Holt and Company, 2001).
Cross, A.W., "Dutch Treat," *Chatelaine* (November 2001) at 135.
Duff, D.G., "Disability and the Income Tax" (2000) 4 McGill L.J. 797.
Duffy, A., and N. Pupo, "Family-Friendly Organizations and Beyond: Proposals for Policy Directions with Women in Mind," in *Family Security in Insecure Times: National Forum on Family Security* (Ottawa: Canadian Council on Social Development, 1996).
—, and N. Mandell, *Few Choices: Women, Work and Family* (Toronto: Garamond Press, 1989).
Eichler, M., *Family Shifts: Families, Policies, and Gender Equality* (Toronto, New York, Oxford: Oxford University Press, 1997).
Elson, D., "The Economic, the Political and the Domestic: Businesses, States and Households in the Organisation of Production" (1998) 3(2) New Political Economy 189.
—, Gender Budget Initiative: Background Papers (London: Commonwealth Secretariat, 1999).
Fineman, M.A., "Cracking the Foundational Myths: Independence, Autonomy, and Self-Sufficiency" (2000) 8 Am. U. J. Gender & L. 13.
Folbre, N., "'Holding Hands at Midnight': The Paradox of Caring Labor" (1995) 1(1) Feminist Economics 73.
—, "Introduction" (1996) 2(3) Feminist Economics ix.
—, *The Invisible Heart: Economics and Family Values* (New York: New Press, 2001).

—, "The Unproductive Housewife: Her Evolution in Nineteenth-Century Economic Thought" (1991) 16(3) Signs 463.

Fraser, N., *Justice Interruptus: Critical Reflections on the "Postsocialist" Condition* (New York and London: Routledge, 1997).

Freiler, C., F. Stairs, and B. Kitchen, with J. Cerny, *Mothers as Earners, Mothers as Carers: Responsibility for Children, Social Policy and the Tax System* (Ottawa: Status of Women Canada, 2001).

Fudge, J. and L. Vosko, "By Whose Standards? Reregulating the Canadian Labour Market" (2001) 22 Economic and Industrial Democracy 327.

Fudge, J., "Flexibility and Feminization: The New Ontario Employment Standards Act" (2001) 16 Journal of Law and Social Policy 1.

—, "Fragmentation and Feminization: The Challenge of Equity for Labour-Relations Policy," in J. Brodie, ed., *Women and Canadian Public Policy* (Toronto: Harcourt Brace and Company, 1996), 57.

Heisz, A., A. Jackson, and G. Picot, "Distributional Outcomes in Canada in the 1990s," in K. Banting, A. Sharpe, and F. St-Hilaire, eds., *The Review of Economic Performance and Social Progress: The Longest Decade: Canada in the 1990s* (Montreal and Ottawa: Institute for Research on Public Policy and Centre for the Study of Living Standards, 2001), 247.

Himmelweit, S., "The Discovery of Unpaid Work: The Social Consequences of the Expansion of Work" (1995) 1(2) Feminist Economics 1.

Hughes, K.D., *Gender and Self-employment in Canada: Assessing Trends and Policy Implications* (Ottawa: Canadian Policy Research Networks, 1999).

Iyer, N., "Some Mothers Are Better Than Others: A Re-examination of Maternity Benefits," in S. Boyd, ed., *Challenging the Public/Private Divide: Feminism, Law and Public Policy* (Toronto: University of Toronto Press, 1997), 168.

Jenson, J., "Part-Time Employment and Women: A Range of Strategies," in I. Bakker, ed., *Rethinking Restructuring: Gender and Change in Canada* (Toronto: University of Toronto Press, 1996), 92.

Luxton, M., "The UN, Women, and Household Labour: Measuring and Valuing Unpaid Work" (1997) 20(3) Women's Studies International Forum 431.

—, and L.F. Vosko, "Where Women's Efforts Count: The 1996 Census Campaign and 'Family Politics' in Canada" (1998) 56 Studies in Political Economy 49.

Macnaughton, A. and T. Matthews, "Is the Income-Splitting Tax Needed? Some Empirical Evidence" (1999) 47(5) Canadian Tax Journal 1164.

Mitchell, O.S., "Work and Family Benefits," in F.D. Blau and R.G. Ehrenberg, eds., *Gender and Family Issues in the Workplace* (New York: Russell Sage Foundation, 1997) 269.

Mossman, M.J. and M. Maclean, "Family Law and Social Assistance Programs: Rethinking Equality," in P.M. Evans and G.R. Wekerle, eds., *Women and the Canadian Welfare State: Challenges and Change* (Toronto: University of Toronto Press, 1997), 117.

—, "'Running Hard to Stand Still': The Paradox of Family Law Reform" (1994) 17(1) Dalhousie L.J. 5.

Neal, M.B. et. al., *Balancing Work and Caregiving for Children, Adults, and Elders* (Newbury Park, London, and New Delhi: Sage Publications, 1993).

Olsen, F.E., "The Family and the Market: A Study of Ideology and Legal Reform" (1983) 96 Harv. L. Rev. 1497.

Philipps, L., "Disability, Poverty and the Income Tax: The Case for Refundable Credits" (2001) 16 J.L. & Soc. Pol'y 77.

—, "Tax Law and Social Reproduction: The Gender of Fiscal Policy in an Age of Privatization," in B. Cossman and J. Fudge, eds., *Privatization, Law and the Challenge to Feminism* (Toronto: University of Toronto Press, forthcoming).

—, "Taxing the Market Citizen: Fiscal Policy and Inequality in an Age of Privatization" (2000) 63(4) Law & Contemp. Probs. 111.

Picchio, A., *Social Reproduction: The Political Economy of the Labour Market* (Cambridge: Cambridge University Press, 1992).

—, "Wages as a Reflection of Socially Embedded Production and Reproduction Processes," in L. Clarke, P. de Gijsel, and J. Janssen, eds., *The Dynamics of Wage Relations in the New Europe* (London: Kluwer Academic Publishers, 1999).

Rochon, C.P., ed., *Work and Family Provisions in Canadian Collective Agreements* (Hull, QC: Human Resources Development Canada, Labour Program, 2000), available at <http://labour-travail.hrdc-drhc.gc.ca/worklife/collective_agreement1/presentation_en.html> (accessed 9 February 2003).

Rutherford, D., *Routledge Dictionary of Economics* (London and New York: Routledge, 1995).

Saskatchewan Labour Standards Branch, *Rights and Responsibilities: A Guide to Labour Standards in Saskatchewan* (Saskatoon: Saskatchewan Labour Standards Branch, undated).

Skrypnek, B.J. and Janet E. Fast, "Work and Family Policy in Canada: Family Needs, Collective Solutions" (1996) 17(6) Journal of Family Issues 793.

Statistics Canada, *Women in Canada 2000* (Ottawa: Minister of Industry, 2000).

United Nations Development Program, *Human Development Report 1999* (New York: Oxford University Press, 1999).

Vosko, L.F., *Temporary Work: The Gendered Rise of a Precarious Employment Relationship* (Toronto: University of Toronto Press, 2000).

Waring, M., *If Women Counted: A New Feminist Economics* (New York: Harper Collins, 1988).

Williams, J., "Is Coverture Dead? Beyond a New Theory of Alimony" (1994) 82(4) Geo. L.J. 2227.

—, "Market Work and Family Work in the Twenty-First Century" (1999) 44 Vill. L. Rev. 305.

—, "Toward a Reconstructive Feminism: Reconstructing the Relationship of Market Work and Family Work" (1998) 19 N. Ill. U. L. Rev. 89.

—, *Unbending Gender: Why Work and Family Conflict and What to Do about It* (New York: Oxford University Press, 2000).

Young, C.F.L., *Women, Tax and Social Programs: The Gendered Impact of Funding Social Programs through the Tax System* (Ottawa: Status of Women Canada, 2000).

# 2

# Private Needs and Public Space: Politics, Poverty, and Anti-Panhandling By-Laws in Canadian Cities

*Damian Collins and Nicholas Blomley*

"Panhandle" means to beg for or, without consideration, ask for money, donations, goods or other things of value whether by spoken, written or printed word or bodily gesture for one's self or for any other person.

— City of Vancouver, *A By-law to Regulate and Control Panhandling*, no. 7885 (30 April 1998)

Panhandling – the act of begging for money and other things of value – closely resembles an economic or "market" activity of the sort that has occupied the heart of the private realm within much liberal thought. It shares many of the characteristics of commercial advertising, requests for charitable donations, and street theatre.[1] Yet, in the context of Canadian cities, this act has increasingly become subject to prohibitive public regulation in the form of by-laws restricting when, where, and how it can occur. This essay asks why such regulation is occurring.

The widespread adoption of anti-panhandling by-laws can be interpreted as part of the purification of public space in North America – a trend that has entailed the removal of the poor and homeless from public view. In the United States, municipal regulations outlawing camping, sleeping, begging, sitting, and "loitering" in public space have proliferated. In Canada, city lawmakers and the representatives of local capital have focused on circumscribing panhandling and the behaviour of "squeegee kids." The imposition of strict controls on street-level requests for spare change points not only to a blurring of the distinction between public and private space but also to the question of what "counts" as a private economic transaction. As we suggest, there is a long history of anxiety about "poor people's money" – in the form of wages, no matter how meagre, as well as in the form of public and private relief – which has prompted various forms of regulation. The assumptions of rationality and trustworthiness that underlie the "private" market economy of classical liberal theory have seldom been extended to the poor.

There appears to be considerable irony in the contemporary criminalization of panhandling. This stems in part from the typically small sums of money that are exchanged. As I. McIntosh and A. Erskine note in the British context, "ten pence dropped in the street as you rush for a bus or a 20p coin sucked into a vacuum cleaner will give little cause for concern for most people but this is generally not the case when being asked for similar amounts from a stranger on the street."[2] The begging encounter in Western cities tends to generate anxieties that initially seem completely disproportionate with the request for "small change."

In addition to their impact on economic transactions, anti-panhandling by-laws have been seen to curtail certain types of private expression. They do so by diminishing the time, place, and manner in which one class of people – the poor and disenfranchised – can communicate most directly their concerns, namely the need for assistance, to members of a broader public. Accordingly, a number of court challenges have argued that such regulations violate the freedom of expression guaranteed by section 2 of the *Canadian Charter of Rights and Freedoms*.[3] Considerable energy has been devoted to establishing that begging is, in fact, a form of expression – as opposed to simply being a form of conduct, or perhaps even misconduct, characterized by "fraud and duress"[4] – and that its prohibition cannot be demonstrably justified under section 1 of the *Charter*. Analogous arguments have been made in the United States, where H. Hershkoff and A.S. Cohen have contended that circumscribing the speech of beggars denies them a "most basic level of recognition" and requires "not only that they must suffer, but also that they will be punished for making direct requests for help."[5]

In this essay, we seek to move beyond the relatively well-established debates about whether begging is or is not a constitutionally protected form of expression. While we have elsewhere supported the argument that anti-panhandling by-laws violate *Charter* rights to speech,[6] we are cognizant of the limitations inherent in such an approach. First, as a result of the way the *Charter* isolates particular rights, speech tends to be treated in isolation. While panhandling is certainly about speech in the broader sense, it is not reducible to it. Other important interpretations, such as the social meanings of money, are also at issue, as we seek to demonstrate in this essay. Second, a focus on speech tends to detach the panhandling encounter from the spaces in which it occurs.[7] Our goal therefore is to spatialize anti-panhandling by-laws, with particular reference to downtown public space, in order to demonstrate that if we want to make sense of such regulations, we need to know something of the dynamic, material contexts in which they are adopted and enforced. In so doing, we hope to contribute to the emergent literature on law and geography.[8]

We begin by detailing the characteristics and status of anti-panhandling by-laws within Canada. We then ask what is so objectionable about panhandling that the practice merits prohibitive regulation. The answer, it is suggested, lies in the fact that it entails *monetary* transactions, involves *poor people*, and occurs in *public space*. To appreciate why panhandling has become such a target for public regulation, it is necessary to undertake a theoretically informed consideration of each of these dimensions. We conclude with a discussion of the implications of anti-panhandling by-laws for the contemporary meaning and redefinition of the public and private spheres in Canadian cities.

It seems clear that it is not requests for money *per se* that cities are worried about, for to walk down the street is to be bombarded with demands for money – in the form of corporate advertising, for example – that are seldom considered problematic, let alone subject to criminal prohibition. Rather, concern appears to centre on the *messenger* – the unsightly and untrustworthy beggar whose presence in public space may variously annoy, frustrate, and disconcert. The physical presence of the homeless and destitute begging for alms on the street is a stark and very public reminder of social marginalization and economic polarization, which potentially undermines carefully crafted urban images.

Yet, at the same time, there is a long-standing anxiety about whether beggars are in fact as marginalized and destitute as they typically appear to be, and how members of the public might distinguish the legitimately needy from those who are "work-shy" on the street "by choice" or simply seeking tax-free income to supplement carefree lifestyles. Moreover, there is considerable concern about the uses to which money given to panhandlers is put – whether it is spent "rationally" to purchase food and accommodation, for example, or whether instead it is diverted to satisfy base cravings and addictions. The "begging encounter" may be problematic for the person approached on the street precisely because it involves making a series of more or less instantaneous moral judgments about the need, sincerity, and trustworthiness of the panhandler.[9] There is little that is novel about such anxieties and uncertainties, for as H. Dean and K. Gale state, "the beggar has always been an ambiguous figure: an ascetic pilgrim or a lawless wanderer; a deserving object of pity or an undeserving scrounger; a hapless victim of welfare retrenchment or a venal representative of an emergent underclass."[10]

We suggest that contemporary moral and legal debates about beggars and begging are linked to the context in which they are typically encountered: public space within downtown cores. The profusion of anti-panhandling by-laws may be interpreted as signalling a growing mistrust of the ideal of a truly inclusive public space and the hegemony of those private interests that assert that if cities are to compete in a global economy, they must "purify" the urban landscape. Thus, just as the privatization of public space (for example, through public–private redevelopment partnerships and private policing and surveillance) is being lauded by urban governments, its use by the homeless and destitute for the purpose of seeking small, seemingly private transactions is being prohibited.

### Anti-Panhandling By-Laws in Canada

A survey of sixteen Canadian cities conducted by the National Anti-Poverty Organization (NAPO) in 1999 revealed that nine had an anti-panhandling by-law of some kind and that seven of these threatened offenders with fines – of up to $10,000 in the case of Calgary.[11] Of the seven cities that did not have a by-law, one (Moncton) has since moved to prohibit "aggressive" and "intimidating" begging, while two others (Toronto and London) have come under the Ontario *Safe Streets Act 1999*,[12] which prohibits "aggressive" panhandling throughout the province. Two by-laws identified by the survey – in Winnipeg and Vancouver, respectively – have since been repealed in light of court challenges contending breaches of *Charter* rights and have been replaced with somewhat less prohibitive regulations governing obstructive solicitation. The net result is that laws (whether municipal or provincial) governing the actions of beggars currently apply in thirteen of the sixteen cities originally surveyed (see Appendix at the end of the chapter for an updated survey of anti-panhandling regulations in Canada).

Anti-panhandling by-laws typically impose restrictions on the time, place, and manner in which panhandling can occur, with few cities imposing an outright ban (Ottawa is the notable exception).[13] First, they seek to control *when* panhandling can occur; generally, by prohibiting it during the hours of darkness. Thus, it is illegal to panhandle in Calgary between 8:00 PM and 8:00 AM, and in Saskatoon between 9:00 PM and 6:00 AM, while Vancouver's recently repealed by-law bans begging from sunset to sunrise. It is seldom made clear by the proponents of such restrictions what it is about panhandling on city streets after dark that is so problematic that it must be prohibited. Presumably, the answer relates in large part to the heightened sense of fear associated with public space at night[14] as well as to cities' desires to re-valorize downtown spaces by making them safe and attractive sites for middle-class leisure and discretionary spending outside of normal working hours. In addition, and as discussed later in this essay, there is widespread concern in Canada about "aggressive" panhandling, and anxiety about threatening and disorderly beggars may become heightened at night as street traffic diminishes, surveillance becomes less readily apparent, and the effects of intoxication possibly become more evident.

Second, the by-laws have imposed restrictions on *where* begging may occur within public space. Many regulations prohibit asking for money at transit stops and shelters; in the vicinity of banks, automated teller machines, and liquor stores; on busy pedestrian walkways; at traffic control signals; and on vehicular roadways. NAPO suggests that such geographical restrictions reflect stereotypes about the inherent criminality of poor and disempowered citizens. In particular, the prohibition on begging near banks and automated teller machines suggests that such individuals are more likely to be thieves than other members of the public.[15] The places specified as "off-limits" to panhandlers tend to be those at which anxiety about their presence is highest. Stories about "elderly persons" and other respectable citizens feeling too scared to use bank machines because of the "risk" of being approached by a panhandler appear periodically in the media.[16] As Richard Moon suggests, however, begging at "prohibited locations" is not *necessarily* aggressive or intimidating, nor even more *likely* to be so than it is elsewhere.[17] Indeed, the fact that some ordinances ban sitting on the sidewalk for the purposes of begging (a typically passive and non-threatening behaviour) suggests that place-restrictions are less concerned with intimidation than they are with avoiding situations where beggars are difficult to evade, ignore, or walk away from without a measure of discomfort or frustration. Not coincidentally, many of the places targeted are sites where financial transactions are executed (for example, the purchase of a bottle of wine, the withdrawal of cash from a bank machine) and where loose change may be readily available upon request.[18]

Third, by-laws seek to regulate the *manner* in which panhandling occurs. The focus in this case is on persistent, intimidating, obstructive, and threatening behaviours, which are commonly considered to constitute "aggressive" panhandling. The Saskatoon by-law, for example, makes it illegal for panhandlers to follow, touch, or obstruct the person solicited, to make persistent requests after a negative response has been given, and to use obscene or abusive language.[19] Similarly, under the City of Vancouver's new regulations, it is forbidden "to continue to solicit from or otherwise harass a pedestrian after that person has made a negative initial response to the solicitation or has otherwise indicated a refusal," "to physically approach and solicit from a pedestrian as a member of a group of three or more persons," and to "solicit in a manner which causes an obstruction."[20] Given that it is already an offence under the *Criminal Code of Canada* to obtain money by force, aggression, or threat,[21] such prohibitions can appear redundant. Certainly, it is seldom explained why existing law is insufficient. The answer to this puzzle appears to lie partly in the fact that, for all the concern expressed by city governments, retailers, and the media about pedestrians being pushed, chased, and insulted by panhandlers, the purpose of the by-laws is less to deter or punish aggression than to facilitate the removal of panhandlers from key downtown spaces. The regulations seek to circumscribe a behaviour that is not *inherently* threatening or dangerous but often proves to be troubling, disconcerting, and frustrating for passers-by.

Such an interpretation appears to be supported by the following comment from the spokesperson for the Vancouver police: "In the past we didn't have anything we could use unless a person became criminally aggressive. Now after a warning we can insist they move along or face consequences."[22]

M-A. Kandrack's reflections on the criminalization of panhandling in Winnipeg are insightful.[23] She contends that there is little, if anything, about the act of asking for money that warrants or necessitates regulation or control. The problem, rather, is that panhandling tends to be conflated with conduct that *is* threatening or disruptive. Discussing the behaviour of three aggressive panhandlers observed in Winnipeg, Kandrack suggests that "the request for money [was] the least problematic aspect of their conduct," which included following passers-by, blocking their paths, harassing them verbally, and threatening them physically.[24] Panhandling was largely incidental to this drunken and belligerent behaviour, which was already subject to legal sanction. In this context, Kandrack concludes, "to construct panhandling as a menace misses the point."[25] One might add that panhandlers are also considerably more likely to be the victims than the perpetrators of violent crime.[26]

Given that panhandling is not synonymous with belligerent conduct and that threatening and violent behaviour is already illegal, the fact that so many Canadian municipalities have deemed it necessary to enact by-laws remains somewhat surprising. We suggest that this legislative trend can be better understood when one considers that the panhandling encounter typically involves a request for *money* made by a *poor person* within *public space*. These three dimensions form the focus for the remainder of our essay.

## The Multiple Meanings of Money

Money, with its dual function as the instrument of exchange and the measure of value, often appears to be an objective, inert phenomenon, which is culturally neutral and socially anonymous.[27] A number of recent studies, however, draw attention to the ways in which money is both constitutive of everyday life and shaped by socio-cultural norms. It acquires multiple meanings that allow us to distinguish between bribes, tributes, wages, gifts, ransoms, bonuses, tips, and dividends, for example.[28] Moreover, people commonly distinguish money based on its source, differentiating earned money (of which the recipient is deserving) from that which is unearned (derived from a windfall), and money acquired in legitimate business from that which is attained through criminal or immoral means.[29] The latter is often referred to as "dirty money," a term that both reflects and reinforces the associated social stigma. It may, however, be "laundered" clean (for example, when governments earmark revenue received from legalized gambling for noble causes such as education).[30]

Money derived from the sale of blood plasma – an important source of income for many homeless people in the United States[31] – is also stigmatized by virtue of its association with an ethically questionable and socially marginal practice. Consequently, sellers often distinguish the money obtained from plasma sales from other funds, reserving the former for quite particular uses.[32] As V.A. Zelizer observes, despite a long history of political and legal initiatives intended to entrench single national currencies, individuals, families, and institutions have continually "introduced new distinctions, invented their own special forms of currency, earmarked money in various ways that baffle market theorists, [and] incorporated money into personalized webs of friendship [and] family relationships."[33]

One of the more problematic examples of such an "incorporation" involves the use of money as a gift. As a result of its close association with impersonal market exchange (and the attendant expectations of commensurability and reciprocity), money represents an "unlikely candidate for gift giving."[34] Money cannot provide an accurate "measure" of the value or significance of a relationship, and, when gifted, it is difficult to personalize. Its "market" connotations appear inescapable, despite the fact that one does not present a friend or relative with gift money in the expectation of immediate reciprocation. Moreover, gifts of money based on genuine interpersonal warmth and friendship have historically proven to be difficult to distinguish from other monetary transfers, such as tips, charity, and tributes.[35] An additional layer of complexity is added by the set of expectations surrounding the use of gift money. Generally, it is considered most appropriate to spend it on non-essential but morally unproblematic goods, such as clothes or books, as opposed to items such as groceries or lottery tickets.

The difficulties associated with the use of money as a gift provide a number of pointers for understanding why panhandlers' requests for assistance – which *prima facie* appear to be expressions of private desires to complete small monetary transactions – have become targets of intensive public regulation. Money, regardless of its material form, is used primarily as an instrument of exchange and a measure of value. When a beggar asks a passer-by for spare change, however, there is generally no expectation that any good or service of commensurate value will be provided in exchange. As McIntosh and Erskine contend, "in contrast to the bulk of interactions in public that we are normally involved in, the begging encounter entails an interaction where the equivalence is not immediately apparent and the norms of obligation are unclear."[36] In market societies where reciprocated exchanges are normal, requests from beggars who apparently want "money for nothing" prove both perplexing and suspicious. Unlike appeals for money that take the form of corporate advertising – which is often viewed as an essential part of Canadian public discourse – beggars' requests neither promise fulfilment through personal consumption nor create fanciful images and associations that mask difficult social and political issues.[37]

At this point, a contrast might be drawn between panhandlers and those who offer goods or services in return for the money they solicit on the street – for example, buskers, pavement artists, newsletter vendors, and "squeegee kids." This distinction often proves difficult to maintain in practice, however, as panhandlers may periodically resort to forms of entertainment (such as the telling of short poems) or take advantage of the opportunity to provide a needed service, such as opening heavy subway-station doors for busy commuters.[38] In this respect, in fact, some poor and destitute city residents behave in relatively entrepreneurial ways, especially when one considers that solicitation may be only one of a diverse set of tasks undertaken each day to secure survival and a basic income.[39]

## Poor People's Money

The begging encounter is problematic not only because the norms of market exchange are not seen to apply[40] but also because the person requesting the money is poor, or at least appears to be.[41] Long-standing anxieties about poor people's money – about how it is obtained, whether it is deserved, and how it is spent – exert considerable influence on the discourses presently surrounding begging in Canada and provide much of the rationale for anti-panhandling by-laws. In particular, connections may be traced between these by-laws and the preoccupation of nineteenth-century relief agencies with distinguishing the deserving from the undeserving poor and ensuring that money received by alms-seekers was put to appropriate uses – not squandered on goods or services that were over-priced, non-essential, or immoral.

In the American context, Zelizer recounts the illustrative story of an impoverished nineteenth-century woman ("Mrs. C."), who was refused a cash allowance by a charitable organization.[42] This decision was made following a home visit by a charity worker, during which time it was "discovered" that Mrs. C. had paid 25 cents for a pound of fresh tomatoes – an extravagant expenditure given that it was possible to obtain "just as good tomatoes at another store for twenty cents a pound."[43] The organization subsequently gave Mrs. C. grocery orders that specified not only *which* goods she could purchase but also *where* she was to buy them. Such a decision was not unusual at the time but rather typified relief agencies' preoccupation with regulating the moral economies of the poor, in part by providing in-kind relief (e.g., food, clothing, heating fuel) and restricted currencies (e.g., purchase orders, food stamps) rather than cash. Notions of consumer sovereignty and autonomy seldom extended to poor households. Indeed, their consumption choices were often dismissed as the "mistaken prejudices" of the irrational.[44] Both public and private relief agencies deemed money in the hands of the poor to be deeply problematic, as indigent persons were thought to be financial incompetents at best and moral bankrupts prone to gambling and intoxication at worst.

In the twentieth century, concerns about the dangers of cash in the hands of the poor have coexisted with a belief in the need for poor people to learn how to learn how to use money rationally and independently. Zelizer notes that this belief in the need for poor families to "do their own buying" informed the development of social security in the United States and that, in the 1930s, public assistance increasingly took the form of monetary payments to which no particular conditions or restrictions were attached, as opposed to in-kind relief or vouchers.[45] More generally, the growth of the welfare state in Western nations also saw the task of distinguishing between the deserving and undeserving poor pass from private charitable organizations to state agencies and an emergent class of professional social workers. Nevertheless, poor people's rationality and consumer competence remained suspect in the eyes of many, and these doubts justified the (re)introduction of restricted currencies for the poor, such as food stamps.[46]

Many of the preoccupations and stereotypes that characterized nineteenth-century debates about poor people's money also feature in contemporary arguments about panhandling. These are often prompted by the "moral judgment" that an encounter with a panhandler appears to necessitate. As several commentators have recently observed, the beggar's request for assistance triggers a series of questions: Why is this person on the street? Is this person genuinely needy? What does this person intend to do with the donated money?[47] As Hartley Dean puts it, "at its simplest the dilemma any of us face when confronted by a beggar is whether to give money or not, yet beneath this dilemma lies the necessity for the kind of classificatory judgments that had supposedly been colonized by social administrators: is the supplicant deserving or undeserving, genuine or fraudulent?"[48] This decision-making process may prove frustrating and disconcerting, not least of all because it involves working with imperfect information. How, for example, can one tell with any certainty why a panhandler is on the street? This is a difficult question, yet it is one that a pedestrian may find him/herself asking several times in the course of a city block.

Many civic politicians, business leaders, and members of the public have expressed concern that some – perhaps most – panhandlers are not "genuine"" – that they are not truly destitute individuals, forced to live on the street through no fault of their own. Considerable credence is given to apocryphal tales of panhandlers who come from lives of considerable privilege, yet choose to wear old clothes and engage in panhandling in order to earn "easy money" or simply for the "thrill" of it.[49] The panhandling population is thought to consist of many people who "choose the lifestyle" as well as those who have fallen on hard times as a result of personal and moral failings, such as alcoholism, drug-use, gambling, criminality, and idleness.[50] Scepticism about panhandlers' reasons for being on the street may be reinforced by a belief that "generous" social security programs ensure that the disadvantaged are provided with benefits, services, treatment, and training. In the words of a former British Home Office minister, Conservative Member of Parliament David Maclean, "there are no genuine beggars. Those who are in need have got all the social benefits they require. Every time we go and check, we find they won't go in hostels. Beggars are doing so out of choice because they find it more pleasant."[51] Moreover, as B. Jordan observes, people in Western countries pay taxes and social insurance contributions with the expectation that they will *not* have to make difficult, individualized judgments about the needs of their fellow citizens, and "hence they resent the serial experience of being asked to decide whether to give."[52]

In addition to raising questions about why the panhandler is on the street, the begging encounter may lead the passers-by to doubt whether the money requested is genuinely needed. First, considerable anxiety surrounds the alleged profusion of "fraudulent" beggars who pretend to be impoverished and/or disabled when in fact they are not.[53] In the contemporary Canadian context, articles in the popular press reveal that certain groups attract particular suspicion: young people who claim to have run away from home, casual and seasonal labourers, and homeless people who theoretically have "every available resource" at their disposal. The preoccupation with fraudulent panhandlers has deep historical roots. B. Gleeson discusses a street vendor in late nineteenth-century Melbourne who wore "a prominent sign around his neck declaring 'I WAS BORN A CRIPPLE' in recognition of the obdurate suspicion of middle-class Victorians that all disabled street traders and beggars were really well-disguised, 'healthy' vagrants imposing on the sympathy of gullible passers-by."[54] Erskine and McIntosh observe similar fears of fraudulence in sixteenth-century Europe, noting that Martin Luther's *Book of Beggars* advised against giving alms to anyone who was not beyond resorting to guile or trickery. The list of suspects was long and included women who looked pregnant, persons who appeared to be suffering from disease, self-proclaimed pilgrims and converts to Christianity, and cripples "who sit at church doors with broken legs or missing limbs, claiming to have been imprisoned by heathens or to have had their limbs chopped off in battle."[55]

A second set of concerns regarding panhandlers' proclaimed need of money relates to the imagined ease with which large sums can be acquired on the street: begging is often represented as something akin to a lucrative profession.[56] Certainly, the mainstream media abounds with stories of beggars who solicit "small fortunes" on the street, some apparently using this tax-free income to purchase mobile phones and mountain bikes and even to maintain expensive cars and homes. Such narratives (many of which surely border on urban legend) also have a long history. Erskine and McIntosh describe the anxieties that existed in Tudor England with vagrants who were deemed too prosperous.[57] Such understandings reinforce the notion that the panhandler is fundamentally untrustworthy, and further complicate the begging encounter by suggesting that, in giving spare change, the "hardworking wage earner" may inadvertently be facilitating a life of unearned luxury.

Related to this concern is a preoccupation with how panhandlers spend the money they receive. Echoing nineteenth-century presumptions about poor people's inherent irrationality and incompetence as consumers, there is a widespread belief that panhandlers beg primarily so that they can purchase alcohol, tobacco, and illegal drugs or so that they can replace money that has already been spent feeding habits and addictions.[58] This perception is fuelled by suggestions that genuinely homeless people already receive adequate food and accommodation free of charge from the various shelters, charities, and agencies that operate in the downtown areas.[59]

Money in the hands of poor people is seldom deemed "morally safe," and, for this reason, various organizations have sought to invent new restricted currencies (in the form of vouchers and coupons) that can be redeemed only for food, transit fares, and other essentials.[60] One of the longer-running initiatives is "Berkeley Cares," a partnership of various public and private agencies, which has sold 25 cent vouchers (which may be used to purchase most everyday goods, excluding alcohol and cigarettes) in Berkeley, California, since 1991.[61] This model was subsequently adopted in Edmonton, where vouchers were promoted as allowing for "guilt-free giving" on the part of citizens, who could be assured that their charity would not be put to "ill-use" and would not facilitate self-destructive behaviours.[62] In Vancouver, the City Council has sought not to create a new currency but rather to remove cash from the outstretched hands of panhandlers. To this end, the anti-panhandling by-law was accompanied by a "Spare Change" program, which entailed "the installation of recycled parking meters that are specially identified and strategically placed for the public to donate spare change to the meter rather than giving it to individuals."[63] The funds collected in these meters ($3,357 in 2000, less $1,150 for installation and repairs) are donated to the United Way charity, which distributes in-kind assistance to the needy. This initiative highlights both the psychological anxiety that surrounds encountering beggars in public space (with the implicit suggestion that pedestrians may feel more comfortable interacting with a machine rather than a person) and the intense concern regarding what panhandlers do when "empowered" to make their own spending decisions. Panhandlers are not, after all, ordinary consumers. The very fact that they are on the street may be seen as *prima facie* evidence of their inability to achieve rational self-government.[64]

## Downtowns

Although a discussion of the ambivalences surrounding "poor people's money" helps to answer our primary question, we argue that we also need to attend to the particular spaces within which both money and anti-panhandling by-laws are operative. While Canadian municipalities' anti-panhandling by-laws are generally city-wide in application, they have typically been drafted in response to particular concerns about begging within the public spaces of the downtown. This geographical specificity reflects pressure from city centre merchants as well as the location of much of the panhandling activity. Most immediately, then, we need to attend to the contemporary dynamics of Canadian downtowns in order to understand the recent upsurge of such by-laws. This topic is difficult, however, as Canadian cities are diverse and characterized by different dynamics. That said, there would seem to be three points of general convergence that bear on the questions of panhandling and its regulation.

### Investment in the Built Landscape

Downtowns have long consumed a significant share of investment in the built environment and, historically, have contained the highest land values. In the postwar Canadian context, downtowns have been shaped by waves of development, with deindustrialization, office expansion, and urban renewal being particularly significant. Reinvestment in the downtown core of many Canadian cities has been marked in the last three decades. G. Gad and M. Matthew document the striking increase in office development, noting, for example, that Toronto core area office space increased by 4.1 million square feet between 1971 and 1996.[65] However, many central areas have also been witness to very significant expansions in other areas, financed by both public and private capital, including hospitals, libraries, sports complexes, art galleries, theatres, restaurants, and waterfront redevelopment. In addition, downtown cores in cities such as Toronto and Vancouver have experienced considerable residential construction and population increase.[66] Calgary's downtown population has also risen: by 12.4 percent (from 9,786 to 11,000) between 1994 and 1997 alone.[67] D. Ley documents the role of the "new middle class" in the "remaking" of the Canadian central city, as gentrification continues, and even some of the most disadvantaged downtown areas are opened up to middle class investment.[68] Sustaining investment in the downtown core, and policing activities – such as panhandling – that might compromise it, have thus become a priority.[69]

Some downtowns have experienced decline, despite extended efforts. Ley notes that Edmonton's downtown experienced a general decline in social status between 1986 and 1991.[70] Similarly, Kitchener's downtown has resisted efforts at revitalization,[71] as has Winnipeg's. Under these conditions, urban elites appear to have targeted panhandlers, seeing them as a visible manifestation of a failing downtown.

**Retail Sales**
Downtown merchants are losing market share. While central city retailers sought to respond to the expansion of the suburban mall with the development of downtown retail malls and speciality shopping districts (for example, Robson Street and Gastown in Vancouver; Crescent and St.-Denis Streets in Montreal), the subsequent growth of big-box and category-killer formats in suburban areas precipitated further decline in downtown retail sales. One recent academic survey estimates that Canada's largest downtowns lost 20 percent of their sales between 1989 and 1996. It found that Edmonton (minus 38.8 percent) and Toronto and Montreal (minus 27 percent) had been particularly hard hit.[72]

Advocates of anti-panhandling by-laws frequently assert that the activities of beggars must be proscribed in order to preserve the economic vitality of downtown areas and, in particular, the viability of retailing.[73] It has been suggested by both city governments and merchants' associations that downtown retailers lose significant numbers of customers as a result of the presence of panhandlers, who deter shoppers from entering particular stores (by standing near their doors), and perhaps from visiting the downtown core altogether (many middle class consumers seemingly prefer the sanctified space of the suburban shopping mall to the risk of encountering beggars in the central city). Although such claims are seldom supported by empirical evidence, they have exerted considerable influence on municipal public policy in Canada[74] and have also shaped the national debate on homelessness in Britain. In the latter context, both Tory and Labour prime ministers have expressed concern about "rough sleepers" and beggars blighting downtown areas. Their very presence has been deemed to damage business by driving away tourists and shoppers.[75]

Such thinking is often translated into the pervasive (and persuasive) language of rights, whereupon it is asserted that beggars' rights to free expression must be balanced with (or possibly trumped by) the rights of retailers to conduct their lawful business, to compete, and to make a profit.[76] Related to this line of argument is the notion that panhandlers also infringe upon the negative right of members of the public to peaceful and uninterrupted enjoyment of public space.[77] Accordingly, the stated purpose of anti-panhandling by-laws in Canadian cities is typically to prevent public nuisances and to ensure that panhandlers do not interfere unreasonably with others' legitimate uses of the streets.[78]

Anti-panhandling by-laws are often enacted in the hope that, by circumscribing certain small private transactions occurring in public space, they will facilitate and protect larger economic exchanges in the downtown environment. D. Mitchell observes:

> Through these laws and other means, cities seek to use a seemingly stable, ordered urban landscape as a positive inducement to continued investment and to maintain the viability of current investment in core areas (by showing merchants, for example, that they are doing something to keep shoppers coming downtown) ... such legislation seeks to bolster the built environment against the ever-possible specter of decline and obsolescence. It actually does not matter that much if this is how capital "really" works; it is enough that those in positions of power believe that this is how capital works.[79]

Corporate and state planners in North American cities have articulated a need to create environments that give security and entertainment priority over interaction, diversity, and politics.

### Social Polarization

S. Sassen has pointed to the "new dynamics of inequality" that are associated with the emergent global city. Such dynamics are characterized by processes of valorization (even over-valorization) of certain spaces and people and the simultaneous, but interlocking, devalorization of those individuals deemed as "other," such as immigrants and the working poor.[80] Canadian cities are, indeed, becoming more socially polarized. Not only do Canadian downtowns contain the increasingly marginalized residents who resort to panhandling but they have also come to attract a more affluent population who may not welcome their presence.

Significant disparities are exhibited within the central city.[81] In inner city Toronto, for example, the range between top and bottom deciles (in 1990 dollars) increased from $31,000 in 1970 to $60,000 in 1990.[82] Newer areas of poverty have been identified within the inner suburbs, often in association with clusters of social housing and socially dependent populations. At the same time, many downtown areas have seen a growing middle class population. By 1996, the decline in relative inner city incomes had been arrested in several instances, including Vancouver and Ottawa-Hull.[83] Fragmented labour and housing markets, fuelled by accelerated globalization and economic restructuring, suggest that "the potential for increased social and spatial inequalities will continue apace."[84] Similarly, L. Bourne and A.E. Olvet argue that although there is considerable variation between cities, and that they are likely to become more unlike, on one front, at least, they will be similar: "they will be more socially unequal internally."[85]

## Review

Recognition of the three dynamics discussed earlier gives the presence of the panhandler in downtown spaces, especially on commercial streets, a particular quality. Much is at stake. Downtowns are "fragile."[86] Millions of dollars have been invested in private and public projects in downtown cores. Yet such investments are seen to be threatened by poor people who, by virtue of their presence in public space, and the ambivalences associated with "poor people's money," can create the "wrong" image. D. Harvey argues that contemporary processes of capitalism have encouraged an "entrepreneurial" approach to urban development, in which downtown spaces in particular are consciously crafted to give out seductive messages to would-be global investors while also, in classical "bread and circuses" style, forging a hegemonic unity among local citizens.[87] Increasingly significant, it seems, is the creation and maintenance of the "correct" urban image to both outside investors and local residents. W. Magnusson has noted the particular importance attached to urban image in Victoria, where "creating the proper ambience in downtown" is seen to be increasingly important: "A concentrated effort is intended to make Victoria into a place that can be consumed as an entertaining spectacle and held in the memory as a place for future retirement. The consumption is organized in such a way that merchants can profit from selling a wide range of goods and services."[88] Anything that detracts from such place-marketing, such as the presence of "the homeless who congregate under the Johnson Street bridge, sleep under the trees in Beacon Park Hill or panhandle on the streets,"[89] is perceived as threatening.

Such infractions would perhaps be less of an issue if downtown investments were a little more secure. However, Canadian central cities remain diverse and dynamic landscapes. Merchants are losing market share. Some downtowns, such as in Winnipeg and Edmonton, have struggled to survive. Even the more economically secure downtowns, such as in Vancouver and Montreal, exist within an uncertain, globalizing, and fast-changing landscape. Thus, urban elites in these places also turn to the panhandler as a potential threat.[90] This perception may also be fuelled by an increasingly "revanchist" attitude toward the urban poor, as has been noted in US cities.[91] As Mitchell notes, the presence of the poor in downtown spaces threatens a loss of control. The solution is to "re-regulate those spaces, annihilate the homeless, and allow the city to once again become a place of order, pleasure, consumption and accumulation."[92] Promoters of anti-panhandling legislation see themselves not as the instigators of a pogrom but rather as the "saviors of cities."[93] Yet the panhandler is as much a product of the contemporary downtown as is the anti-panhandling by-law. As we have seen, downtowns have become increasingly socially polarized places. Shifts in urban land and labour markets have further disadvantaged many segments of urban society, squeezing some people into poverty, homelessness, and begging.

## Public Space

The dynamics of contemporary downtowns provide a partial answer to our question of why so many Canadian cities have deemed panhandling to be a problem of pressing public concern. However, it is necessary to contextualize further the begging encounter by considering its location within public space. While it has been argued that panhandling's "publicity" gives it normative worth as a form of communication,[94] it also renders it problematic.

To speak of public space is to speak of the public sphere. We can define the latter as "a sphere which mediates between society and state, in which the public organises itself as the bearer of public opinion."[95] J. Habermas, in *The Structural Transformation of the Public Sphere*, lays out the most influential treatment, clarifying both the analytical and normative qualities of the public sphere.[96] For Habermas, the public sphere makes a truly democratic politics possible, by carving out a site within which free, rational discourse can occur between citizens, distanced from the particularities of the state, the economy, and the private domain. Within the public sphere, which Habermas first locates in eighteenth-century Western Europe, informed, robust conversations on the common good and constructive commentaries on political life and citizenship can occur. The public sphere allows for a politics in the richest sense.

However, membership in the public sphere is not a given, as the scholarship of both Habermas and H. Arendt illustrate.[97] Historically, white, propertied men alone were recognized as valid members of the "public." Women, workers, "aliens," and racial and sexual minorities have all engaged in struggles to be included as citizens and acknowledged as legitimate contributors to the democratic debate of the public sphere. These battles have been hard won – powerful interests have consistently fought to restrict membership. The political history of Canada has, in large measure, centred on this struggle. First Nations, Chinese Canadians, women, trade unionists, and others have all been caught up in it. And it is a struggle that is consequential in several ways. To be excluded from the public sphere is not only to be silenced politically but also to be denied standing as a member of a political community.

It is tempting to think of the public sphere in abstract terms. However, geographers have argued convincingly that the public sphere needs to be grounded in public space – that is, the material location where the social interactions and political activities of the "public" occur. While public space is not exclusively "publicly owned," the streets, parks, and plazas of the contemporary city are its most obvious manifestation. The fact that the public sphere is to be found, in part, in public space is significant. It is in public space that the conversations and encounters of public life become physical and real:

> Politics ... is a matter of people sharing a common world and a common space of appearance in which public concerns can emerge and be articulated from different perspectives. For politics to occur it is not enough to have a collection of private individuals voting separately and anonymously according to their private opinions. Rather these individuals must be able to see and talk to one another in public, to meet in a public space so that their differences as well as their commonalities can emerge and become the subject of democratic debate.[98]

Yet interacting and engaging with diverse others in public space can also be unnerving, unpredictable, and disruptive of established social boundaries.[99] Indeed, there is a long history of legal attempts to police and regulate public space (often accompanied by re-designs of the built environment) in an effort to counter its perceived "disorder." "Vagrants" and beggars, in particular, have long been targets for those who seek to cleanse public space of individuals and classes deemed threatening to dominant values. Canadian municipal by-laws regulating panhandling thus have a long pedigree.

Many commentators note a pervasive redefinition of public space whereby "interactive, discursive politics have been effectively banned from the gathering points of the city."[100] Urban design increasingly turns its back on the street with the creation of "analogue" spaces, such as the enclosed pedestrian walkways of Calgary and the tunnels of Montreal, which for T. Boddy constitute a conscious attempt to sanitize, separate, and simulate.[101] In such "dignified" settings, the "human contact, conflict and tolerance"[102] that give public life its density and texture is typically denied. Shopping malls, the chosen site of social interaction for many people driven indoors by pervasive fear-mongering about public space, routinely deny access to those deemed "other."[103] Such environments reject public space, with its perceived risks, at the same time as they simulate the street, creating "an idealized public space, free, by virtue of private property, planning and strict control, from the inconvenience of the weather and the danger and pollution of the automobile, but most importantly from the terror of crime associated with today's urban environment."[104] Merchants' associations in retail districts such as Vancouver's Gastown and Chinatown employ private security guards who, according to some commentators, harass panhandlers and the poor in an attempt to create a tourist-friendly milieu. Gated communities exclude the diversity of the street, promising their residents a secure, homogenous living space. Planning and zoning criteria, in combination with the working of the marketplace, have tended to homogenize and separate spaces.[105]

In addition, an increasing number of cities have enthusiastically embraced by-laws and design tactics that seem designed to remove all signs of the poor and the homeless from public space.[106]

For some commentators, this privatization of public space must be seen as part of a longer-term trend, whereby "the messy vitality of the metropolitan condition, with its unpredictable intermingling of classes, races, and social forms is rejected, only to be replaced by a filtered, prettified, homogenous substitute."[107] Why? The presence of the poor and destitute on the streets does not *necessarily* constitute an imminent threat to public safety. As J. Wardhaugh and J. Jones note, "it is not marginality per se that is dangerous; rather it is the *visible* presence of marginal people within prime space that represents a threat to a sense of public order and orderliness."[108] Sennett, in *The Fall of Public Man*, points to the deep-seated aversion within modern Western culture toward both diversity and the public realm. He locates this aversion within contemporary understandings of the psychology of the self, in which the individual psyche is treated as *sui generis*, and an "intimate society" predicated on "warmth, trust and open expression of feeling" is given priority.[109] The public realm, which cannot yield these psychological rewards, is thus seen to be threatening. D. Sibley also draws on psychoanalytic understandings of purification and dirt to argue that the desire to exclude groups such as beggars from public space reflects the "polluting" threat they pose to the dominant social order.[110]

From a related angle, T. Cresswell argues that spatial arrangements, such as the division between public and private space, serve as a vital – if taken-for-granted – means of classification. The ostensible inertia of space may render such classification natural and pre-ordained such that places "appear to have their own rules, not the rules constructed for them."[111] Space, he reminds us, comes with particular and deeply encoded classifications of appropriate behaviour: "There are places to play, pray, sleep, eat, make love ... The built environment materializes meanings – sets them in concrete and stone."[112] Behaviours and people that challenge such classifications are deemed "out of place" and may be properly subject to regulation. This is certainly the case with respect to anti-homeless legislation, whose advocates contend that streets and subways are for commuting from home to office (not for sleeping or begging) and that parks are for recreation and orderly consumption (not for cooking or loitering).[113] Even apparently minor acts performed in public view, such as panhandling by the homeless, can be seen as a threat to order and normalcy.[114]

## Conclusion

J. Weintraub observes that the distinction between public and private "has long served as a point of entry into many of the key issues of social and political analysis, of moral and political debate, and of the ordering of everyday social life."[115] He notes that one of the many ways in which the public–private distinction has been employed is in the "liberal-economistic model," which asserts that the difference between public and private mirrors the distinction between state administration and the market economy. Within this model, there is a preoccupation "with demarcating the sphere of the 'public' authority of the state from the sphere of formally voluntary relations between 'private' individuals."[116] With the ascendancy of neoliberalism, most financial transactions have been seen as falling into the latter category and, consequently, as being properly exempt from interference by the public, *qua* the state. Such discourse has helped to legitimate, extend, and protect the much-heralded "free movement" of capital. Pro-business urban governments have actively embraced a reduced role for state intervention into the private domain.

What, then, does a study of anti-panhandling by-laws tell us about the meanings and definitions attached to the public–private distinction in the contemporary Canadian polity? While it is tempting to view such regulations as further privatizing public space, this conclusion is not completely satisfactory. Certainly, the by-laws constitute an attempt to regulate and order that which frequently appears to be disordered. Nevertheless, more careful reflection suggests that the very categories of public and private are at issue.

There appears to be considerable irony in the contemporary criminalization of panhandling. Downtown corporate complexes, which facilitate the movement of billions of dollars, are seen to be threatened by a few modest financial exchanges. At the same time that capital flows of billions of dollars are proceeding relatively unregulated by the state, begging on the streets of North America for dimes and quarters is increasingly subject to governmental sanction. When the local state responds to such anxieties with intensive regulation, thereby circumscribing the beggar's ability to initiate relatively minor monetary transactions, an additional layer of irony may be added. This irony is linked to the fact that money has occupied a central role within the private sphere of classical liberalism – the school of thought that many contemporary governments claim as their ideological heritage.[117] Habermas contends that in the era of classical liberalism, the private sphere consisted of a civil society centred upon a market economy in which freely contracting individuals engaged in trade and acquired property, facilitated by various forms of currency. These individuals established a "bourgeois public sphere" in large part to secure and extend the freedom of the market *from* the state. Through rational-critical debate, the bourgeoisie sought the negative liberties that would guarantee the privacy of their transactions of money, goods, and property (for example, the rights to freedom of contract, trade, and inheritance). In regulating panhandling, then, the state would seem to be in violation of a foundational liberal tenet.[118] How can we make sense of this?

One option, drawing from critical legal studies, is to point to the essentially contradictory character of liberal categories, such as the public–private duality. While the maintenance of such distinctions serve vital ideological functions, many critics would argue that they are practically unsustainable. Thus, for example, "'free contract' could never be defined without an implicit vision of the boundaries of duress and fraud."[119] An alternative, more "external" in orientation,[120] is to recognize that state action can successfully navigate a variety of contradictions. For example, New Right ideologies, such as Thatcherism, can combine anti-statism with a call for "discipline."[121] The state "is to be simultaneously rolled back and rolled forward. Non-interventionist and decentralized in some areas, the state is to be highly interventionist and centralized in others."[122] If we accept that a New Right ideology has a continuing influence upon political discourse in Canada, this claim is a useful one.

Our argument, however, is slightly different and relates to the traffic between law and society more generally. In their discussion of this relation, A. Sarat and T.R. Kearns remind us that "society's normative resources are not entirely dictated by law; on the contrary law's constitutive powers might easily awaken nonlegal commitments that will prove to be law's undoing."[123] In other words, we must be cautious about ascribing liberal-legal categories, such as the public–private divide, a determinative and straightforward influence upon social life. Our discussion suggests that they can be put to work in complicated, contradictory, and partial ways in material social contexts. Liberal-legal categories are not autonomous, but can be cross cut by other understandings, ethics, and practices. While the public–private divide is useful in an understanding of anti-panhandling by-laws – for example, by making possible the very idea of public space – it neither explains their recent prevalence, nor maps neatly onto their operation. Indeed, as noted, the by-laws actually appear to violate the liberal economists public–private divide. To understand the by-laws, we also need to look to other anxieties that are only partly captured by liberal categories, such as apprehensions concerning public sociability, social understandings of the meaning of money, or the rapid transformation of downtown spaces.

Put more generally, to understand the everyday workings of law and its associated dualities, we need to be careful of adopting either an instrumental or a constitutive analysis.[124] Instead, we need to adopt situated and resolutely empirical readings of law's relation to social life. In order to achieve this, and this is our final point, we must attend to the simultaneous spatiality of law.[125] Situating an abstraction, such as the public–private divide, in social space alerts us to its contradictory and ambiguous purchase on everyday life. This is important analytically because it raises questions about the public–private divide itself. Yet it is also important ethically. The actual adoption and implementation of anti-panhandling by-laws reveal important distinctions and dynamics – for example, the differential treatment of begging and advertising or the politics of downtown transformation – which speak both to the conditional and deeply political nature of liberal categories as well as to the specific politics of panhandling regulation.

**Appendix:**
Survey of anti-panhandling regulations in Canada

| Jurisdiction | Complete ban | Time of day restriction | Specific area restriction | Aggressive panhandling banned | Obstructive panhandling banned | Specific fine Min./Max. |
|---|---|---|---|---|---|---|
| Fredericton | | | | × | | 0/$70 |
| Moncton | | | | × | | 0/$50 |
| Quebec City | | | | | × | 0/$500 |
| Ottawa | × | | | | | 0/$5,000 |
| Kingston | | | | × | | |
| Hamilton | | | | × | × | |
| Sudbury | × | | | | | |
| Windsor | × | | | | | 0/$1,000 |
| Ontario | | | | × | | 0/$1,000 |
| Winnipeg | | | × | × | × | |
| Saskatoon | | × | × | × | × | 0/$2,000 |
| Edmonton | | | | | × | |
| Calgary | | × | × | × | × | 0/$10,000 |
| New Westminster | × | | × | × | × | 0/$2,000 |
| Vancouver | | | × | × | × | 0/$2,000 |

*Note:* This survey updates and modifies that undertaken by the National Anti-Poverty Organization in 1999. See NAPO, *infra* note 11 at 20.

**Notes**

1  R.B. Horwitz, "Begging the Question: Consistency and 'Common Sense' in the First Amendment Jurisprudence of Advertising and Begging" (1993) 13 Studies in Law, Politics, and Society 213.

2  I. McIntosh and A. Erskine, "'Money for Nothing'? Understanding Giving to Beggars" (2000) 5 Sociological Research Online 1 at 1.5.

3  *Canadian Charter of Rights and Freedoms,* Part I of the *Constitution Act, 1982*, being Schedule B of the *Canada Act 1982* (U.K.), 1982, c. 11.

4  R.C. Ellickson, "Controlling Chronic Misconduct in City Spaces: Of Panhandlers, Skid Rows, and Public-Space Zoning" (1996) 105 Yale L.J 1165 at 1231.

5  H. Hershkoff and A.S. Cohen, "Begging to Differ: The First Amendment and the Right to Beg" (1991) 104 Harvard L.R. 896 at 903, 897.

6  N.K. Blomley, "Panhandling and Public Space" (2000), submitted as expert opinion to the British Columbia Supreme Court in *Federated Anti-Poverty Groups of BC* v. *Vancouver (City)* 2002 B.C.S.C. 105, as part of a case against City of Vancouver By-Law 7885: A By-law to Regulate and Control Panhandling.

7  *Ibid.* Compare with Horwitz, *supra* note 1 and Hershkoff and Cohen, *supra* note 5. For important, and radically counterposed, exceptions to the neglect of space in the discussion of municipal regulation of poor people's behaviours, see Ellickson, *supra* note 4; and

D. Mitchell, "The Annihilation of Space by Law: The Roots and Implications of Anti-Homeless Laws in the United States" (1997) 29 Antipode 303

8  See N.K. Blomley, D. Delaney, and R.T. Ford, eds., *The Legal Geographies Reader: Law, Power and Space* (Oxford, UK: Blackwell, 2001).

9  A. Erskine and I. McIntosh, "Why Begging Offends: Historical Perspectives and Continuities," in H. Dean, ed., *Begging Questions: Street-Level Economic Activity and Social Policy Failure* (Bristol, UK: Policy Press, 1999), 27.

10  H. Dean and K. Gale, "Begging and the Contradictions of Citizenship," in Dean, *supra* note 9 at 13 [citation omitted].

11  National Anti-Poverty Organization [hereinafter NAPO], *Short-Changed on Human Rights: A NAPO Position Paper on Anti-Panhandling By-Laws* (Ottawa: NAPO, 1999).

12  *Safe Streets Act*, 1999, S.O. 1999, c. 8.

13  NAPO, *supra* note 11.

14  R. Pain, "Space, Sexual Violence and Social Control: Integrating Geographical and Feminist Analyses of Women's Fear of Crime" (1991) 15 Progress in Human Geography 415.

15  NAPO, *supra* note 11.

16  C. Sankar, "Vancouver Panhandling Bylaw Faces Constitutional Challenge: Anti-Poverty Activists Claim That the Year-Old Statute Impinges on the Poorest People's Freedom of Speech," *Vancouver Sun* (20 May 1999) at B1. R. See also R. Wicksen, "Panhandling By-Law Must Change," *Business Examiner* (2 October 2000) n.p.

17  R. Moon, "Begging as Expression – Poverty and the Charter of Rights," address to the Mid-Winter Law and Society Conference, Green College, University of British Columbia, 25 January 2001 [unpublished].

18  NAPO, *supra* note 11.

19  City of Saskatoon, By-Law no. 7850, *The Panhandling By-Law* (10 May 1999), s. 3(c)(i-v).

20  City of Vancouver, By-Law no. 2849, *Street and Traffic By-Law* (31 July 2001), s. 70A(1)(b-c) and (2).

21  NAPO, *supra* note 11. See *Criminal Code of Canada*, R.S.C. 1985, c. C-46.

22  P. Shafer, "Bums and Beggars Will Be Busted: Vancouver and New Westminster Pass Anti-Panhandling Bylaws," *British Columbia Report* (25 May 1998) at 28.

23  M-A. Kandrack, *What's Panhandling Got to Do with It?: The Criminalization of Poverty* (Winnipeg: Public Interest Law Group, 1997).

24  *Ibid.* at 20.

25  *Ibid.* at 23.

26  G. Fooks and C. Pantazis, "The Criminalisation of Homelessness, Begging and Street Living," in P. Kennett and A. Marsh, eds., *Homelessness: Exploring the New Terrain* (Bristol, UK: Policy Press, 1999), 123 at 126.

27  V.A. Zelizer, *The Social Meaning of Money* (New York: Basic Books, 1994).

28  *Ibid.* See also W.E. Baker and J.B. Jimerson, "The Sociology of Money" (1992) 35 American Behavioral Scientist 678.

29  Baker and Jimmerson, *supra* note 28. B.G. Carruthers and W.N. Espeland, "Money, Meaning, and Morality" (1998) 41 American Behavioral Scientist 1384.

30  Carruthers and Espeland, *supra* note 29.

31  D.A. Snow *et al.*, "Material Survival Strategies on the Street: Homeless People as *Bricoleurs*," in J. Baumohl, ed., *Homelessness in America* (Phoenix: Oryx Press, 1996), 86.

32  Carruthers and Espeland, *supra* note 29.

33  Zelizer, *supra* note 27 at 2.

34  *Ibid.* at 82.

35  *Ibid.* at 73.

36  McIntosh and Erskine, *supra* note 2 at 1.3.

37  J. Bakan, *Just Words: Constitutional Rights and Social Wrongs* (Toronto: University of Toronto Press, 1997) at 107-9. See also Moon, *supra* note 17.

38  P. Curran, "Door Shut on Enterprise," *[Montreal] Gazette* (25 May 1999) at A3. H. Dean, "Introduction," in Dean, *supra* note 9 at 5.

39  Snow *et al.*, *supra* note 31.

40 M. Adler, "Public Attitudes to Begging: Theory in Search of Data," in Dean, *supra* note 9 at 165.

41 Evidence suggests that while Canadian panhandlers are diverse, they are generally poor and engage in panhandling as a survival strategy. See Blomley, *supra* note 6.

42 Zelizer, *supra* note 27 at 120-21.

43 *Ibid.* at 120.

44 *Ibid.* at 175.

45 *Ibid.* at 144-93.

46 *Ibid.* at 193-97.

47 Erskine and McIntosh, *supra* note 9; B. Jordan, "Begging: The Global Context and International Comparisons," in Dean, *supra* note 9 at 43; and McIntosh and Erskine, *supra* note 2 at 5.4 and 7.4.

48 Dean, *supra* note 38 at 3-4.

49 McIntosh and Erskine, *supra* note 2 at 5.3. One such legend from Victoria, BC, involved a group of affluent, well-dressed suburbanites travelling to the downtown, using public washrooms to change into "grunge clothes" carried in Adidas bags, and proceeding to beg on the street. When sufficient monies were received, this so-called "Adidas crowd" would change back into their expensive clothes and return to the suburbs to party. See "Canada's Amsterdam: Victoria Achieves Notoriety as a Haven for Beggars," *Western Report* (6 May 1996) at 24.

50 Jordan, *supra* note 47 at 55; and P. Shafer, "Don't Feed the Bears: Protected by the Courts, Beggars Forage for Cash and Threaten to Despoil Vancouver," *British Columbia Report* (16 March 1998) at 21.

51 Cited in Dean and Gale, *supra* note 10 at 14.

52 Jordan, *supra* note 47 at 56.

53 McIntosh and Erskine, *supra* note 2 at 4.3-5.3.

54 B. Gleeson, "The Social Space of Disability in Colonial Melbourne," in N.R. Fyfe, ed., *Images of the Street: Planning, Identity and Control in Public Space* (London, UK: Routledge, 1998), 92 at 104.

55 Cited in Erskine and McIntosh, *supra* note 9 at 33.

56 McIntosh and Erskine, *supra* note 2 at 5.3.

57 Erskine and McIntosh, *supra* note 9 at 30.

58 Shafer, *supra* note 50 at 21; and McIntosh and Erskine, *supra* note 2 at 5.3.

59 D. Lindsay, "Easy Pickings for Transients in Kelowna: Young Drifters and Job-Seekers Take Advantage of the Okanagan City's Charity," *British Columbia Report* (4 August 1997) at 15. See also Shafer, *supra* note 22.

60 Zelizer, *supra* note 27 at 197.

61 K. Shue, *Public Health and Social Welfare: Berkeley Cares* (Berkeley: University of California at Berkeley, 1999) at 1.

62 "Guilt-Free Panhandling Voucher System," *Western Report* (7 June 1993) at 16.

63 City of Vancouver, *Administrative Report: "Spare Change" Meters* (Vancouver: City of Vancouver General Manager, 2001) at 1.

64 See Jordan, *supra* note 47 at 57. Zelizer, *supra* note 27 at 123.

65 G. Gad and M. Matthew, "Central and Suburban Downtowns," in T. Bunting and P. Filion, eds., *Canadian Cities in Transition: The Twenty-First Century* (Don Mills, ON: Oxford University Press, 2000), 248 at 259.

66 L. Bourne and A.E. Olvet, *New Urban and Regional Geographies in Canada: 1986-91 and Beyond,* Major Report 33 (Toronto: Centre for Urban and Community Studies, University of Toronto, 1995).

67 P. Hope, "Reviving Downtown Calgary" (1997) 24 Alberta Report 14.

68 D. Ley, The New Middle Class and the Remaking of the Central City (Oxford: Oxford University Press, 1996).

69 Mitchell, *supra* note 7.

70 Ley, *supra* note 68 at 103. See also S. McKeen, "Edmonton's Downtown Dreams Derailed: Core Languishes," *Financial Post* (21 June 1999) at C3.

71  T. Bunting and H. Millward, "A Tale of Two CBDs I: The Decline and Revival(?) of Downtown Retailing in Halifax and Kitchener" (1998) 7 Canadian Journal of Urban Research 139.

72  J. Simmons, *Retail Sales and Retail Location* (Ryerson: Centre for Study of Commercial Activity, 2000).

73  G. LePage, "The Underlying Problem with Panhandlers," *Ottawa Citizen* (27 June 1999) at A17. Lindsay, *supra* note 59; Wicksen, *supra* note 16; and Shafer, *supra* note 22.

74  NAPO, *supra* note 11 at 11.

75  Fooks and Pantazis, *supra* note 26 at 126-28.

76  LePage, *supra* note 73; and NAPO, *supra* note 11 at 11.

77  Jordan, *supra* note 47 at 55.

78  NAPO, *supra* note 11 at 12.

79  Mitchell, *supra* note 7 at 316.

80  S. Sassen, "The Global City: Strategic Site/New Frontier," in E.F. Isin, ed., *Democracy, Citizenship and the Global City* (London: Routledge, 2000), 48 at 52.

81  R.A. Murdie and C. Tiexeira, "The City as Social Space," in Bunting and Filion, *supra* note 65 at 198.

82  *Ibid*. at 209-10.

83  *Ibid*.

84  *Ibid*. at 219.

85  Bourne and Olvet, *supra* note 66 at 65.

86  P. Brent, "Big Box Stores Thump Retailers Downtown: Flight to Suburbs as Sector Becomes Americanized," *Financial Post* (7 July 2000) at D3.

87  D. Harvey, *The Condition of Postmodernity: An Enquiry into the Origins of Cultural Change* (Oxford: Blackwell, 1989).

88  W. Magnusson, "Victoria Regina: Social Movements and Political Space," in J. Caulfield and L. Peake, eds., *City Lives and City Forms: Critical Research in Canadian Urbanism* (Toronto: University of Toronto Press, 1996), 324 at 328.

89  *Ibid*. at 329.

90  Compare with Mitchell, *supra* note 7.

91  N. Smith, *The New Urban Frontier: Gentrification and the Revanchist City* (London: Routledge, 1996).

92  Mitchell, *supra* note 7 at 310.

93  *Ibid*. at 312.

94  Blomley, *supra* note 6. M. Young, "Begging as Expression – Poverty and the Charter of Rights: Commentary," address to the Mid-Winter Law and Society Conference, Green College, University of British Columbia, 25 January 2001) [unpublished].

95  P. Howell, "Public Space and the Public Sphere: Political Theory and the Historical Geography of Modernity" (1993) 11 Environment and Planning D: Society and Space 303 at 309.

96  J. Habermas, *The Structural Transformation of the Public Sphere: An Inquiry into a Category of Bourgeois Society* (Cambridge, MA: MIT Press, 1989).

97  *Ibid*. See also H. Arendt, *The Human Condition* (Chicago: University of Chicago Press, 1958), 22.

98  Howell, *supra* note 95 at 314.

99  R. Sennett, *The Fall of Public Man: The Forces Eroding Public Life and Burdening the Modern Psyche with Roles It Cannot Perform* (New York: Knopf, 1977).

100  D. Mitchell, "The End of Public Space? People's Park, Definitions of Public, and Democracy" (1995) 85 Annals of the Association of American Geographers 108 at 119.

101  T. Boddy, "Underground and Overhead: Building the Analogous City," in M. Sorkin, ed., *Variations on a Theme Park: The New American City and the End of Public Space* (New York: Noonday Press, 1992), 123. For a Toronto-based study, see J. Hopkins, "Excavating Toronto's Underground Streets: In Search of Equitable Rights, Rules, and Revenue," in J. Caulfield and L. Peake, eds., *City Lives and City Forms: Critical Research in Canadian Urbanism* (Toronto: University of Toronto Press, 1996), 63.

102  Boddy, *supra* note 101 at 123.

103  J. Goss, "The 'Magic of the Mall': An Analysis of Form, Function, and Meaning in the Contemporary Retail Built Environment" (1993) 83 Annals of the Association of American Geographers 18.

104  *Ibid.* at 24.

105  Sennett, *supra* note 99.

106  M. Davis, *City of Quartz: Excavating the Future in Los Angeles* (New York: Verso, 1990). H. Simon, "Municipal Regulation of the Homeless Public Space," in J. Baumohl, ed., *Homelessness in America* (Phoenix: Oryx Press, 1996), 149. Simon provides a detailed description of this phenomenon in Santa Ana, California, where the city council passed a succession of ordinances in its attempt to remove "all vagrants and their paraphernalia" from public places (at 154). See also Mitchell, *supra* note 7.

107  Boddy, *supra* note 101 at 126.

108  J. Wardhaugh and J. Jones, "Begging in Time and Space: 'Shadow Work' and the Rural Context," in Dean, *supra* note 9 at 112 [our emphasis]. This phenomenon places the poor in a difficult situation. They are expected to remain hidden, but the pursuit of economic survival through begging requires them to enter into public view.

109  Sennett, *supra* note 99 at 5.

110  D. Sibley, *Geographies of Exclusion* (London: Routledge, 1994).

111  T. Cresswell, *In Place/Out of Place: Geography, Ideology and Transgression* (Minneapolis: University of Minnesota Press, 1996) at 159.

112  *Ibid.* at 47.

113  J. Waldron, "Homelessness and the Issue of Freedom" (1991) 39 U.C.L.A. L. Rev. 295.

114  In the contemporary context, negative perceptions may be underscored by the mass media, which constantly invite us to view public spaces and its inhabitants as inherently threatening and violent. When teenagers venture into public space, for example, they are frequently represented as an inherently problematic and dangerous presence, and efforts to remove them from the streets (for example, through juvenile curfews) have been linked to media images of youth as both the perpetrators and victims of crime. See D.C.A. Collins and R.A. Kearns, "Under Curfew and under Siege? Legal Geographies of Young People" (2001) 32 Geoforum 389. Street crime and public disorder are viewed with considerable apprehension by Canadians, despite declines in violent crime, and statistics suggesting women and children are most likely to experience violent assaults in the home (the quintessential private space) at the hands of someone they know. See Pain, *supra* note 14.

115  J. Weintraub, "The Theory and Politics of the Public/Private Distinction," in J. Weintraub and K. Kumar, eds., *Public and Private in Thought and Practice* (Chicago: University of Chicago Press, 1997), 1 at 1.

116  *Ibid.* at 8.

117  There are, of course, other ironies here. For example, the attempt by the state to "responsibilize" welfare recipients by encouraging them to be more entrepreneurial and self-directed (with the assumption that public support can give way to private independence) could also be said to conflict with panhandling by-laws that punish precisely this behaviour.

118  Habermas, *supra* note 96.

119  M. Kelman, *A Guide to Critical Legal Studies* (Cambridge, MA: Harvard University Press, 1987).

120  N.K. Blomley, *Law, Space and the Geographies of Power* (London: Guildford Press, 1994) at 15

121  S. Hall, "The Great Moving Right Show," in S. Hall and M. Jacques, eds., *The Politics of Thatcherism* (London: Lawrence and Wishart, 1983), 19.

122  A. Gamble, *The Free Economy and the Strong State: The Politics of Thatcherism* (Basingstoke: MacMillan, 1988).

123  A. Sarat and T.R. Kearns, "Beyond the Great Divide: Forms of Legal Scholarship and Everyday Life," in A. Sarat and T.R. Kearns, eds., *Law and Everyday Life* (Ann Arbor: University of Michigan Press, 1995), 21.

124  *Ibid.*

125  Blomley, *supra* note 120.

## Bibliography

Adler, M., "Public Attitudes to Begging: Theory in Search of Data," in H. Dean, ed., *Begging Questions: Street-Level Economic Activity and Social Policy Failure* (Bristol: Policy Press, 1999), 163.

Arendt, H., *The Human Condition* (Chicago: University of Chicago Press, 1958), 22.

Bakan, J., *Just Words: Constitutional Rights and Social Wrongs* (Toronto: University of Toronto Press, 1997).

Baker W.E., and J.B. Jimerson, "The Sociology of Money" (1992) 35 American Behavioral Scientist 678.

Blomley, N.K., "Panhandling and Public Space" (2000), expert opinion to the British Columbia Supreme Court case, *Federated Anti-Poverty Groups of BC* v. *Vancouver (City)* 2002 B.C.S.C. 105.

—, *Law, Space and the Geographies of Power* (London: Guildford Press, 1994).

Blomley, N.K., D. Delaney, and R.T. Ford, eds., *The Legal Geographies Reader: Law, Power and Space* (Oxford, UK: Blackwell, 2001).

Boddy, T., "Underground and Overhead: Building the Analogous City," in M. Sorkin, ed., *Variations on a Theme Park: The New American City and the End of Public Space* (New York: Noonday Press, 1992), 123.

Bourne L., and A.E. Olvet, *New Urban and Regional Geographies in Canada: 1986-91 and Beyond,* Major Report 33 (Toronto: Centre for Urban and Community Studies, University of Toronto, 1995).

Brent, P., "Big Box Stores Thump Retailers Downtown: Flight to Suburbs as Sector Becomes Americanized," *Financial Post* (7 July 2000) at D3.

Bunting T., and H. Millward, "A Tale of Two CBDs I: The Decline and Revival(?) of Downtown Retailing in Halifax and Kitchener" (1998) 7 Canadian Journal of Urban Research 139.

"Canada's Amsterdam: Victoria Achieves Notoriety as a Haven for Beggars," *Western Report* (6 May 1996) at 24.

*Canadian Charter of Rights and Freedoms,* Part I of the *Constitution Act, 1982*, being Schedule B of the *Canada Act 1982* (U.K.), 1982, c. 11.

Carruthers B.G., and W.N. Espeland, "Money, Meaning, and Morality" (1998) 41 American Behavioral Scientist 1384.

City of Saskatoon, By-Law no. 7850, *The Panhandling By-law* (10 May 1999).

City of Vancouver, By-Law no. 7885, *A By-law to Regulate and Control Panhandling* (30 April 1998).

City of Vancouver, *Administrative Report: "Spare Change" Meters* (Vancouver: City of Vancouver General Manager, 2001).

City of Vancouver, By-Law no. 2849, *Street and Traffic By-law* (31 July 2001).

Collins D.C.A., and R.A. Kearns, "Under Curfew and under Siege? Legal Geographies of Young People" (2001) 32 Geoforum 389.

Cresswell, T., *In Place/Out of Place: Geography, Ideology and Transgression* (Minneapolis: University of Minnesota Press, 1996).

Curran, P., "Door Shut on Enterprise," *[Montreal] Gazette* (25 May 1999) at A3.

Davis, M., *City of Quartz: Excavating the Future in Los Angeles* (New York: Verso, 1990).

Dean, H., "Introduction," in H. Dean, ed., *Begging Questions: Street-Level Economic Activity and Social Policy Failure* (Bristol: Policy Press, 1999), 1.

—, and K. Gale, "Begging and the Contradictions of Citizenship," in H. Dean, ed., *Begging Questions: Street-Level Economic Activity and Social Policy Failure* (Bristol: Policy Press, 1999), 13.

Ellickson, R.C., "Controlling Chronic Misconduct in City Spaces: Of Panhandlers, Skid Rows, and Public-Space Zoning" (1996) 105 Yale L.J. 1165.

Erskine A., and I. McIntosh, "Why Begging Offends: Historical Perspectives and Continuities," in H. Dean, ed., *Begging Questions: Street-Level Economic Activity and Social Policy Failure* (Bristol: Policy Press, 1999), 27.

Fooks G., and C. Pantazis, "The Criminalisation of Homelessness, Begging and Street Living," in P. Kennett and A. Marsh, eds., *Homelessness: Exploring the New Terrain* (Bristol: Policy Press, 1999), 123.

Gamble, A., *The Free Economy and the Strong State: The Politics of Thatcherism* (Basingstoke: Macmillan, 1988).

Gleeson, B., "The Social Space of Disability in Colonial Melbourne," in N.R. Fyfe, ed., *Images of the Street: Planning, Identity and Control in Public Space* (London, UK: Routledge, 1998), 92.

Goss, J., "The 'Magic of the Mall': An Analysis of Form, Function, and Meaning in the Contemporary Retail Built Environment" (1993) 83 Annals of the Association of American Geographers 18.

"Guilt-Free Panhandling Voucher System," *Western Report* (7 June 1993) at 16.

Gad G., and M. Matthew, "Central and Suburban Downtowns," in T. Bunting and P. Filion, eds., *Canadian Cities in Transition: The Twenty-First Century* (Don Mills, ON: Oxford University Press, 2000), 248.

Habermas, J., *The Structural Transformation of the Public Sphere: An Inquiry into a Category of Bourgeois Society* (Cambridge, MA: MIT Press, 1989).

Hall, S., "The Great Moving Right Show," in S. Hall and M. Jacques, eds., *The Politics of Thatcherism* (London: Lawrence and Wishart, 1983), 19.

Harvey, D., *The Condition of Postmodernity: An Enquiry into the Origins of Cultural Change* (Oxford: Blackwell, 1989).

Hershkoff H., and A.S. Cohen, "Begging to Differ: The First Amendment and the Right to Beg" (1991) 104 Harvard L. Rev. 896.

Hope, P., "Reviving Downtown Calgary" (1997) 24 Alberta Report 14.

Hopkins, J., "Excavating Toronto's Underground Streets: In Search of Equitable Rights, Rules, and Revenue," in J. Caulfield and L. Peake, eds., *City Lives and City Forms: Critical Research in Canadian Urbanism* (Toronto: University of Toronto Press, 1996), 63.

Horwitz, R.B., "Begging the Question: Consistency and 'Common Sense' in the First Amendment Jurisprudence of Advertising and Begging" (1993) 13 Studies in Law, Politics, and Society 213.

Howell, P., "Public Space and the Public Sphere: Political Theory and the Historical Geography of Modernity" (1993) 11 Environment and Planning D: Society and Space 303.

Jordan, B., "Begging: The Global Context and International Comparisons," in H. Dean, ed., *Begging Questions: Street-Level Economic Activity and Social Policy Failure* (Bristol: Policy Press, 1999), 43.

Kandrack, M-A., *What's Panhandling Got to Do with It?: The Criminalization of Poverty* (Winnipeg: Public Interest Law Group, 1997).

Kelman, M., *A Guide to Critical Legal Studies* (Cambridge, MA: Harvard University Press, 1987).

LePage, G., "The Underlying Problem with Panhandlers," *Ottawa Citizen* (27 June 1999) at A17.

Ley, D., *The New Middle Class and the Remaking of the Central City* (Oxford: Oxford University Press, 1996).

Lindsay, D., "Easy Pickings for Transients in Kelowna: Young Drifters and Job-Seekers Take Advantage of the Okanagan City's Charity," *British Columbia Report* (4 August 1997) at 15.

Magnusson, W., "Victoria Regina: Social Movements and Political Space," in J. Caulfield and L. Peake, eds., *City Lives and City Forms: Critical Research in Canadian Urbanism* (Toronto: University of Toronto Press, 1996), 324.

McIntosh I., and A. Erskine, "'Money for Nothing'? Understanding Giving to Beggars" (2000) 5 Sociological Research Online 1.

McKeen, S., "Edmonton's Downtown Dreams Derailed: Core Languishes," *Financial Post* (21 June 1999) at C3.

Mitchell, D., "The End of Public Space? People's Park, Definitions of Public, and Democracy" (1995) 85 Annals of the Association of American Geographers 108.

Mitchell, D., "The Annihilation of Space by Law: The Roots and Implications of Anti-Homeless Laws in the United States" (1997) Antipode 303.

Moon, R., "Begging as Expression – Poverty and the *Charter of Rights*," address to the Mid-Winter Law and Society Conference, Green College, University of British Columbia, 25 January 2001 [unpublished].

Murdie R.A., and C. Tiexeira, "The City as Social Space," in T. Bunting and P. Filion, eds., *Canadian Cities in Transition: The Twenty-First Century* (Don Mills, ON: Oxford University Press, 2000) 198.

National Anti-Poverty Organization (NAPO), *Short-Changed on Human Rights: A NAPO Position Paper on Anti-Panhandling By-laws* (Ottawa: NAPO, 1999).

Pain, R., "Space, Sexual Violence and Social Control: Integrating Geographical and Feminist Analyses of Women's Fear of Crime" (1991) 15 Progress in Human Geography 415.

*Safe Streets Act*, 1999, S.O. 1999, c. 8.

Sankar, C., "Vancouver Panhandling Bylaw Faces Constitutional Challenge: Anti-Poverty Activists Claim That the Year-Old Statute Impinges on the Poorest People's Freedom of Speech," *Vancouver Sun* (20 May 1999) at B1.

Sarat A., and T.R. Kearns, "Beyond the Great Divide: Forms of Legal Scholarship and Everyday Life," in A. Sarat and T.R. Kearns, eds., *Law and Everyday Life* (Ann Arbor: University of Michigan Press, 1995), 21.

Sassen, S., "The Global City: Strategic Site/New Frontier," in E.F. Isin, ed., *Democracy, Citizenship and the Global City* (London: Routledge, 2000), 48.

Sennett, R., *The Fall of Public Man: The Forces Eroding Public Life and Burdening the Modern Psyche with Roles It Cannot Perform* (New York: Knopf, 1977).

Shafer, P., "Bums and Beggars Will Be Busted: Vancouver and New Westminster Pass Anti-Panhandling Bylaws," *British Columbia Report* (25 May 1998) 28.

—, "Don't Feed the Bears: Protected by the Courts, Beggars Forage for Cash and Threaten to Despoil Vancouver," *British Columbia Report* (16 March 1998) at 21.

Shue, K., *Public Health and Social Welfare: Berkeley Cares* (Berkeley: University of California at Berkeley, 1999).

Sibley, D., *Geographies of Exclusion* (London: Routledge, 1994).

Simmons, J., *Retail Sales and Retail Location* (Ryerson: Centre for Study of Commercial Activity, 2000).

Simon, H., "Municipal Regulation of the Homeless Public Space," in J. Baumohl, ed., *Homelessness in America* (Phoenix: Oryx Press, 1996), 149.

Smith, N., The New Urban Frontier: Gentrification and the Revanchist City (London: Routledge, 1996).

Snow, D.A., L. Anderson, T. Quist, and D. Cress, "Material Survival Strategies on the Street: Homeless People as *Bricoleurs*," in J. Baumohl, ed., *Homelessness in America* (Phoenix: Oryx Press, 1996), 86.

Waldron, J., "Homelessness and the Issue of Freedom" (1991) 39 U.C.L.A. L. Rev. 295.

Wardhaugh J., and J. Jones, "Begging in Time and Space: 'Shadow Work' and the Rural Context," in H. Dean, ed., *Begging Questions: Street-Level Economic Activity and Social Policy Failure* (Bristol: Policy Press, 1999), 101.

Weintraub, J., "The Theory and Politics of the Public/Private Distinction," in J. Weintraub and K. Kumar, eds., *Public and Private in Thought and Practice* (Chicago: University of Chicago Press, 1997), 1.

Wicksen, R., "Panhandling By-Law Must Change," *Business Examiner* (2 October 2000) n.p.

Young, M., "Begging as Expression – Poverty and the Charter of Rights: Commentary," address to the Mid-Winter Law and Society Conference, Green College, University of British Columbia, 25 January 2001 [unpublished].

Zelizer, V.A., *The Social Meaning of Money* (New York: Basic Books, 1994).

# 3
# Private Life: Biotechnology and the Public–Private Divide

*Nathan Brett*

A case recently before Supreme Court of Canada involves the extension of patents to mammals, asking the question of whether a genetically altered mouse can be patented.[1] The Canadian Patent Office had denied Harvard University's (and DuPont's) claim on grounds that the mouse was not an invention. The decision was upheld on its first appeal, but then reversed on appeal to the Federal Court (thereby allowing the patent). The US-based Geron Corporation has recently sought and obtained an English patent on a genetically altered human embryo.[2] In another well-publicized case, the Myriad Corporation has held patents for several years on naturally occurring genes that predispose women to breast cancer.[3] Each of these cases involves patent protection of intellectual property rights in living things or the constituents of living things. They are salient examples of what has become a huge industry (and a rapidly expanding source of work for lawyers).[4] Many different claims can be involved in a single patent application – for instance, three enterprises that are at work on the human genome project have submitted patent applications that involve over three million claims of intellectual property.[5]

As the recent attempt of pharmaceutical companies to enforce their patents on AIDS-related drugs in South Africa reveals, the protection of such intellectual property rights can have very serious consequences. These companies recently dropped their legal case because of the public opinion costs of openly litigating a policy that would cost many thousands of lives.[6] Such cases (as well as the recent developments cited earlier) require us to reflect on the political morality that has led us in these directions. What, if anything, might justify these forms of privatization? This essay addresses this question by looking at justifications for the lines between public and private that are embedded in liberal-democratic theory.

The arguments in this essay are designed to question the shift of the line between public and private that is represented by biological patents. The first section offers some general reflections on the various contrasts between public and private. It argues that the normative structures that we characterize as "private" support forms of exclusion and partiality that are ruled out where matters are deemed to be public. It does not deny, of course, that some matters are properly private. In the relevant sense, loyalty and friendship are virtues that relate to private matters. They are not evils to be eradicated. However, a social world constructed entirely out of private relations would be one from which justice had disappeared. The second section of the essay focuses on the creation of private property. It considers how one might go about justifying the removal of something from a realm where it is publicly accessible by making it into private property. The section begins by outlining a theory of "original acquisition" as an account of what is necessary to justify this form of "privatization." It then considers whether this account applies to the justification of patents. The final section takes up this question of privatization in relation to living things. The discussion concerns the characterization of living things (and genes) as "inventions" – a question that is central to the Harvard Onco-mouse case. The discussion utilizes some thought experiments to explore and defend the view held by Canada's patent examiner that mice are *not* inventions. The essay concludes by raising some doubts about the notion that these forms of privatization are justified by their social utility.

## Analyzing the Public and Private "Spheres"

### Some Public–Private Dichotomies

> Public. adj. In general, and in most of the senses, the opposite
> of private. The varieties of sense are numerous and pass into each
> other by many intermediate shades of meaning. The exact shade
> often depends upon the substantive qualified, and in some
> expressions more than one sense is vaguely present.
>
> — *Oxford English Dictionary*[7]

I begin this section with a list of some of the divisions that one encounters in the literature on the public and private:

1 **Autonomy:** The private sphere of autonomous action and decision versus the domain appropriately governed by public law and policy.
2 **Privacy:** The right to privacy regarding information and observation versus the public right to know.
3 **Property:** Private property in resources and enterprise versus (i) resources held in common (public roads, parks, knowledge in the public domain) and (ii) public services (public schools, hospitals).

4  **Family:** The private or domestic sphere of (family life) versus (i) the public world of business and (ii) the public sphere within the reach of governmental and legal intervention.
5  **Government:** The sphere of private (that is, domestic) politics and state sovereignty versus that of international law, including[8] (i) international public law (for example, as developed under human right agreements) and (ii) international private law (for example, as developed under free trade agreements).[9]

This list is not, of course, an exhaustive catalogue of the different divisions between public and private. (It does not include, for example, a possible division between public and private morality.) Moreover, these categories can overlap. Private or domestic matters, which are contained in the fourth category (family), are areas protected as matters of (1) decisional autonomy, and (2) informational privacy. Historically, private property relations, which are contained in the third category (property), have figured in connections among the adult persons comprising families (that is, one person having in some respects ownership of another). This is still an aspect of the relations between parent and child, which battles over custody make salient.

These categories of public and private can also exist in opposition, in the sense that the same item can be public in relation to one category and private in relation to another. Thus, aspects of business relations can be "private enterprises," which come under the third category (property) and involve certain immunities from government regulations, but they are also "public" in the sense that contrasts with the "private sphere" of family life. The metaphor of public and private "spheres" itself suggests a simplicity of division that makes it difficult to grasp the complexity of these distinctions. Even the study of changes in the lines between public and private is affected by the ambiguities that result from this diversity. For example, the recent ascendancy of international law through trade agreements is a shift toward a public, international standard of world commerce. However, at another level, it has clearly involved privatization, including the shift of many items from an "information commons" to a regime of private intellectual property rights.

## Privacy and Equality
There is a perception that, in general terms, matters in the public realm are subject to judgments of fair and equal treatment in a way that matters in the private realm are not. Indeed, one might wonder how it could be otherwise – since judgments of both formal and substantive equality require interpersonal comparisons, which can be blocked by rights to privacy or by the relegation of decisions to a sphere of private judgment. In an era of

tax-cutting politics, where we are moving away from the government pursuit of substantive equality, we also see shifts in the lines between public and private. There is in Canada, for example, a legitimate worry that moves toward privatization of (some) medical services will mean a loss of equal access to medical treatment. There is a comparable worry about the effects of a proliferation of private primary and secondary schools. Government reductions of public funding to postsecondary education have also raised concerns about the equality of access. Feminist critiques present a different kind of case, but they have a similar point when they argue that the relegation of the family to a private realm is one of central ways in which male domination and gender inequality are maintained.[10]

These examples illustrate a strong association between public and equal on the one hand, and private and unequal on the other. Other cases reveal, however, that the relation between equality and privacy is more complex than this equation suggests. Clearly, many items on the private side of these dichotomies (from individual autonomy to freedom from surveillance, ownership of a private home, and so on) are themselves highly prized and should be equitably distributed. Some level of autonomy must be protected from state interference if we are to lead recognizably human lives.[11] Were, for example, the state to demand a code of heterosexual conduct, it would be failing to treat its citizens as equally autonomous. Again, a person who is constantly under the surveillance of others will not be free in ways that are necessary to develop the capacity for autonomy or individuality. Feminists have also made clear the price that may be paid by those people whose right to privacy is denied. The intrusion of social service agents prying into the lives of welfare recipients can be one of the instruments through which social oppression is maintained.[12] Moreover, the enforcement of codes of privacy can be one of the mechanisms utilized to advance the goal of substantive equality. By treating certain types of information (for example, information about a person's genetic make-up) as private, the state can seek to impose a "veil of ignorance" to protect individuals from discriminatory decisions regarding, for example, employment and insurance.

These cases demonstrate that we cannot defend a *simple* link between the dichotomies of public and private on the one hand and equality and inequality on the other. Nonetheless, I will argue that there is a link between inequality and privacy at the conceptual level. It is important to set the stage for this discussion of "privatization" by highlighting this constitutive feature of the domains that we refer to as "private." In this respect, partiality (as opposed to impartiality) is an essential feature of "private" domains. This means that we should be particularly vigilant when social and legal changes involve moving the line between public and private by privatizing what has heretofore been a public matter.

## Two Analytical Hypotheses

What, if anything, do the divisions between public and private have in common? Some authors have argued that these categories have so little to do with each other that our best strategy is to select a central sense and stop using the public–private distinction for the rest.[13] The heteronomy and relativity of the divisions listed earlier may also suggest this strategy. Yet we would lose sight of some important connections if we adopted it. A private domain or area of privacy is one in which – in *some* respect – a person or group is to be left free from interference and free from public review or scrutiny. Focusing on the private, I will suggest two common features, in the belief that these features will help us to understand the legitimate worries about shifts of the various lines between public and private. I will not try to show that each is a necessary condition or that they are jointly sufficient for all forms of "privacy."

### Exclusion

My first point should seem obvious in relation to the first three categories. Part of what is going on when the public–private distinction is used normatively has to do with the descriptive meaning of the terms. What is private in this latter sense is away from people – secluded and exclusive. When we use the contrast normatively to mark the sphere of individual autonomy, the private sphere consists of those types of decisions and actions from which the control of the state *ought* to be excluded. Likewise, the right to privacy is the right to exclude others from information about ourselves, either as individuals or as members of groups.[14] The right to privacy excludes certain forms of investigation and observation as well. Private property also involves this right to exclude. In fact, the most obvious connections between privacy and exclusion are those involved in private property. Property is private when it involves the right to use and control something, together with the right to exclude others from its use. Although I believe that forms of exclusion are involved in the other forms of privacy that I have listed, I shall not stop to defend that thesis in this essay.[15]

### Partiality

I want to introduce a further general hypothesis about these divisions that is related to the exclusivity of that which is private. Private matters are, in some respect, also immune from generalization tests that apply to public matters. Within some dimensions of decision making it is permissible, in the various private spheres, to *treat like cases differently*. In other words, the various private spheres involve relations of *partiality* among persons.

This type of partiality needs to be explained by means of examples. Let me take the relations of family and friends as paradigms of private relations. In being part of a family, I am connected with specific other people in ways that I am not related to others. In befriending a person, I enter into normative relations with this person that I will not have with others. These relations between certain specific people and myself are relations of partiality. If I treat my friends and family as if they matter to me no more than anyone else, I *mistreat* them. I can recognize that two children are equally needy and still be obliged to treat one preferentially because one child is *mine*. In the same way, I am partial to my friends and rightly so, according to the moral outlook that prevails in most societies. In entering into promises and contracts, I establish further relations of partiality: I can no longer treat the interests of A and B as being of equal importance in all respects, if I have a promised something to A but not to B.

Much of our normative world is comprised of such relations of partiality. A good chair of an academic department will act in a way that favours her department over others, just as a good leader of a corporation will work for its goals and those of its shareholders over others. A loyal citizen promotes the good of his political community, and the head of a state works in ways designed to favour its citizens over others. From the perspective that the privacy of property establishes (taken by itself), the owner of private property need not concern himself with the fact that others have far greater need for these resources than he does.

All of these partial viewpoints exist in contrast with, and often in tension with, public viewpoints that demand impartiality. In some contexts, the types of loyalties that define the relationships just considered become matters of unfairness and injustice. A judge cannot take pride in giving lighter sentences to his friends. A teacher treats his students unfairly if he or she plays favorites. There is a vantage point of public reason from which all specific relations of partiality can appear to be vices. This viewpoint has sometimes been thought to define the outlook of reflective morality.[16] Yet, in my view, it is a mistake to suppose that partiality can be eliminated from a defensible reflective morality. It is true that loyalties can easily be, and often have been, taken to excess. A normative world constructed entirely from such partial relations would be one from which justice has disappeared. The holocaust was built (in part) out of a morality of loyalties that left no room for an impartial point of view. However, the partialities involved in friendship and citizenship are not (like Nazism or racism) something that we should strive to overcome. A world of wholly utilitarian impartiality, in which people are rendered free from commitments to specific others and in which caring (in this sense) and loyalty disappear, is itself not a worthy ideal of human perfection.

I said earlier that private matters are *in some respects* immune from generalization tests that apply to public matters. This qualification should be explained in a way that heads off a misunderstanding. While I am claiming that partiality is a constitutive feature of the private spheres that are the focus of our concern, I am not saying that impartiality plays no role within them. It has often been said that a good parent treats her children equally. We also think that the citizens of a state should be treated with equal concern and respect. Yet this is not to deny that relations of partiality are constitutive of the family and the sovereign state. My contention is that such relations of partiality are essentially involved in the social constructions of the private spheres under discussion. Partialities may also be involved in the "public" spheres that comprise our social world (how could it be otherwise, given the overlaps between categories)? However, partiality is not a defining feature of what is public, and it is not what we are after when we designate some matter as a public interest or responsibility.[17]

It seems clear that we can end up with the lines drawn in the wrong places. We are prepared to condemn a totalitarian state in which there is little in the way of protected spheres of autonomous decision-making or informational privacy or in which no property is private property from which others can be excluded. The special relationships of partiality are important aspects of any life worth living. Yet a social world built entirely (or predominantly) out of partialities, in which there is no public perspective from which human actions and possessions are constrained by reference to public and impartial standards, is also a vision of dystopia.

In the discussion that follows, I focus on one of the divisions between public and private listed earlier – that is, the division between private and common property. My aim is to examine one of the current ways in which this division between public and private is shifting. This shift involves the privatization of what would otherwise belong to the public world of objects and information, treated as resources held in common. I will begin by considering the problem of "privatization" in its general form.

## Taking Property Out of the Commons

### Original Acquisition

Why should *any* resources be privatized? The problem of appropriating things (whether concrete or abstract) from an unowned state is an interesting and complex issue. As is usual in human affairs, considerations of desert and utility are both involved in the plausible justifications of this form of privatization. There is no doubt that *some* system of private property is useful to us. In order for beings such as ourselves, with needs and other interests, to have any level of security, there must be some degree of control over some of the things we depend upon. We can sometimes avoid tragedies of the commons,[18] in which a resource is lost (or not developed adequately to meet our needs), by parcelling out what has been held in common. It also seems that people sometimes have rights to things because what they have done entitles them to control them. John Locke gives an account of appropriation that is based (in part) on intuitions about what people deserve for their efforts.[19] However, it is an account that requires us to take into consideration the equal importance of the interests of other persons. Let me begin with a simple Lockean scenario, which we can then complicate by thinking about intellectual property.

Suppose that someone (call her Alice) finds some seeds, cultivates a small area of land, and grows tomatoes. It seems plausible to say that she is entitled to the fruits of her labour. Other things being equal – she is not harming anyone else by growing them – the tomatoes are properly deemed to be hers because she produced them. We would not give Alice sufficient respect as a human agent, if we supposed that others were free to take what she has produced. Alice has assumed some risks and costs and expended some effort in growing this crop. These factors lie behind the intuition that she deserves control over them in the sense that she is entitled to exclude others from their use. She is also free to utilize them in ways that involve partiality: to feed her children, for example, and to let others fend for themselves. Yet this entitlement to what she has produced seems to require the support of further entitlements. For one thing, Alice cannot produce anything without utilizing resources. What about the land that she utilizes for her garden? Does her crop also give her entitlement to exclude others from the use of this land? If we deny that it does, then we leave others free to use this garden plot in ways that are incompatible with the respect for Alice that we have just endorsed. Others cannot be free to hold their dances or dig for gold in Alice's garden. Maintaining our intuition about respect for her as a person requires us to expand her (limited) right to exclude others. She is entitled to the necessary land as a resource, although there must be limits to this sort of appropriation.

Locke provides two such limits in discussing the possibility of converting the resources that one finds into private property.[20] In the first place, Alice cannot collect property to the point where she wastes resources that others need. Viewed in terms of the land's utility, this is an obvious and plausible constraint. If Alice stakes out four times as much property as she needs for her crop in order to keep others from utilizing the resource, nothing about desert or respect for persons will justify these extra holdings. The second constraint that Locke imposes seems to throw the whole business of acquisition into doubt. After Alice makes her appropriation, there must be "enough and as good left in common for others."[21] It would seem that this theory presupposes conditions of *abundance*. How could one possibly leave enough *and as good*, under conditions of scarcity? What use is a theory of acquisition that becomes inapplicable as soon as things are in short supply?

Two contemporary theorists, Robert Nozick and David Gauthier,[22] have developed a solution to this problem that involves a consequentialist element. Alice can acquire the (scarce) resources that she needs for her crop without leaving others worse off, as long as she is productive in some way that offsets what she has taken from the commons. If, for example, she is willing to trade what she produces, she may even make their situation better. Given the efficiencies of a division of labour, her neighbour might work fewer hours for more tomatoes than if he had grown his own. Alice need not provide this sort of benefit, but she cannot (justifiably) make public resources into private property if she is making other people *worse* off.

The Lockean proviso (enough and as good left) allows one to acquire what would otherwise continue to be held in common as long as one is not making oneself better off by imposing burdens on others. Under this interpretation, the proviso is nicely consistent with a main principle in John Rawls's theory of justice: losses to some people cannot be justified by gains accruing to others.[23] One can also take this theory to be a specific application of the standard liberal constraint on individual autonomy (deriving from John Stuart Mill). Individual liberty is limited by the obligation not to cause harm to others.[24] Acquisition within the limits of the Lockean proviso allows people – and presumably groups that form corporations – to privatize (scarce) resources only where this privatization is linked to production, in the sense that it leaves others as well off as they were before.[25] This theory provides what I regard as a liberal basis for "privatization." It makes possible a world of private commerce in which there will be competition and winners and losers, although this commerce will require further controls in order to maintain the conditions of justice.

### Patents and Appropriation

A patent is a form of private property. To be patentable under existing law (in Canada and internationally), an invention must be something that is *novel*; it must be something *non-obvious* to those knowledgable in the relevant area of inquiry and technology; and it must have *utility*. "Utility" is not used in the wide sense that is assumed by utilitarianism – that is, it is not a matter of weighing overall costs and benefits. The question of whether an invention has utility is generally reduced to the question of whether it has some industrial application. Patenting requires the inventor to fully disclose the design of the product or process that he seeks to patent. In return for this disclosure, the patent holder is granted a twenty-year[26] monopoly on producing the type of object that is patented.

A justification for *intellectual* property rights, such as patents, may seem rather far from the theory of appropriation that was just summarized. Intellectual property is unlike ordinary property in two ways that deserve our attention:

1  The objects of patents are abstract. Intellectual property is never simply rights to particular things, although patents do extend control over

particular items that fall within protected categories. The rights conferred by patents relate to a certain *type* of object – one that is deemed an invention. Patenting involves securing a monopoly right to the use of the design embedded (actually or potentially) in a whole class of particulars. If one has patented a mousetrap, the patent extends to all instances of this design.

2  Generally speaking, intellectual discoveries are non-rival. That is, one person's use of a design, recipe, or procedure (or a research paper) is ordinarily compatible with the (simultaneous) use of this resource by others. As Joseph Raz points out, some goods are contingently public (non-rival), in this sense; and some are inherently so.[27] Municipal water supplies and public hospitals are only contingently public resources or goods.[28] On the other hand, a language is essentially a public good. One person's use of English or French, for instance, does not use it up, leaving less for others.[29]

Intellectual property involves knowledge or information, ways of presenting information, and the products that utilize this information. This information is usually a non-rival good, in the sense that a language is a public good. Unless they are *artificially* introduced, scarcities in this resource occur when needed information has not yet been discovered or when information is not being used and, hence, not being transferred to others. The monopolies conferred by patents can create artificial barriers to scientists' using needed information. Holders of patents are granted the right to exclude others from the unlicensed use of the information about their inventions that they are required to make public.

The fact that patents are only granted on *inventions* suggests an objection to the line of inquiry that I am developing. I will be considering the patenting of life forms as cases in which something is moved from a public to a private domain. However, if the object of a patent is always an invention, then (it might be said) it did not exist in any domain, public or private, prior to its invention. And, if inventions are additions to the total set of available resources, then there is no sense in which something is being "privatized" by being moved from a public to a private domain.

This is an important objection. Conferring the status of "invention" on an object or process, and thereby identifying it as something new, is essential to its patentability. The Lockean proviso gives us one interpretation of the importance of this distinction. If an invention is a useful addition to the total set of resources that the people of a community can rely on, then not only will a patent give deserved recognition, it will do so under conditions that cannot violate the proviso. The addition of something useful cannot itself be a way of imposing a loss on others. It would seem, then, that no harm could be done by the state's recognition of private property rights in inventions. Consider an example. There was no cure for polio prior to Dr. J.E. Salk's putting together (or isolating) what was necessary for a vaccine. Using the historical point prior to this invention as a baseline, one can determine that Salk would have made no one worse off, even if he had entirely withheld the vaccine from others. If he patented and marketed it at prices people were eager to pay, he could hardly be guilty of reducing the resources remaining for others. And, if (like the pharmaceutical companies in the South African market) he sold it at a price that many could not possibly afford, it still could not be said that he had made anyone worse off.

If inventions were pure resource additions for which individual (or corporate) responsibility could be assigned, as this application of the proviso implies, this objection would be unassailable. However, there are several factors rendering this claim dubious:

- One is the image of the inventor working in isolation. In fact, of course, scientists do not proceed in isolation from each other. Progress and discoveries in science depend very heavily on a shared community of investigators and theorists. Even the verification of theories is such that no one person is ever in possession of evidence for all of the relevant claims. It is only as an interdependent social project that discoveries and inventions are made. Moreover, the image of the solitary intellectual discoverer is particularly at odds with the sorts of inventions that are products of biotechnology, where various genome projects have involved massive coordination. Even privately funded labs have depended very heavily on research that they have been able to garner from a domain of public (and publicly funded) research. Why, then, should we regard any particular individual or firm as deserving full credit for an invention? Edwin Hettinger puts the point in this way: "A person who relies on human intellectual history and makes a small modification to produce something of great value should no more receive what the market will bear than should the last person needed to lift a car receive full credit for lifting it."[30]
- Judged in terms of desert, it would be arbitrary to treat the last person needed to lift a car as if he had sole responsibility for lifting it. The same is surely true in relation to modern technological innovation, which draws heavily on the resources of the community. Yet, despite this arbitrariness (from the desert perspective), it might be useful to organize our activities so that we treat the agent who relies on the resources of others to complete an innovation *as if* he were solely responsible. (Of course, there is an element of freeloading embedded in this mode of justification that we would have to be prepared to overlook.) It might be that treating individual agents as if they were responsible for inventions (and therefore entitled to privatize them) is the best way to stimulate the completion of social processes of innovation. As soon as we shift entirely to this

utilitarian justification, however, we open up the possibility that it is *not* the best way to organize the complex processes that are required for research-based solutions to our goals.

Suppose a jigsaw puzzle is being put together by a group. If our goal is to get the puzzle built as efficiently as possible, it may be an ineffective strategy to divide up the pieces and distribute control over them to individual members of the group. Similarly, coordinating the various human enterprises necessary to understand, prevent, and perhaps cure cancer involves pulling together a huge number of intellectual resources. Assigning proprietary rights over the various pieces of this puzzle may be a very poor way to organize this process.[31] Under competitive market conditions, this dispersion may give rise to situations in which progress is blocked because researchers are unable to gain access to each of the various elements needed to reach individual solutions. Researchers may also be hesitant to proceed for fear of being accused of utilizing a piece of the puzzle that belongs to others. (In one respect, the jigsaw puzzle analogy is misleading. As we have seen, patents are in categories or types of things, which cannot literally be distributed to different players.) To the extent that progress toward the goals of such research is impeded by the privatization of the resources necessary to reach solutions, there are costs and harms associated with such patents.[32] The Lockean proviso should not be applied in a way that misses these costs by ignoring the collective aspects of the process of innovation. The question of whether anyone is made worse off by privatization of the evolving resources of technology depends on a judgment about how lives would have gone without the introduction of these forms of privacy. One will miss these costs in making a simple comparison of available resources before and after an invention.

- Patent protection involves a fine and troublesome line between invention and discovery. Every inventor discovers procedures for doing something. In some sense, these ways of doing things are there to be found and utilized. When an invention is patented, the procedures are still there to be found (by independent inventors), but what one finds at this latter point is someone's private property. In recognizing this point, Robert Nozick argues that the duration of a patent should be no longer than the length of time, under prevailing circumstances, that we could reasonably expect it to take others to come up with a comparable solution.[33] In the world of modern technology, this period may be negligible.[34]

- In the cases that particularly concern us in this essay, patents are being requested and granted on living creatures and genes. As the following discussion is designed to show, these patent rights extend far beyond what has actually been invented. It can hardly be true that a living creature *as a whole* is an invention. Nor is it true that a newly isolated, but naturally occurring, gene (for example, one that predisposes toward breast cancer) is an invention. There are reasons to think that what is really patented in such cases are scientific discoveries. Officially speaking, however, scientific discoveries are deemed to belong to the domain of public knowledge and are immune from patent protection: "Anything that is merely a discovery is not patentable subject-matter."[35] A worrisome feature of patents in biotechnology is that they contribute to the process of blurring this line between invention and discovery.

## Patents on Life

### Inventing Living Things
The Canadian Federal Court case, *Harvard College* v. *Canada (Commissioner of Patents)*, considers whether Harvard University can patent a mouse.[36] The case concerned the so-called "Onco-mouse," a genetically altered rodent especially prone to cancer and, therefore, an unusually good subject for certain studies of the disease. The question was whether the genetically engineered version of the mouse could itself be patented. A patent had already been granted in the United States,[37] but the Canadian Patent Office did not accept that the mouse was an "invention" in the sense required by the law governing patents. The trial division of the Federal Court agreed that it was not an invention. However, as we have noted earlier, this decision was reversed on appeal.[38] The attorney-general has appealed the case to the Supreme Court of Canada.[39] The Harvard mouse case is important because it will establish whether (in Canada) higher life forms can be treated as patentable property.

It is true, of course, that there is a public interest in cancer research and hence, in the development of ideal living models for the study of cancer. The patenting of the Harvard mouse is defended on the grounds that such patenting will provide the funding incentive for the research that may lead to the prevention and cure of this disease. If the case is successful (as it already has been in the United States and Europe), it will set a precedent that will provide lucrative control over living things that are used as research tools. Let us consider, then, what could justify the patent holder's claim of proprietary rights over whole categories of living things.

It is certainly true that even the earliest forms of property permitted the ownership of particular living things. In our earlier example, Alice seems entitled, at least within the limits set by the Lockean proviso, to ownership of the plants that she has cultivated. Moreover, there is no doubt about the possibility of owning particular animals under current (or ancient) rules. We would not suppose, however, even if she were the first to cultivate tomatoes, that Alice's action entitles her in any way to control *all* of the tomatoes that anyone might produce. Yet, as we have seen, a patent of the sort in question would involve temporary (twenty-year or limited) ownership of whole categories of living things. What could justify this claim? Did DuPont, acting through its agents at Harvard,[40] actually invent the cancer-mouse that it seeks to patent?

An official of the Canadian Patent Office who first considered this question, the Canadian Commissioner of Patents who reviewed this decision, and the trial division judge to whom the case was first appealed all held that, although the process through which the Onco-mouse was produced was patentable, the mouse itself was not. They accepted, in accord with the criteria for patents, that the mouse was something new, that it was non-obvious, and that it would be useful in the study of cancer. However, they denied that the mouse was an invention.[41] These decision-makers held that the claim to have invented the mouse highly inflates the degree to which the researchers were responsible for the existence of the mouse. A single sequence in the genetic material had been changed. Why should this change be sufficient to warrant the claim that the resulting mouse as a whole should be taken as Harvard's invention and that it must be withdrawn from the public domain?

We would never suppose that the changing of a single line in a work by Shakespeare or in a Microsoft Word program (assuming that they are both in the public domain) would gain one status as the author or programmer of the works that resulted. Why is a comparable claim plausible in relation to the mouse? The Canadian Patent Office was prepared to accept Harvard's claim that it was the inventor of the specific gene insertion process and even of the transformed gene itself, but it denied the claim that the mouse as a whole was Harvard's invention because so little of the development of the mouse was attributable to the manipulation of this particular gene sequence.

The Federal Court was not impressed with this argument.[42] The Onco-mouse is useful as a cancer research tool precisely, and only, because of the transgenic modification that Harvard had introduced. Of course, the mouse cannot exist without a myriad of other traits. Harvard was not dictating the length of the tail or the eye colour of these mice, for example. However, these properties have nothing to do with the usefulness of these mice in the research context. It is true that this cancer research depends on a whole range of genetic factors for the development of the animal itself with organs susceptible to cancer. In this respect, the Harvard researchers are not unlike other inventors who must *always* rely heavily on the laws of nature to produce their inventions. Every invention, whether it is a Franklin stove or a gravity pump is dependent upon causal conditions of which the inventor is not the author. There is no such thing as invention *ex nihilo*.

If one were seeking an ideal case to open the door to patents on higher forms of life (and no doubt DuPont was), this one looks like a good bet. There is no question that cancer research is (and is perceived to be) important. The Onco-mouse is engineered to be an ideal tool for certain kinds of drug research. Moreover, this mouse would seem to have little value apart from this research context. There is no other reason for such a mouse to exist. We routinely dispose of mice as pests, are unlikely to want cancer-prone mice as pets, and so on. The fact that this type of mouse is both new and not obvious we can take for granted. The fact that the utility of this type of mouse appears to be confined to its use as a research tool *seems* to be sufficient reason to collapse the question "Is it invented?" into the question "Is its usefulness a product of invention?"

Nonetheless, I share the intuition of the earlier decision-makers who were unwilling to open the door on this kind of privatization. Let us reconsider the argument. It is certainly true that inventors are always heavily dependent on the "laws of nature" – no one invents *ex nihilo*. In this respect, the processes that were integral to developing a living Onco-mouse were not different from those involved in any sort of invention. There is also a significant difference between re-writing a single line in *Othello* or in Microsoft Word and adding an altered gene to the myriad of information carriers embedded in the cells of a mouse. Unless we adopt a particular theological view of the gene sequence of the mouse, the remaining encoded information is not assignable to some human (or super-human) agent. The "information" encoded in the genes consists simply of very complex causal potentials. There is no author/programmer, analogous to William Shakespeare or Bill Gates's team, who can be identified as the source of the genetic potential of the mouse.

It is not necessary, however, to anthropomorphize natural genetic processes in order to raise doubts about the claim that DuPont's research team at Harvard has invented the mouse. We are certainly not constrained by metaphysics to say that the mouse as a whole is invented. Consider another analogy. A river runs beside a community that (we will suppose) already has an ample alternative water supply. Andrew, a woodcutter, discovers that the river can be made to move logs from the mountains to the community, where there is a market for his lumber. In order to do this, however, he finds it necessary to divert another stream into the river, thereby giving it sufficient flow. By this process, he creates a new and very useful "mixture of matter," one that was, at the time, not obvious to others who are knowledgeable about forestry and transportation. Andrew has provided a highly useful innovation. Being the first to do this, he now claims to be the inventor of the river itself and applies for a patent.

In this case, there is no question of anthropomorphism. We will assume that the river does not have an author, as *Othello* does. And, unlike tomatoes and mice, it does not have a complex information-carrying program, analogous to that of a Microsoft product, which might tempt us toward a design hypothesis. There is also no reason to think that the river is already owned by someone. As with categories of living things, accepting the patent on a river would involve a move toward the private possession of a type of thing previously held in common. However, the claim that Andrew invented the river itself seems clearly false. Still, one might wonder why it should matter. By hypothesis, the community only cares about Andrew's river as a way of carrying its lumber. He has invented the only thing that (at the time of his innovation) makes the river useful.

One reason that it should matter is that the imagined inventor, who is claiming a patent on the river itself, would be (for the duration of the patent) in a position to exclude or tax others for their own new developments and uses of the river. Second, the claim extends not only to *this* river. It is a matter of *intellectual* property rights. Any unused river that other individuals contemplate connecting to tributaries (in places governed by his community's patent laws and those with whom it has trade agreements) will be subject to Andrew's veto – unless his permission has been granted. Third, he is not just free to charge those who want to use these rivers as conduits for lumber. Other potential users cannot alter their rivers in this way (by connecting a stream for irrigation purposes, for example) without licensing agreements, because this *type* of river has already been assigned to someone. It does not matter whether others stumble on the idea of connecting tributaries or learn by reading Andrew's statement of disclosure. Finally, it may not matter whether they find *other* ways of making shallow rivers work to carry their logs, since it is not just the process that Andrew has patented but the (flow-increased) type of river itself.

The claim that Andrew invented this river is itself preposterous. He changed it. He changed it in a way that, for a community and at a given time, was highly useful. Given the circumstances, it was the only use that they had found for the river. Such a change is not a sufficient reason for saying that all such rivers are his inventions. One might object that the analogy is misleading because it is easy to imagine other uses for these rivers but difficult to see how the transgenic mouse could be good for anything but research on cancer. This may be a plausible response, in relation to the intrinsic merits of the case – although I have no reason to exclude the possibility that these mice could become useful in relation to research on other diseases. However, the threat that is posed by the case being taken as a precedent is another matter. Inevitably, companies seek to extend their control over resources that are necessary (or useful) to consumers of various sorts. In this "knowledge economy," they are keen to establish intellectual property rights. Since intellectual property involves control over whole categories of things, it is a much more efficient mode of acquisition than material property in objects appropriated as particulars, gained one at a time. Intellectual property in living things is especially attractive since they come equipped with natural processes of manufacture (or replication). Conversely, for those likely to be affected by these exclusionary rights, these same factors constitute powerful reasons against allowing such patents.

There are other reasons for apprehension. The Onco-mouse that Harvard seeks to patent is a "research tool," although it is not a research tool in the same way that test tubes and calculators are instruments of research. One can expect research to be done *on* the mice as they are utilized in cancer research. The distinction between research that is conducted on (as opposed to with) a patented tool is important in understanding what is at stake in this case. One would never suppose that holders of patents on test tubes or calculators have entitlements that "flow through" from the use of the instruments to a research output. However, that inference is much more tempting when the research is being conducted on a patented object. Since the mouse is itself claimed as an "invented" object of study, it can be argued that intellectual property rights *do* flow through from research using the mouse to the therapeutic techniques and products that result from this research. (If the mouse is my invention, then I am at least partly responsible for the inventions that are based on my invention.)

According to M.A. Heller and R.S. Eisenberg,[43] this transitivity of patent rights is just what DuPont claims in relation to the Onco-mouse, which was produced through research that it funded:

> DuPont has offered noncommercial research licenses and sublicenses on terms that seem to require licensees to return to DuPont for further approval before any new discoveries or materials resulting from the use of licensed mice are passed along to others or used for commercial purposes. DuPont thereby gains the right to participate in future negotiations to develop commercial products that fall outside the scope of their patent claims. In effect, the license terms permit DuPont to leverage its proprietary position in upstream research tools into a broad veto right over downstream research and product development.

Once again we see the stark difference between the private property rights in question and those that we are prepared to accept as governing our relations with Alice's tomatoes or an invention such as a mousetrap. We can easily find a basis for saying that respect for the gardener or inventor requires that we treat their output as products that belong to a private realm of property (in different ways). We would take unfair advantage of Alice if we failed to acknowledge any such entitlement. These intuitions do not easily extend to the kind of leverage that DuPont seeks in claiming this mouse as its invention. On the contrary, this is a kind of control that takes unfair advantage of those "downstream" researchers who find that the products of their own research are controlled by DuPont's patent rights. This "leveraging" of patent protection also illustrates an important way in which patent rights can function to produce a "chilly climate" for research. If other parties will end up with patent rights to new products of research, then proceeding with research will bring new patent liabilities with little benefit. Indeed, this is the main point of the above quotation.

In this case, we are looking at a form of appropriation that resembles putting up a flag to claim a continent. Such claims will inevitably outstrip any plausible justification in terms of what is deserved for the effort and risks involved. If we are to justify this form of appropriation, we will need to show that greater utility can be obtained from playing the social game in this way. Inevitably, the form of privatization that biological patents involve will exclude some persons from resources that would otherwise become available to them. If it does not make up for this limitation by generating greater opportunities and resources than would be available without privatization, it is imposing costs and leaving those excluded worse off than they would otherwise be. Thus, this form of privatization would fail to meet the *proviso* that (as I have argued earlier) a liberal theory of acquisition requires.

### Genes as Patentable Inventions

Before turning to the utility calculation that this claim requires, I want to consider (much more briefly) a related issue concerning the patenting of genes. Patents on whole living organisms are controversial enough to give rise to the court case that we have just been discussing. However, both within and outside Canada, and for some time, corporations have been applying for, and obtaining, patents on genes. Such patents not only include the new genetic sequences generated by the processes of implantation. Many gene patents that are the result of research on the human genome project concern naturally occurring genes. Some well-known examples include patents on genes that appear to carry a predisposition for breast cancer and patents on a rare gene that may provide immunity from the AIDS virus.[44] On the surface, there seems little question that these genes are discovered, not invented. How could such genetic discoveries be patentable? In discussing gene patents, Richard Gold gives the following answer to this problem:

> The simple response to this question about the newness of genes is that genes, as they occur in our bodies, are not patentable. After all, if they were, no one would be permitted to grow new skin let alone have children. Genes, as they exist naturally within our bodies, cannot be patented for the simple reason that they have been around for a very long time ... [However,] isolated genes that have been removed from the body and copied many, many times constitute something that can potentially be patented if they otherwise meet the criteria for patentability. This is because, in all the eons that

have passed since our genes came into existence, they have never come neatly in isolated and purified form. This is one of the hallmarks of an invention: that it would not have existed but for human intervention. In fact, anything taken from a human, animal, or plant and put into isolated form can potentially be patented.[45]

So, this answer states that genes are patentable when they are isolated and copied. Since the latter is not a way of generating something new, it must be that it is in isolating the gene that innovation occurs. Once again, the distinction between a process and its product becomes significant. There is no doubt (in my mind) that one can claim to have invented the process through which the isolation of a particular gene is made possible. Gold claims, however, that the gene itself is patentable because, prior to the use of this technique, it had not existed in isolation. He also suggests that it is only the *gene in isolation* that can be patented.[46]

Although I do not doubt that Gold has captured an official rationale for allowing gene patents, the argument does not strike me as unproblematic. From the fact that something (G) is newly isolated, it clearly does not follow that G is new. At least from the realist view, which is presupposed by the court's distinction between discovery and invention, G had to exist prior to its isolation. Moreover, the techniques of isolation are pervasive in science – consider, for instance, the processes that led to the discovery of elements, atoms, species, or the reasoning involved in statistical and causal analysis. It is hard to know what discovery could not be re-cast as a patentable invention on this basis. (In general, to find something is to isolate it from its surroundings.) The acceptance of isolation as a legitimate basis for the patenting of discoveries would provide a wide and slippery slope toward the privatization of whatever scientists find.

Of course, it is true that a company that has patents on genes that are present in your cells does not thereby own you. A patent does not constitute that kind of ownership. Yet a patent may well affect what one can do in relation to the genes in one's body. If a woman wants tests to determine whether she has a gene that involves a predisposition for breast cancer, she may have to wait until the company with the patent on this gene has time to process her tissue sample. It also may turn out that she cannot afford it. Moreover, if another company invents a simpler and more effective technique for isolating this gene, they may not be able to use it without violating the first company's patent. This latter point shows one of the practical differences between patenting the process and patenting the gene itself. It also indicates why one might worry that this kind of patenting, instead of functioning as a powerful incentive for investigation, could create a bottleneck that is inimical to scientific progress. Research aimed at finding a more efficient way to produce or detect a gene is blocked by the fact that the gene has been patented.

## Biological Appropriation and Utility: Concluding Remarks

If the conclusions drawn from the above discussion of appropriation are ultimately defensible, then the discoveries/inventions that emerge within modern science and technology cannot be assigned individual (or even corporate) responsibility. This means that desert-based arguments will not lead us to a justification of patents on the (largely social) products of modern technology. The arguments of the next sections were designed to raise doubts about the claim that some of the specific products of biotechnology are appropriately categorized as inventions. Once again, the supposed inventors are making inflated claims as to their responsibility for the objects over which they would claim patent rights. In the process, they are downloading the costs of missed opportunities on those who are excluded by the assignment of such rights. The question remains, however, as to whether these forms of property can be justified in terms of their overall utility.

When the argument for biological patents is put directly in terms of utility it is open to sources of doubt that would not be in place if desert and compensation were the basis of claims to appropriation. Short of conducting a huge research project, of course, it is not possible to provide an adequate assessment of the overall utility of this practice. Given that much has been written about the benefits of the patent system, I will end this discussion by raising some difficulties with arguments for patents based on overall gains in utility.

Some of the main questions that we need to answer are obviously empirical:

- We need evidence, not of the effectiveness of patents as incentives (this we can take for granted, I think), but rather of their being more effective than the alternatives (such as public funding of research).
- We need to enter into our calculation the disutility involved in restricting the use of patented products. This is the sort of consideration that came to the surface when drug companies tried to enforce their patents on AIDS-related drugs and, to cite another example, when patent protections delay the entry of generic drugs and thereby impose heavy costs on health care systems.
- There are, by now, huge transaction costs involved in obtaining and enforcing patents. The average cost of a patent in this area of study is US $10,000, and "it typically costs US $1.5 million to litigate a patent."[47]
- Research opportunities are lost and discoveries not made because the licensing fees relating to patents on necessary research tools are too high

or because there is some likelihood that patents will be violated inadvertently. The Bristol Meyers Corporation has recently given up more than fifty cancer-related research projects because of fears of patent violations.[48]

Proponents of patents in the area of biotechnology often provide little more than speculative answers to the cost/benefit question. We are told, for example, that

> the Canadian patent system benefits not only the individual patent holder, but society as a whole as well. The prospect of reaping economic rewards from patented innovations spurs people and companies to invest their time and money in novel areas of scientific research. Consequently, new and better products become available to the public at a faster pace.[49]

This conclusion may be right. It is clear that huge private investments,[50] are currently being made in biotechnology and research and that there are many new applications for patents on the products of biotech research every day. Yet the main argument for these sweeping claims is generally phrased in terms of such "economic indicators" as the numbers of jobs or dollars involved. One must bear in mind, however, that a great deal of economic activity – which will be impressive from this confined economic viewpoint – may not in fact be productive. If a corporation discovered a way to remove much of the oxygen from the earth's atmosphere and sell it to us in canisters, they would engender a huge amount of economic activity in the process of privatizing a resource that we have held in common. However, in doing this, the company would have made our lives considerably worse.[51] Since the patenting of biological discoveries also involves the privatization of resources (research tools and information) that might otherwise be held in common, we should be especially vigilant in assessing the "economic indicators" generated by the prospect of patents. Patents necessarily reduce some forms of competition that would otherwise exist, sometimes reserving whole categories of research to particular companies. Clearly, the assessment of the fact that biotechnology is a multi-billion dollar industry depends on looking carefully at these figures in relation to the risks and harms that are associated with the business of granting companies the monopolies that patents involve.

Not all questions about a utility-based defense of patents on living things and their constituents are empirical. To be a plausible basis for social justification, the pursuit of utility itself must be constrained by considerations based on individual rights. The framework of liberalism that I have assumed in this essay includes such basic rights as those relating to freedom of expression and inquiry. Moves toward the privatization of scientific inquiry exist in fundamental opposition to the emphasis on freedom of inquiry and expression that are at the core of liberal democracy. Privatization is always suspect in this respect for it involves the confinement of what would otherwise be held in common to a sphere of decision-making that, by its very nature, is exclusive and partial. We have every reason to worry that the forms of partiality that are introduced when various forms of inquiry are privatized will be corruptions of the projects that they are expected to stimulate. We have recently seen some of the ways in which privately funded research can exhibit this partiality, in the questions that are investigated, in the ways that the data is analyzed, and in the results that are publicly reported. The patenting of the Harvard mouse is a small, but very important, step in the direction of a form of partiality that is fundamentally at odds with the spirit of free inquiry upon which liberal democracy depends.

**Notes**

1  *Harvard College* v. *Canada (Commissioner of Patents)*, [2000] 4 F.C. 528, rev'g [1998] 3 F.C. 510. [hereinafter *Harvard College*]. While this paper was in press, the Supreme Court of Canada (*Harvard College* [2002] S.C.J. No. 77) reversed the Federal Court of Appeal decision in a five to four judgment. In the Supreme Court case, the majority rejects the Harvard's claim to have "invented" the Onco-mouse. That conclusion is also defended in this essay.

2  "Britain Grants Embryo Cloning Patent," *New York Times* (24 January 2000), available at <http://www.gene.ch/genet/ 2000/Jan/msg00083.html>.

3  "Myriad Genetics Reinforces Its Strong Intellectual Property Position with the Award of Two More Patents in Breast Cancer," press release from *Myriad Genetics*, available at <http://www.myriad.com/pr/20000425.html>.

4  "Since 1995 in the USA, the number of intellectual property lawsuits reaching federal courts has risen ten times faster than any other legal action ... Twelve of every one hundred biotech patents end up in court. Forty-six percent of all US biotech patents that are challenged are overturned." P.R. Mooney, "The Impetus for and Potential Alternatives Mechanisms for the Protection of Biotechnological Innovations," report prepared for the Canadian Biotechnology Advisory Committee, 2001, 4, available at <http://www.CBAC-CCCB.ca./ documents/ Mooney_English.pdf>.

5  *Ibid.* at 5.

6  *London Financial Times* (19 April 2000). The editorial goes on to say that "South Africa is to the global pharmaceuticals industry what Vietnam was to the US military. Nothing will ever be quite the same again." This piece is quoted in "Drug Companies Drop Lawsuit Preventing South Africa from Importing Generic AIDS," available at <http://www.hivandhepatitis.com/hiv_and_aids/public/041901.html>.

7  From the *Oxford English Dictionary*, CD-ROM version 1.02 (Oxford: Oxford University Press, 1992). The etymological note is also interesting: "The change to *publicus* [from *poplicus*], appears to have taken place under the influence of *pubes*, in the sense 'adult men,' 'male population.'"

8  Susan Boyd considers the public–private dichotomy in relation to domestic and international politics in her introduction to the edited volume *Challenging the Public/Private Divide* (Toronto: University of Toronto Press, 1997). The essay in this volume that is focused on in this dichotomy is by Doris Buss, "Going Global: Feminist Theory, International Law, and the Public/Private Divide" at 360-84.

9  In this discussion, I will not attempt to deal with the complexities involved in the legal taxonomy of public and private law.

10  This is a dominant theme of feminist critiques of the public/domestic dichotomy. See, for example, Chapter 6, "Justice from Sphere to Sphere: Challenging the Public/Domestic Dichotomy," in Susan Moller Okin, *Justice, Gender and the Family* (New York: Basic Books, 1989).

11  A useful source is Zillah Eisenstein, "Equalizing Privacy and Specifying Equality," in Nancy Hirshmann and Christine DiStefano, eds., *Revisioning the Political* (Boulder: Westview, 1996) at 181-207.

12  See Martha Acklesberg and Mary Shanley, "Privacy, Publicity, and Power," in Hirshmann and DiStefano, *supra* note 11 at 222-23.

13  See Hyman Gross, "Privacy and Autonomy," in J. Chapman and J.L. Pennock, eds., *Nomos XIII (1971) Privacy* (New York: Lieber-Atherton, 1971) at 169-82; and W.A. Parent, "Privacy, Morality, and the Law" (1983) 12 Philosophy and Public Affairs at 269-88. These articles are reprinted in J. Feinberg and H. Gross, eds., *Philosophy of Law,* 3rd edition (Belmont: Wadsworth, 1986) at 291 and 297, respectively.

14  While most writers on privacy rights concentrate on the protection of individuals, Ferdinand Schoeman emphasizes the importance of the protection of associations in *Privacy and Social Freedom* (Cambridge: Cambridge University Press, 1992).

15  Affairs of domestic government and sovereignty seem to fit in an obvious way. To the extent that a government is sovereign, it can exclude other decision-makers. The privacy of the domestic sphere in relation to the state is once again clearly a matter of exclusion. The division between the domestic sphere and the world of commerce, on the other hand, appears to break the pattern. In this case, the exclusion seems to run the other way: those assigned to the domestic sphere were excluded from the forms of commerce that provided compensation for labour.

16  Kurt Baier articulates this claim in *The Moral Point of View* (Ithaca: Cornell University Press, 1958). It represents a tradition that includes most of moral philosophy, including philosophers as diverse as Plato and Hume. For a critique of this view, see, for example, Bernard Williams's discussion of integrity in "A Critique of Utilitarianism," in J.J.C. Smart and B. Williams, eds., *Utilitarianism: For and Against* (Cambridge: Cambridge University Press, 1973); and Thomas Nagel, *Equality and Partiality* (Oxford: Oxford University Press, 1991). This view has also been questioned by some feminists who defend an ethic of care, for example Carol Gilligan, *In a Different Voice: Psychological Theory and Women's Development* (Cambridge, MA: Harvard University Press, 1982).

17  I am also not arguing or assuming that partiality (and, hence, privacy) necessarily connects with egoism and the pursuit of self-interest. Not all forms of partiality involve the promotion of self-interest, though, of course, this is a highly important manifestation of partiality. The kind of partiality that is involved in care – for example, care for the members of one's family – can involve great sacrifices of time and energy, which might have been devoted to one's own projects. The chair of a department can impose costs on herself for the sake of the department. In times of conflict, the partiality of loyalty to a state can cost a person his life.

18  Garrett Hardin, "The Tragedy of the Commons" (1968) 162 Science 1243.

19  John Locke, *Two Treatises of Government,* Book II, edited by P. Laslet, 2nd edition (Cambridge: Cambridge University Press, 1967), Chapter 5.

20  *Ibid.* at sections 27 and 33.

21  *Ibid.* at sections 33-36. This has come to be known as the "Lockean proviso." Robert Nozick's main commentary on the proviso is in *Anarchy, State, and Utopia* (New York: Basic Books, 1974) at 174-82.

22  Nozick, *supra* note 21 at 177; Gauthier, *Morals by Agreement* (Oxford: Oxford University Press, 1986), Chapter 7.

23  John Rawls, *A Theory of Justice* (Cambridge, MA: Harvard University Press, 1971) at 28: "Each member of society is thought to have an inviolability founded on justice, or as some might say, natural right, which even the welfare of society or of every one else cannot override. Justice denies that the loss of freedom for some is made good by a greater good shared by others." Nozick put the point as follows: "Locke's proviso that there be 'enough and as good left in common for others' (sect. 27) is meant to ensure that the situation of others in not worsened" (at 175).

24  J.S. Mill, "On Liberty" in *The Essential Works of John Stuart Mill,* Max Lerner, ed. (New York: Bantam Books, 1971) at 263.

25 Nozick, *supra* note 21 at 179, allows that, in a limited sense the proviso "runs with the title," that is, applies to the justice of transfers. However, much of what Nozick says indicates that once one has entitlement via original acquisition, one is free to utilize this in competitions with others, where there will be losers, as well as winners. Using this interpretation, one is never justified in reducing the circumstances of individuals to a condition worse than what one would have obtained in the "state of nature" – that is, before such appropriations and the consequent organization of trade and production began. Yet if I am right, this is not a legitimate move. Appropriation from a supposed ancient "state of nature" misrepresents the situation. Appropriation from resources held in common is an ongoing social process.

26 In Canada, prior to 1989, a patent lasted for a period of seventeen years. Since that time, a patent's life has been extended to twenty years. Twenty years appears to be the norm now under international agreements.

27 Joseph Raz, *The Morality of Freedom* (Oxford: Oxford University Press, 1986) at 198: "A good is a public good in a certain society if and only if the distribution of the good is not subject to voluntary control by anyone other than each potential beneficiary controlling his share of the benefit."

28 As we are all too aware, such resources can be funded and administered in such a way that they become rival goods: there may not be enough beds to go around in our hospitals.

29 In fact, the problems with language are almost the reverse of those that face us in relation to food or housing. A language can be dissipated – destroyed as an effective medium of communication – by its *disuse*. This fact has motivated a great deal of expenditure and regulation in the province of Québec.

30 E. Hettinger, "Justifying Intellectual Property" (1989) 18 Philosophy and Public Affairs 38.

31 The possibility of a "tragedy of the anti-commons" is now important in discussions of biotech patents. The anti-commons arises when ownership is dispersed in a way that blocks those who would make a contribution to human welfare (for example, through research into life-saving therapies). See M.A. Heller and R.S. Eisenberg, "Can Patents Deter Innovation? The Anticommons in Biomedical Research" (1998) 280 Science 698: "Anticommons property can best be understood as the mirror image of commons property. A resource is prone to overuse in a tragedy of the commons when too many owners each have a privilege to use a given resource and no one has a right to exclude another. By contrast, a resource is prone to underuse in a "tragedy of the anticommons" when multiple owners each have a right to exclude others from a scarce resource and no one has an effective privilege of use."

32 See the final section of this chapter ("Biological Appropriation and Utility") for further discussion of this problem.

33 Nozick, *supra* note 21 at 182. See also the discussion in Hettinger, *supra* note 29 at 44.

34 In practice, the holder of a patent may not even be a first discoverer. This point would seem to be ruled out by the criteria for patents – because the design would not be *new*. However, novelty can be treated as a question of whether anyone already holds a patent. The question, in practice, is who is first to stake a claim and whether this discovery is still non-obvious to the appropriate research community.

35 Justice Nandon, in *Harvard College*, F.C., *supra* note 1 at para. 26. This view is frequently expressed in the literature and cases involving patents.

36 *Harvard College*, F.C., *supra* note 1.

37 The US patent actually covers *all* "non-human mammals" whose cells have been modified by the oncogene sequence. See US Patent no. 4736866, claim number 1. See Rebecca Eisenberg, "Patenting Research Tools and the Law," available at <http://www.nap.edu/readingroom/books/property/2.html>.

38 Two out of three Federal Court judges agreed on reversing the denial of the patent on the Onco-mouse.

39 The appeal established that higher forms of life are not patentable under current law. Legislative changes to allow for such patents were not ruled out. See *supra* note 1.

40 It is important to remember that a big corporation has a financial stake in this case.

41   A part of their reasoning concerned the unreliability of the technology. Only about 7 per-
      cent of the mice developed through this procedure (and therefore only 3.5 percent of their
      offspring) would have the characteristic in question. The unreliability argument is dis-
      missed in Federal Appeal (*Harvard College*, F.C., *supra* note 1 at para 68-78). This might be a
      reason for not patenting the *process*. However, the examiner had allowed that the process
      was patentable. Having accepted gene insertion as a process of making something new, he
      was in no position to use this argument against the product of the process. Moreover, this
      question is really about the utility of the invention, and the earlier decisions had accepted
      that the technology was useful as well.
42   *Harvard College*, F.C., *supra* note 1 at para. 49.
43   Heller and Eisenberg, *supra* note 30 at 700.
44   "Feud over Gene Patents,"ABC News, 28 February 2000, available at <http://www.abcnews.
      com>.
45   Richard Gold, "Patents in Genes," CBAC Consultation Document, 2000, 2-3, available at
      <http://www.cbac-cccb.ca>.
46   On this theory, it is specific genes, in physio-chemical isolation, that are the invented
      objects that can be treated as private property. The theory is not plausible: the sequences of
      nucleotides that comprise genes cannot be isolated from their normal habitats in cells and
      then utilized as a resource. In this respect the isolation of genes is quite unlike the isolation
      of substances like adrenaline, with which gene isolation is sometimes compared (because
      adrenaline was patented).
47   Mooney, *supra* note 4 at 4.
48   *Ibid*. at 13.
49   Mona Frendo, "Intellectual Property Protections for Biological Innovations," prepared for
      the Canadian Biotechnology Advisory Committee, January 2001, available at <http://www.
      cbac-cccb.ca>.
50   "Canada's biotechnology industry consists of 360 firms." It employs 10,000 people "and
      generates 1.9 billion [annually] in sales." Biotechnology is "one of the world's fastest grow-
      ing industries, with global demand expected to move from $20B in 1995 to $50B in 2005."
      "Biotechnological Intellectual Property and the Patenting of Higher Forms of Life," CBAC
      Consultation Document, 2001, 5, available at <www.cbac-cccb.ca>.
51   To cite a real world example, industrial pollution contributes to the economy by generat-
      ing a demand for bottled water – a multi-million-dollar industry. We *could* include this as
      one of the ways in which industry contributes to the economy, but in so doing, we would
      have missed the fact that this revenue is generated by imposing immense costs.

## Bibliography

### Jurisprudence
*Harvard College* v. *Canada (Commissioner of Patents)*, [2000] 4 F.C. 528.
*Harvard College* v. *Canada (Commissioner of Patents)*, [1998] 3 F.C. 510.

### Books and Articles
Acklesberg, Martha, and Mary Shanley, "Privacy, Publicity, and Power," in Nancy Hirshmann
      and Christine DiStefano, eds., *Revisioning the Political* (Boulder: Westview, 1996), 213.
Baier, Kurt, *The Moral Point of View* (Ithaca: Cornell University Press, 1958).
Boyd, Susan B., ed., *Challenging the Public/Private Divide* (Toronto: University of Toronto
      Press, 1997).
Buss, Doris, "Going Global: Feminist Theory, International Law, and the Public/Private
      Divide," in Susan B. Boyd, ed., *Challenging the Public/Private Divide* (Toronto: University of
      Toronto Press, 1997) at 360.
Eisenstein, Zillah, "Equalizing Privacy and Specifying Equality," in Nancy Hirshmann and
      Christine DiStefano, eds., *Revisioning the Political* (Boulder: Westview, 1996), 181-207.
Gauthier, David, *Morals by Agreement* (Oxford: Oxford University Press, 1986).
Gilligan, Carol, *In a Different Voice: Psychological Theory and Women's Development* (Cam-
      bridge, MA: Harvard University Press, 1982).

Gross, Hyman, "Privacy and Autonomy," in J. Chapman and J.L. Pennock, eds., *Nomos* XIII (1971) *Privacy* (New York: Lieber-Atherton, 1971), 169.

Hardin, Garrett, "The Tragedy of the Commons" (1968) 162 Science 1243.

Heller, M.A., and R.S. Eisenberg, "Can Patents Deter Innovation? The Anticommons in Biomedical Research" (1998) 280 Science 698.

Hettinger, E., "Justifying Intellectual Property" (1989) 18 Philosophy and Public Affairs 31.

Hirshmann, Nancy and DiStefano, Christine eds., *Revisioning the Political* (Boulder: Westview, 1996).

John Locke, *Two Treatises of Government*, edited by P. Laslet, 2nd edition (Cambridge: Cambridge University Press, 1967).

Mill, John Stuart, "On Liberty," in Max Lerner, ed., *The Essential Works of John Stuart Mill* (New York: Bantam Books, 1971).

Nagel, Thomas, *Equality and Partiality* (Oxford: Oxford University Press, 1991).

Nozick, Robert, *Anarchy, State, and Utopia* (New York: Basic Books, 1974).

Okin, Susan Moller, *Justice, Gender and the Family* (New York: Basic Books, 1989).

Parent, W.A., "Privacy, Morality, and the Law" (1983) 12 Philosophy and Public Affairs 269.

Rawls, John, *A Theory of Justice* (Cambridge, MA: Harvard University Press, 1971).

Raz, Joseph, *The Morality of Freedom* (Oxford: Oxford University Press, 1986).

Schoeman, Ferdinand, *Privacy and Social Freedom* (Cambridge: Cambridge University Press, 1992).

Williams, Bernard, "A Critique of Utilitarianism," in J.J.C. Smart and B. Williams, eds., *Utilitarianism: For and Against* (Cambridge: Cambridge University Press, 1973).

**Internet Sources**

"Britain Grants Embryo Cloning Patent," *New York Times*, 24 January 2000, <http://www.gene.ch/genet/ 2000/Jan/msg00083.html>.

"Biotechnological Intellectual Property and the Patenting of Higher Forms of Life," Canadian Biotechnology Advisory Committee, 2001, <http://www.cbac-cccb.ca>.

"Drug Companies Drop Lawsuit Preventing South Africa from Importing Generic AIDS," <http://www.hivandhepatitis.com/hiv_and_aids/public/041901.html>.

"Feud over Gene Patents," ABC News, 28 February 2000, <http://www.abcnews.com>.

"The Impetus for and Potential Alternatives Mechanisms for the Protection of Biotechnological Innovations," P.R. Mooney, Canadian Biotechnology Advisory Committee, 2001, <http://www.cbac-cccb.ca./documents/Mooney_English.pdf>.

"Intellectual Property Protections for Biological Innovations," Mona Frendo, Canadian Biotechnology Advisory Committee, January 2001, <http://www.cbac-cccb.ca>.

"Myriad Genetics Reinforces Its Strong Intellectual Property Position with the Award of Two More Patents in Breast Cancer," press release of *Myriad Genetics*, <http://www. myriad. com/pr/20000425.html>.

"Patents in Genes," Richard Gold, CBAC Consultation Document, 2000, 2-3, <http://www.cbac-cccb.ca>.

# 4
# Invasions of Publicity: Digital Networks and the Privatization of the Public Sphere

*Darin Barney*

The widespread deployment of digital information and communication networks has renewed popular concern and scholarly reflection on the relationship between the private and public spheres of human existence. The digitization of increasing volumes and varieties of social and personal information, escalating mediation of human activity by vulnerable public and proprietary network technologies, and the development and use of highly sophisticated data management and surveillance techniques by state and commercial actors have all contributed to an urgent sense that privacy is under considerable threat in postindustrial liberal democracies. Accordingly, a great deal of attention has been devoted recently to describing the nature of the digital threat to privacy as well as to considering how legal and regulatory regimes might be configured to secure individuals against its advance. This attention has taken many forms, including scholarly and trade books,[1] popular (and often alarmist) treatment in the periodical press and mass media,[2] privacy policy-making and legislation,[3] the growth of privacy organizations, and even the emergence of a nascent privacy "industry."[4]

This article is intended to sketch some theoretical avenues towards consideration of the other side of this dynamic: the impact of digital technologies on the character of publicity, or the public sphere of democratic citizenship. I will draw upon two accounts of the public sphere and its fate under modern conditions – Hannah Arendt's theorization of the ancient Greek *polis*[5] and Jürgen Habermas's account of the bourgeois public sphere[6] – in order to isolate some critical questions that we might fruitfully bring to bear in considering the status of the democratic public sphere under the regime of digital technology. These include questions regarding the relationship between economics and politics, the material basis of a viable public sphere, the democratic role of media technologies, and the character and practice of citizenship.

Contrary to popular imaginings about its inherently democratic character, and despite both considerable technical potential as an instrument of democratic participation and exciting – but still exceptional – cases of counter-hegemonic applications, I will argue that as currently deployed in the context of liberal capitalism, digital technology forms part of a general condition in which politics has been eclipsed by economic activity in markets, rational-critical debate has been supplanted by consumer choice, and the public sphere, understood as a site of citizenship, remains conspicuous by its relative absence. In sum, the argument is that rather than mediating a rejuvenation of the public sphere, digital technology is part of the trajectory of mass, technological modernity in which the political character of the public sphere has largely decomposed.

## Rise and Fall of the Ancient Public Sphere

The notion of a public sphere as distinct from the private is an ancient one, rooted in the practices of Athenian democracy and expressed in the political philosophy developed in response to these practices. We receive what is arguably the clearest theorization of the contours of this distinction in Hannah Arendt's *The Human Condition*, wherein Arendt attempts to specify the status of the public realm in terms of the *vita activa*, or "the basic conditions under which life on earth has been given to man."[7] These basic conditions are divisible into three fundamental activities – labour, work, and action – which together comprise the totality of a human life.

By labour, Arendt means the activity that attends to the vital necessities of individual and species survival. Among these necessities we might list nourishment, rest, shelter, and procreation. By work, she means activities that prosecute useful arts, practices that fabricate the artificial world of objects and things in the midst of which human beings live, the crafting of natural materials into durable, useful forms that are not provided in or by nature itself. Finally, by action, Arendt refers to the exercise of a human being's political capacities in common with a plurality of others, the collective pursuit of public justice through reasoned speech (*logos*) and practical deeds (*praxis*). Action, in this sense, includes (but is not exhausted by) political discussion, judgment, and citizenship. Together, labour, work, and action manifest the conditions of human existence, although their character, relationship, and relative status may vary geographically or historically.

Within the categories of the *vita activa*, it is in exercising the political capacity of action that humans express and realize their essential and distinctive nature as political beings – beings singularly capable of reasoned speech about common justice and practical action toward achieving that end. As Aristotle taught and Arendt affirms, human beings are certainly social, but this sociability, this mere *living* together, does not distinguish them from other creatures in the way that their capacity for expressly political action does (as we will see later in this essay, Arendt identifies the collapse of politics into the category of society as marking the degeneration of the modern public sphere). No other creature besides the human combines *logos* (reasoned speech) and *praxis* (practical action) in a single practice whose end is justice amongst fellows. In their capacity for political action, human beings excel beyond other beings, thus politics is a particularly human excellence, and a life without it is other than adequately human. It is in this sense that Aristotle stipulated that a person who does not partake in politics "is either a poor sort of being, or a being higher than man" and, in a slightly different formulation, Arendt writes that "action alone is the exclusive prerogative of man; neither a beast nor a god is capable of it."[8] Furthermore, within the *vita activa*, it is in political action alone that a human being achieves freedom, conceived in Aristotelian terms as a life freely chosen, a life emancipated from the demands of necessity and utility (that is, from labour and work). As Arendt writes, "neither labor nor work was considered to possess sufficient dignity to constitute a *bios* at all, an autonomous and authentically human way of life; since they served and produced what was necessary and useful, they could not be free, independent of human needs and wants."[9] As Arendt points out, the political life of action "escaped this verdict" precisely because its substance, in attending exclusively to justice, was indifferent to the needful and the useful, and therefore free.[10] Thus, the three elements of the *vita activa* exist in a hierarchy, with action at the crown, labour at the base, and work mediating between the two.

The base of labour and the crown of action correspond roughly to the distinction between the private and public spheres, which, not incidentally, also entails a distinction between economics and politics. As Arendt puts it: "the distinction between a private and public sphere of life corresponds to the household and political realms, which have existed as distinct, separate entities at least since the rise of the ancient city-state."[11] The domestic household (*oikia*) comprises the private realm and is the site of laborious attention to the biological necessities of survival and reproduction. Economics – which combines *oikia* with *nomos* for "law" to yield the "law of the household" – is the servile, apolitical art of managing necessity. As Arendt writes, "according to ancient thought on these matters, the very term 'political economy' would have been a contradiction in terms: whatever was 'economic' related to the life of the individual and the survival of the species, was a non-political, household affair by definition."[12] The private realm, as a realm wholly defined by its status as a site for the economic management of necessity, is necessarily incapable of yielding human freedom. This incapacity is manifested in the rule of masters over women and slaves in the household, which is violent, despotic, and apolitical. Even in exercising this despotism, "men of the house" themselves express an attention to necessity that eliminates their own freedom in that realm.[13] Bereft of freedom, the private sphere of the household could not contain distinctly human excellence, nor could economics express it (indeed, in this view, economics expresses precisely an absence of human excellence).

The human capacity for action, understood specifically as reasoned speech and practical deeds pursuant to justice, requires for its exercise a sphere that is not corrupted by base necessity or the imperatives of utility; a common realm that is not exhausted by consumption or by markets for the exchange of material goods; a site of genuine citizenship. The public sphere is that formation in which the particularly human excellence of political action is freely undertaken. In the ancient Greek context, this public sphere was institutionalized as the *polis,* the space where base, despotic, beastly masters of households (that is, economists) assumed the crown of their essential humanity and acted as public-spirited citizens. In contrast to the violence of the private sphere, and the money of the markets, the currency of the *polis* was persuasive speech. "To be political," Arendt explains, "to live in a *polis*, meant that everything was decided through words and persuasion, and not through force and violence," and the political life was "a way of life in which speech and only speech made sense and where the central concern of all citizens was to talk with each other."[14] Politics, in this understanding, is reasoned speech about justice by equal citizens, combined with practical attempts to achieve this end. It is a form of activity that simply demands a public sphere of freedom for its exercise: "Action needs for its full appearance the shining brightness we once called glory, and which is possible only in the public realm."[15] Human excellence, as it is manifest in political action, is possible only in the public realm, and its role as the site of political activity distinguishes the public from the private sphere.

It should be noted that the public realm in which humans act as political beings is not at all abstract. It is, instead, the sphere in which human beings are related concretely in a "common world of things."[16] Politics is intersubjective because it is activity comprised of speaking and acting with others. It is to this point that Arendt refers when she writes: "The *polis*, properly speaking, is not the city-state in its physical location; it is the organization of the people as it arises out of acting and speaking together, and its true space lies between people living together for this purpose, no matter where they happen to be ... action and speech create a space between the participants which can find its proper location almost anytime and anywhere."[17] Nevertheless, she also emphasizes that the public sphere in which this political activity takes place is constructed and objective, or it is not at all. For Arendt, "the term 'public' signifies the world itself in so far as it is common to all of us" – the world that "relates and separates men at the same time." Arendt is careful to point out that this "world" that is the public sphere is not equivalent to mere nature: "It is related rather, to the human artifact, the fabrication of human hands, as well as to affairs which go on among those who inhabit the man-made world together. To live together in the world means essentially that a world of things is between those who have it in common."[18] These "things" that comprise the public sphere or world of politics are the product of human work, and it is in this sense that work occupies a middle ground between the private sphere of labour and the public, political sphere.

Corresponding to Arendt's estimation of the public sphere as the site of human fulfilment is an estimation of the private sphere and its concerns as a site of fundamental deprivation. Within the *vita activa*, the private management of necessity is the requisite material foundation for a public life of politics, but confinement, or excessive attention, to the private sphere and its needs yields a life that is less than completely human: "In ancient feeling the privative trait of privacy, indicated in the word itself, was all-important; it meant literally a state of being deprived of something, and even of the highest and most human of man's capacities. A man who lived only a private life ... was not fully human."[19] In this view, the life of complete privacy was, by definition, the life of an idiot (from *idios*, for "one's own" – an *idiotēs* was a private person). Arendt's forceful articulation of the substance of this idiocy merits extended quotation:

> To live an entirely private life means above all to be deprived of things essential to a truly human life: to be deprived of the reality that comes from being seen and heard by others, to be deprived of an "objective" relationship with them that comes from being related to and separated from them through the intermediary of a common world of things, to be deprived of the possibility of achieving something more permanent than life itself. The privation of privacy lies in the absence of others; as far as they are concerned, private man does not appear, and therefore it is as though he did not exist. Whatever he does remains without significance and consequence to others, and what matters to him is without interest to other people.[20]

Later she writes that "a life without speech and action ... is literally dead to the world; it has ceased to be a human life because it is no longer lived among men."[21]

There is much to consider in this account of the ancient separation and relative valuation of the public and private spheres. In the first place, it suggests that those who are confined, by inclination or by force, to the private, domestic sphere of labour and necessity are somehow inhuman. In the Athenian context, women and slaves were denied the privilege of citizenship and so were arbitrarily confined to the private sphere. This fact – coupled with Aristotle's insupportable claim that women and slaves, comprehensively lacking the natural capacity for reasoned speech, were fitted by their very nature for summary relegation to the private sphere in roles that excluded citizenship (slaves for life as living instruments of production; women for a life of home economics) – has led to persuasive criticisms of the ancient construction of the public–private divide as irretrievably gendered and discriminatory, the beginning of a trajectory of social relations in which women and "others" have been consistently and systematically denied political rights of access to the public sphere as equals. In this view, Athens is the fountain of a discourse in which "public" means male, private means "female," and in which the private sphere, where countless women in Western history have been forced to live their lives, is a realm without politics (that is, without the practice that would qualify women as fully human), despite the obvious operation of power there.[22] These criticisms effectively eliminate Athens as an adequate model for a just society. They do not, however, eliminate the need to consider the possibility that a public, political life is essential to human fulfilment in a way that an exclusively economic life is not. Indeed, it could be argued that it is precisely this conviction that has motivated centuries of opposition to the injustices engendered by Athens: western women and "others" have sought to overcome the arbitrary socioeconomic conventions of Athens and its progeny precisely because they understand that access to the public sphere of citizenship is as necessary to their completion as it is to that of any male.

Beneath the irrational and arbitrary gendering of the ancient divide between public and private is perhaps a more enduring truth: namely, that a public sphere of political action freed from laborious attention to necessity requires as its material foundation a private sphere of economics capable of producing the leisure required for citizenship. The fact that the arrangements struck by Athens (and by too many subsequent political communities) to accomplish this fundamental requirement of political life were unjust does not negate or eliminate it. Slaves and servile women may not be the answer, but the question remains, and it is a question not just about productivity in the private sphere but also about the place of economics in public life. In the Athenian understanding outlined by Arendt, it is clear that economics was meant to serve politics in the sense of making it possible by freeing citizens from necessity and labour. Thus, "household life exists for the sake of the 'good life' in the *polis*."[23] However, it is also the case that this conception entailed a definite exclusion of basic economic activities from the public sphere of citizenship: "No activity that served only the purpose of making a living, of sustaining only the life process, was permitted to enter the political realm."[24] Matters of necessity were by definition a private concern, unfit for the attention of a free citizen seeking completion, as well as distinction from lesser beings, in the *polis*. The public sphere was reserved for politics – an activity that, unlike labour, was particular to humans. And it was not only the economic activity of labouring for necessity that was to be excluded from public life, but also those activities concerned with private property and the accumulation of surplus. Labour and property found their purpose in being used to release citizens from necessity. Any expenditure of labour or accumulation of property beyond this represented an abstention from the higher activities of the *vita activa* – a choice for economics over politics, a diminution rather than a fulfilment of one's humanity. As Arendt recounts: "To be prosperous had no reality in the Greek *polis* ... If the property owner chose to enlarge his property instead of using it up in leading a political life, it was as though he willingly sacrificed his freedom and became voluntarily what the slave was against his own will, a servant of necessity."[25] Thus, neither the economics of labour/necessity nor the economics of property/prosperity were fit to occupy the public sphere. This is not to say that matters of common economic concern (that is, distribution, planning, conservation, and so on) were not fit subjects for political deliberation amongst free and equal citizens. It is rather to say that the public sphere simply was not an arena for the pursuit of private economic interests. To the extent that the pursuit of such interests manages to invade the public sphere, the latter is drained of the political character that defines it as being distinct from the private sphere, effectively resulting in the disappearance of that space in which the higher elements of the *vita activa* can be realized.

In Arendt's estimation, this colonization of the public, political sphere by private interest is one aspect of the degeneration of the public sphere under the auspices of liberal, capitalist, and social-welfare democracy. In general, this degeneration is captured by a collapse of the distinction between the private/economic and the public /political spheres into a single, essentially apolitical, category of "society." As characterized by Arendt, "society is the form in which the fact of mutual dependance for the sake of life and nothing else assumes public significance and where the activities connected with sheer survival are permitted to appear in public."[26] This modern "social realm" is, according to Arendt, "neither private nor public" – not private because it is unconcealed and not public because it is devoid of politics. Instead, in modern society (which corresponds, not incidentally, to an escalation in the scale of organization from city-state to nation-state), we witness the rise of "a gigantic, nation-wide administration of housekeeping,"[27] wherein the economic concerns and practices of the household are extended into what was previously the public realm. Politics is replaced by the collective management of individual necessity, and the economic logic of the household – idiocy, force, despotism, and violence – overwhelms the persuasive, reasoned speech and practical action that characterized the public sphere, which was once free of economics.

The collapse of the ancient public–private distinction into the modern category of "society" and the corresponding eclipse of politics by economic activity are not without consequences for the *vita activa*. In the first place, the public sphere – "the only place where men could show who they really and inexchangably were"[28] – disappears, and with it goes the possibility of expressing meaningful individuality and distinction via political activity. To the extent that is possible in the modern context, distinction is reduced to the esteem gathered in exchanging products and accumulating material wealth. Accordingly, the public place (*agora*) shifts emphasis from constituting a meeting place for citizens to providing a marketplace for producers and consumers.[29] Similarly, fabrication or work no longer fulfils the primary task of building a common, enduring world of objects that provides a stable dwelling place for mortal beings, and, instead, it is directed towards the more efficient production of items of exchange. As a consequence, the common world of things, which formed the architecture of the public sphere and which related and separated men concretely, dissolves into the ephemerality and alienation of commercial trade in private interests. Human beings, thrown from their common world, sink into themselves.[30] What remains of politics – once the crown of the *vita activa* in which the uniquely human capacities for reasoned speech and practical action combined to pursue justice – is a phantom contained within the "modern concept of government, where the only thing people have in common is their private interests," and government is "appointed to shield the private owners from each other in the competitive struggle for more wealth."[31] The ancient relationship, whereby economics served political citizenship by releasing it from necessity, is thus precisely reversed. At this point, Arendt writes, "both the public and the private spheres of life are gone, the public because it has become a function of the private and the private because it has become the only common concern left."[32]

### Rise and Fall of the Bourgeois Public Sphere

Arendt's concern is to specify how particular constructions of the public sphere either succeed or fail to establish the conditions for human fulfilment. Jürgen Habermas's more modest aim is to trace the contours of the modern public sphere as it has evolved and to hold it against liberal democracy's own criteria of legitimacy.[33] Habermas's concern is with the rise and fall of the public sphere that emerged in conjunction with European bourgeois capitalism and parliamentary democracy from the late seventeenth to the early nineteenth century. As Habermas describes it, this was a "public of private people engaged in rational-critical debate,"[34] and it is most clearly defined in contrast to its immediate historical predecessor – the "representative publicness" of medieval absolutism – which Habermas insists did not constitute a public "realm" or "sphere" distinct from the private. Instead, in this context, "public" speaks to a status attribute that denotes elevation relative to the commonness of "private" persons. To the extent that something public did exist in feudal societies, it was embodied in those persons – monarchs, members of court, nobility – who, by their very person, represented absolute authority before the common, private persons over whom it was exercised. Thus, according to Habermas, "representation pretended to make something invisible visible through the public presence of the person of the lord."[35] Publicity, in this sense, was staged and represented before private people – it did not emerge from or between them.

Representative publicness corresponded to a feudal economy in which private material interest was forcibly minimized or, at the very least, assimilated into that of the feudal estate. The emergence of early bourgeois capitalism – expanded rights to accumulate private property; finance and trade; free markets for the exchange of commodities – established the conditions under which the modern public sphere emerged. In this period, the material basis of individual autonomy shifts from managing need in closed households to exchanging property (including labour) in open markets: "Modern economics was no longer oriented to the *oikos*; the market had replaced the household, and it became 'commercial economics.'"[36] This economic shift entailed a corresponding shift in the meaning of "private" and "public," with private referring to individual or corporate interests derived from "free power of control over property"[37] in a capitalist economy and public referring to the space in which those interests are articulated, appear, and compete for security. Markets are shared by their participants, and they require the coercive authority of states for the enforcement of contracts. Thus, the economics of private interest and exchange, released from the household, become a political matter, and the exercise of public authority in regard to these practices becomes a subject of consideration and vigilance by those private persons (property holders without formal public title) whose interests are at stake. The public sphere reconstitutes as the realm in which this vigilance and consideration is exercised. As Habermas explains, "the bourgeois public sphere may be conceived above all as the sphere of private people come together as a public; they soon claimed the public sphere regulated from above against the public authorities themselves, to engage them in debate over the general rules governing relations in the basically privatized but publicly relevant sphere of commodity exchange and social labor."[38] Under the medieval regime of representative publicness, it was enough for the state to represent itself before obedient subjects. However, under the modern regime of the bourgeois liberalism, state authority is compelled to legitimate itself before the private citizens who authorize it. Habermas describes the bourgeois public sphere as "a forum in which the private people, come together to form a public ... to compel public authority to legitimate itself before public opinion."[39]

The bourgeois public sphere evolved as a key element in the assumption of sovereign political control in Europe by private, popular forces and the movement to eliminate arbitrary domination from political and economic life. Other elements in this dynamic included the strengthening of parliaments and the entrenchment of constitutional guarantees of the political rights of citizens. According to Habermas, the definitive quality of the bourgeois public sphere was its democratic "publicity," a complex distinction entailing three crucial characteristics: the public use of critical reason; debate; and accessibility. The sovereignty of public reason de-personalized authority and undermined arbitrary domination. Debate – "the public competition of private arguments [pursuant to] consensus about what was practically necessary in the interest of all"[40] – replaced compliance with consent. Universal access qualified the public sphere as genuinely public. "The public sphere," according to Habermas, "stood or fell with the principle of universal access. A public sphere from which specific groups would be *eo ipso* excluded was less than merely incomplete; it was not a public sphere at all. Accordingly, the public ... viewed its sphere as a public one in this strict sense; in its deliberations it anticipated in principle that all human beings belonged to it."[41] This is not to say that citizenship and its benefits were truly generalized (as is well known). Rather, admission to the bourgeois public sphere in the nascent European liberal democracies of the eighteenth and nineteenth centuries was typically contingent on education and property ownership – qualifications that effectively excluded the labouring classes and women from citizenship (a sociological fact shared by the ancient and the bourgeois public spheres). Clearly, it was not universal access in this sense that lent publicity to the bourgeois public sphere. Instead, in this context, universal access meant that no individual or group within the class of citizens could be arbitrarily excluded and that the class of citizens identified itself with universal humanity as such.[42]

The bourgeois public sphere, in its ideal, was therefore that space wherein private citizens could engage in the process of rational-critical debate that generates public opinion – the "critical reflections of a public competent to form its own judgments"[43] – which, in turn, constitutes the ruling principle of liberal democratic political authority. On these terms, a "public of private people engaged in rational-critical debate" is a core requirement of modern democracy: "Publicity was, according to its very idea, a principle of democracy not just because anyone could in principle announce, with equal opportunity, his personal inclinations, wishes, and convictions – opinions; it could only be realized in the measure that these personal opinions could evolve through the rational-critical debate of a public into public opinion."[44] Invoking M. Guizot's classic formulation, Habermas thus identifies in publicity that spirit whereby citizens "seek after truth and ... tell it to power."[45]

The bourgeois public sphere emerged in polities whose scale had long since exceeded the immediacy of the *agora* of city-states. Hence, communication mediated by technology played a crucial role in in their establishment and maintenance. Late-seventeenth- and early-eighteenth-century "technologies" through which publicity was mediated included British coffee-houses, French *salons,* and German table societies, in which "critical debate ignited by works of literature and art was soon extended to include economic and political disputes."[46] However, more than any other medium, it was the press that "turned society into a public affair" in a sense that was specifically political.[47] In Habermas's estimation, the political press was "the public sphere's preeminent institution," in so far as it mediated on a large scale the qualities of publicity that gave the public sphere its substance: universally accessible, rational-critical debate aimed at generating public opinion.[48] Independent journalism, a daily press, publication of the debates of representative assemblies and of state budgets, the *Encyclopedia* in France, reading societies in Germany – each affirmed the central role of print communication in the infrastructure of a rationally debating critical public of private persons. As Habermas points out, the indispensability of print communication to the bourgeois public sphere was codified in the French constitution of 1791, which explicitly guaranteed the right of citizens to "speak, write and print freely" and again in the constitution of 1793, which entrenched "the right to communicate one's ideas and opinions, whether through the press or in any other manner."[49] That being said, the widespread availability of printed communication – a "free press" – did not solely establish the public sphere as public: "The formation of a public opinion in the strict sense is not effectively secured by the mere fact that anyone can freely utter his opinion and put out a newspaper."[50] Under certain conditions, a medium such as the press can be as privatizing, manipulative, and de-politicizing as it is publicizing. Habermas's point is that under the conditions of early bourgeois capitalism and the historical challenge to absolutism that existed in Europe at the time, print media mediated the key ingredients of publicity.

The capitalist mode of production, having in its infancy supplied the material motivation for the development of the bourgeois public sphere, matured into a form that led to the decomposition of that sphere and its publicity. The classical era of competitive capitalism, which formed the material basis of the bourgeois public sphere, was, as Habermas characterizes it, "a mere episode."[51] The transformation during the late nineteenth and twentieth centuries to oligopolistic, industrial capitalism, which concentrated capital and power in ever-fewer hands and which required increasing levels of state intervention (in forms ranging from protectionist trade policies to social welfare programs) for its maintenance – the constellation that is often described as "Fordism" – dramatically transformed the liberal democratic public sphere. As Habermas writes, "for about a century the social foundations of this sphere have been caught up in a process of decomposition. Tendencies pointing to the collapse of the public sphere are unmistakable, for while its scope is expanding impressively, its function has become progressively insignificant."[52] This curious dialectic of simultane-ously expanding reach and contracting substance is the particular mark of the breakdown of the public sphere under the regime of industrial capital-ism. Describing this transformed public sphere, Habermas writes: "While it penetrated more *spheres* of society, it simultaneously lost its political *func-tion*, namely: that of subjecting the affairs that it had made public to the control of a critical public."[53] The decomposition of the political function of the public sphere corresponds to what Habermas would later describe as the "colonization of the lifeworld" by the non-communicative rationality of economic and administrative systems.[54] In their ideal configuration, pri-vate and public orders of the lifeworld are structured by discursive commu-nication that is aimed at common understanding and normative consensus on the basis of shared rationality. Under the conditions of an expanding but concentrating capitalist economy and a bureaucratized state, the lifeworld is overrun by the formal logic of market and administrative sys-tems that replace rational conversation with mediation by money and power to secure performance/obedience in place of agreement.[55]

Having lost its political function as a sphere for rational-critical debate, the public sphere takes on new roles in modern society. Among these roles is that of providing a field for socializing private persons into their systemic roles as employees and consumers.[56] In the process, rational-critical debate by private persons who have come together as a public is usurped by the employment and consumption activity of individuals artificially generated as a mass, which is itself ultimately constituted as a commodity whose at-tention as an audience is bought and sold by economic and political inter-ests. As Habermas writes: "The public sphere assumes advertising functions. The more it can be deployed as a vehicle for political and economic propa-ganda, the more it becomes unpolitical as a whole and pseudo-privatized."[57] Just as print media played a central role in the elaboration of the bourgeois public sphere, so too have mass electronic media played a decisive role in its transformation – in a society that "invites its public to an exchange of opinion about articles of consumption and subjects it to the soft compul-sion of constant consumption training."[58] Even the press – which has turned from "a journalism of conviction to one of commerce,"[59] as it takes the form of a highly concentrated and centralized capitalist industry funded by advertising – ceases to play its traditional role in mediating rational-critical debate and becomes yet another "gate through which privileged private interests invade the public sphere."[60]

What remains of political publicity in the modern public sphere assumes forms that are highly technical, manipulative, and privatized. Bureaucratic formalization "disempower[s] and dessicate[s] spontaneous processes of opinion- and will-formation," and so the public sphere is reduced to an arena for the "engineering of mass loyalty."[61] Individuals, exhausted by their duties as employees and consumers in the private realm, defer their role as critically debating public citizens to an inter-organizational network of corporations, political parties, interest groups, and trade unions, which between them manage the execution of sovereign authority. Publicity takes on a new aspect in this constellation: it ceases to be something before which power presents itself to seek legitimacy, but rather becomes something that powerful interests seek to manipulate.[62] Publicity no longer entails "the exposure of political domination before the public use of reason,"[63] and, instead, it is replaced by public relations geared to "engineering legitimation."[64] Even the public opinion that is generated around the clash of corporate interests is managed and mobilized "for the purposes of supporting or securing compromises negotiated nonpublicly."[65] Thus, the modern sphere of public relations evinces a dual "uncoupling": political decision making is uncoupled from the "concrete, identity forming contexts of [individual] life"; and symbolic exchange between representative elites is "largely uncoupled from real decision-making processes within the political system."[66] The modern public sphere, so constructed, is therefore deeply de-politicizing. Left with no space in which to exercise their rational-critical capacities, citizens recede into the only function for which their truncated public life provides – that of client. As Habermas explains: "Citizens entitled to services relate to the state not primarily through political participation but by adopting a general attitude of demand – expecting to be provided for without actually wanting to fight for the necessary decisions. Their contact with the state occurs essentially in the rooms and anterooms of bureaucracies; it is unpolitical and indifferent, yet demanding."[67]

For better or for worse, the scale of contemporary societies seems to necessitate that whatever public sphere exists be mediated by technologies of mass communication. As Habermas observes, "in a large public body [democratic] communication requires specific means for transmitting information and influencing those who receive it. Today, newspapers and magazines, radio and television are the media of the public sphere."[68] To this list, we might now fairly add the Internet. Decades of critical theory and communication studies have argued quite persuasively that the primary function of mass media in advanced capitalist societies is hegemonic, anti-democratic, and corrosive of the public sphere.[69] It should be noted that Habermas himself is not entirely convinced by this interpretation. In his view, mass communication technologies have an "ambivalent potential": they can act as "steering media," which "take the place of those communication structures that had once made possible public discussion and self-understanding by citizens," or they can constitute "generalized forms of communication, which do not replace reaching agreement in language but merely condense it, and thus remain tied to lifeworld contexts."[70] According to Habermas, "the mass media belong to these generalized forms of communication."[71] It is here that he locates the potential for a recovery of the principle of the public sphere – the exposure of political power before universally accessible, rational-critical debate amongst a public of private persons – under modern conditions.

## Digital Public Sphere

The purpose of reviewing the categories set out by Arendt and Habermas is not to suggest that their work captures the dynamics of the modern public sphere comprehensively, nor is it to promote either of their respective accounts of the ancient and bourgeois public spheres as an adequate, comprehensive ideal toward which we might strive in the contemporary context. As feminist scholars have pointed out, appeals to Athens risk valorizing a public sphere predicated on the subjugation of women and slaves, just as Habermas's account can encourage idealizing a bourgeois public sphere to which only a male, property-holding minority had access. Postmodern theorists point out that such conceptions of the public sphere are compromised by an overt "logocentrism": insofar as they privilege rational speech (*logos*) as the definitive content of politics (such accounts exclude from the "political" and the "public" a variety of practices and sites of power contestation that ought to be so considered).[72] Finally, it can be argued that Arendt and Habermas contribute (wittingly or not) to a tradition that conceives of public and private as an abstract binary, describing clearly demarcated, self-contained spheres characterized respectively by state/compulsory and market/voluntary relations. In fact, the distinction between public and private in contemporary liberal capitalist democracies is not nearly so clear or objective. Instead, in this context, the public–private distinction takes on a primarily normative character – as a discursive device that supports exemption of select activities from the attention of sovereign public authority. As many of the studies in this volume show, these designations consistently correspond to prevailing configurations of socioeconomic power. Thus, unpaid domestic caregiving and environmental standards are deemed private, voluntary matters, which are not properly subject to public authority, while the market transactions of panhandlers are somehow construed as public acts meriting strict regulation by the state.[73]

For reasons both theoretical and practical, neither Arendt nor Habermas provide us with the final, definitive word on the public sphere. However, what they do provide is a minimalist starting point from which we can begin thinking about the possibilities of a public sphere mediated by digital technology. For both Arendt and Habermas, the public sphere is, at a minimum, a place for active engagement in politics. In Arendt's terms, this entails the clash in speech and action of reasoned accounts of the demands of justice – unconstrained and uncorrupted by material necessity – between equals related in a concrete world of common things. In Habermas's terms, a political public sphere is one in which private individuals engage in rational-critical debate over the general interest, in the process yielding a public opinion in relation to which the legitimacy of power is established or denied. To meet the conditions of publicity, these media must resist devolution into a means for managing commercial consumption, social diversion, and superficial consent. The question is whether digital media succeed in these terms.

American cultural critic Neil Postman has written that "a wise man must begin his critique of technology by acknowledging its successes."[74] Digital communications media are still in their infancy as technologies, but even preliminary considerations of their impact must begin by recognizing their obvious potential to facilitate dialogue between citizens, and, in so doing, their contribution to the construction of a democratic public sphere. Indeed, interpersonal communication mediated by networks seems to meet readily some of the conditions laid out by Arendt and Habermas as basic to the constitution of a public sphere. When Arendt describes the *polis* as being not a physical location but rather a *space* that exists between people living together for the purpose of speaking and acting, she could be talking about the Internet. Similarly, Habermas describes the democratic potential of mass media in general terms that now seem particularly evocative of the digital mediascape: "They free communication processes from the provinciality of spatio-temporally restricted contexts and permit public spheres to emerge, through establishing the abstract simultaneity of a virtually present network of communication contents far removed in space and time and through keeping messages available for manifold contexts."[75] Were this statement not written in 1981, one might think Habermas was referring specifically to digitally mediated virtual communities.

There is certainly reason to be hopeful that the digital sphere is, or will be, a highly public and democratic one. A portion of this hope resides in the technical configuration of the medium itself, especially its dialogic applications: its interactive capacities mean that every passive receiver is at least potentially an active conversant; its decentralized architecture undermines the capacity of centralized interests to control outright communication between private persons; and its reach enables communication, and the circulation of information, between large numbers of people who would otherwise be isolated from one another. Still greater hope is derived from the explicitly political and democratic activities that either take place in the digital space or use digital technologies. These activities include communication between constituents and representatives, mediating direct engagement in civic decision-making, on-line political discussion groups, and the use of digital media by politicized individuals, interest groups, and parties for the purposes of information gathering, deliberation, publication, organization, and mobilization.[76] There is little doubt that digital technology has the capacity to mediate significant public activity and that there presently exist substantial examples of cases and movements in which this capacity is being exploited. The question, in terms of a preliminary diagnosis of the fate of the public sphere under the auspices of digital technology, is whether these capacities are likely to be generalized under the broad conditions of this technology's development and whether we have reason to believe that publicist applications of this technology do, or are likely to, represent the norm in terms of its deployment and use.

We might start by asking whether the digital sphere we inhabit is oriented primarily toward economics or politics. Is it occupied by labour bound to necessity or by the liberated action of individuals exercising their capacity for reasoned speech and practical action in pursuit of justice? There are certainly some, perhaps even many, people who inhabit part of the digital sphere as free citizens engaged in political dialogue and action. It should be kept in mind, however, that these citizens represent just a portion of the users of a portion of the digital sphere. As will be detailed later in this essay, recent evidence in the North American context does not support the proposition that "political engagement" is the best way to describe what most people are doing most of the time they are connected to the Internet and the World Wide Web. In any case, these dialogic and interpersonal communication applications do not nearly exhaust the manner in which digital technologies mediate life activity in postindustrial societies. The digital sphere is comprised of more than websites and mailing lists – it consists of the broad range of life practices, mediated by devices such as digital and cellular telephones, voice-mail, portable and wireless computing machines, digitized transactional registers at retail checkouts (which mediate the labour of both the shopping consumer and the wage-earning employee), automated teller machines, call centres, proliferating databanks and proprietary networks, electronic public service kiosks, digitized entertainments, and computers on the desks, laps, and dashboards of work sites across occupational and industrial categories. These are all elements of what I have described elsewhere as the "standing-reserve of bits,"[77] which forms the core of the digital sphere. It is in this broader mediation of human activity – broader than just the personal and mass communications enabled by the Internet and the World Wide Web – that the digital sphere is constructed, and it is via these activities that we most deeply inhabit that sphere.

For the most part, this broader digital sphere is not populated by citizens: the digital sphere is a sphere of labour and necessity for most people, not one of political action. We inhabit the digital sphere primarily in the course of attending to necessity by making a living, either as jobholders or when doing the unpaid "shadow work" of consumption.[78] The public sphere collapses into the private via these technologies not primarily because increasing numbers of people have computers in their homes that are connected to the Internet, but more because our collective encounter with these technologies is overwhelmingly characterized by its economic nature. In terms of the activities that characterize it, the digital sphere is more *oikia* than *polis*. And far from yielding increased leisure, which is a basic condition of citizenship, these technologies, in their ubiquity and proliferating connectivity, yoke people to the private sphere of labour almost incessantly. Under the ancient distinctions articulated by Arendt, this means that the digital sphere is not a public sphere at all, but rather a deeply private, and, therefore, also a privative, realm – a realm for collective housekeeping, which includes socializing and recreation but leaves little room for the virtues of a political life.

It is also a realm in which the modern tendency to dissolve the "common world of things," which both unites and separates people, is accelerated. Arendt's description of this aspect of the modern condition resonates quite deeply with the digital present:

> What makes mass society so difficult to bear is not the number of people involved, or at least not primarily, but the fact that the world between them has lost its power to gather them together, to relate and to separate them. The weirdness of this situation resembles a spiritualistic séance where a number of people gathered around a table might suddenly, through some magic trick, see the table vanish from their midst, so that two persons sitting opposite each other were no longer separated but also would be entirely unrelated to each other by anything tangible.[79]

In Arendt's account, the proper role of work is to fabricate a common world of enduring objects – a permanent and stable dwelling place that both gathers people to, and sets them apart from, their fellows. It is in this sense that work and its products mediate between the public and private realm. Arendt sees the modern condition as having replaced work oriented toward crafting useful, enduring objects of dwelling with the production of valuable commodities for exchange between privately interested individuals, in the process reducing the public sphere to a market. While adequate models of advertising and transaction remain to be established, it seems safe to say even at this point that perhaps the greatest promise of digital technology lies in its capacity to mediate commercial activity of various kinds. The Internet is not responsible for the conversion of public space into commercial space, but – despite the hostility to commerce that is expressed by the medium's pioneers and the reluctance of consumers to trust it – neither is it likely to reverse this dynamic. People certainly work with and via this medium, but the work they do is characteristically oriented toward exchange relations rather than toward the fabrication of a common, enduring world.

There are other ways in which this technology contributes to the evapo-
ration of the common world of concrete things. Much has been made of
the potential for digital networks to support "virtual" environments that
are indifferent to the physical demand of spatial proximity that sometimes
prevents people from communicating. The progressive potential of so-called
"virtual communities" has been the subject of considerable hope and debate.[80] It is too early to say with finality what sort of communities these
digitally mediated formations might actually constitute, but one issue they
raise is the fate of the non-digital sphere when communal relationships
cohere around shared appetites, experience, identity, ideals, and ideology
rather than a shared world of objects and a shared place of dwelling. Phrased
differently, we might wonder about what will become of the concrete world,
in which our bodies are unavoidably grounded, as it becomes progressively
disconnected from social relationships that are increasingly abstract and
technologically distanced from a common world of things.[81]

One consequence of the "vanishing table," identified by Arendt – the loss
of a common world that unites and separates us –is the tendency for individuals thrown from the common world of things to sink into themselves
and turn from matters of general interest and the politics of the public sphere
to the aesthetics of personal identity. The spirit of personalization and
"customization" runs deep in the culture of digital communications. As
Nicholas Negroponte has enthused, the Internet makes possible the reduc-
tion of the information environment – both what one consciously contributes to it and what one draws from it – to "the daily Me."[82] The consequences
of such personalization for the possibility of a viable public sphere are potentially profound, as it reduces the likelihood of people encountering, and
adapting to, the concrete plurality of the world in which they live – a dynamic that Robert Putnam has labelled "cyberbalkanization."[83] In a related
vein, Michele Willson has raised the possibility that what are often presented as technologies of community may actually operate more as "technologies of individuation," isolated and detached insofar as they promote
individual aesthetic choice-making over concrete grounding in a shared
world of things. Capturing the essence of virtual association, Willson writes:

> The emphasis is on fluidity and choice of associations in a social space.
> Interaction is abstracted from more concrete and embodied particularities
> and takes place within an environment shaped by the actors themselves. A
> "loosening" of connections may appear liberating ... liberatory and
> postmodern claims about virtual communities are precisely based on the
> promotion of an anonymity which enables flexible, multiple and anony-
> mous identity construction, and the alteration of spatial and time experi-
> ences ... I would suggest that the dissolution or fragmentation of the subject

and the instantaneous, transient nature of all communication disconnect or abstract the individual from physical action and a sense of social or personal responsibility to others ... While virtual communities may be interactive, they do not require either physical commitment or moral, political or social extension beyond the network.[84]

David Holmes characterizes the present situation similarly when he describes on-line associations as "community through personalization and simulation" and suggests that this serves as an apt metaphor for a contemporary condition "in which it becomes difficult, if not meaningless, to map our place, or social location in the world."[85] Under these conditions, digital technology, "offers us the option of experiencing space in perhaps the most social way we can, which is paradoxically a retreat to individuality."[86] Rather than constituting a public place where individuals can "show who they really and inexchangably [are],"[87] the possibility looms that the digital sphere will simply provide individuals with yet another place to hide while still enjoying social contact. Though certainly not thinking specifically of virtual community, Arendt has already observed in 1958 that "for a society of laborers, the world of machines has become a substitute for the real world, even though this pseudo world cannot fulfil the most important task of the human artifice, which is to offer mortals a dwelling place more permanent and more stable than themselves."[88]

There is a deep resonance between this personalization of social space and the spirit of exchange relationships in markets. We might recall that for Arendt, the colonization of the *vita activa* by market relations marked the absence of a public sphere in which political activity might be undertaken by free citizens. Todd Gitlin has described the digitally mediated customization of sociability and identity as part of a more general transformation of the public sphere into "public sphericules," which, while ripe for organization as "targeted markets and consumption subcultures," do not necessarily fulfil the democratic functions of a public sphere.[89] As Gitlin writes, "the diffusion of interactive technology surely enriches the possibilities for a plurality of publics – for the development of distinct groups organized around affinity or interest. What is not clear is that the proliferation and lubrication of publics contributes to the creation *a* public – an active democratic encounter of citizens who reach across their social and ideological differences to establish a common agenda of concern and to debate rival approaches."[90] Digital media increase the ease with which individuals can partake in disaggregated, personalized, virtual *publics* and, in so doing, simultaneously undermine the possibility of an integrated public sphere. It is in this sense that Gitlin describes digital media as technologies of "secession, exclusion, and segmentation"[91] – dynamics that are not typically identified with a robust, democratic public sphere.

Nevertheless, as Willson points out in the passage reproduced earlier in this essay, those who see digital technologies as forming the infrastructure for a distinctly postmodern and highly democratic public sphere often seize on its capacity to mediate alternative practices of identity negotiation. Mark Poster, for example, argues that digital media de-stabilize identity by enabling its free construction, re-construction, combination, and multiplication in the very act of communicating, and so the Internet constitutes a public sphere characterized by the "diminution of prevailing hierarchies of race, class, and especially gender."[92] In Poster's analysis, modern theories of the public sphere, such as Habermas's, are ill-suited to understanding the digital sphere because they are predicated on assumptions about coherent rational subjects engaging in transparent critical discourse that have been thoroughly undermined by this technology. Drawing on accounts of identity play in computer mediated multi-user domains (MUDs), Poster describes the postmodern digital sphere as a place "not of the presence of validity claims or the actuality of critical reason, but of the inscription of new assemblages of self-constitution."[93] In this sphere, says Poster, MUDs and other digitally mediated environments "serve the function of a Habermasian public sphere without intentionally being one."[94]

This claim raises the question of the digital sphere's standing in relation to the categories set out by Habermas. Postmodernists such as Poster are keen to point out that politics comes in forms other than rational dialogue and that the Internet has vast potential as a medium for alternative subjectivities and identities that are political by virtue of their very expression. Thus, insofar as MUDs and Internet chat rooms "function as places of difference from and resistance to modern society,"[95] they implicitly constitute public spheres in which domination is exposed and critiqued. Even if this is conceded, it is not clear that such alternative practices make the Internet – let alone the broader scope of digital mediation – a public sphere of Habermasian proportions. To be sure, Habermas himself thought that mass media could serve this purpose, provided they act to condense rather than to replace or manipulate discursively generated political consensus. There is no reason to dismiss, out of hand, the potential of digital media to accomplish this end – but the technology's success in this regard will be established on the basis of the activity that it mediates for the great majority of those who encounter and use it, rather than by virtue of what it enables for a marginal, self-consciously "alternative" few. The pertinent question is not what the Internet is on its margins but, rather, what digital technology is, and what it does, for the mainstream of "public" life under the socio-economic constitutions of advanced liberal capitalism.

Setting aside for a moment the fact that the Internet and the World Wide Web far from exhaust our encounter with these technologies, if we are to find even signs of a rejuvenated public sphere of significant proportions, it is likely that it would be in the use patterns of these particular applications. Recent evidence from the 2000 General Social Survey by Statistics Canada proves useful in this regard.[96] In the year 2000, roughly 53 percent of Canadians reported having access to and using the Internet. The group with the highest representation of users was aged fifteen to nineteen, with percentages declining regularly for every five-year increment in age bracket. Rates of Internet use correlate strongly to the level of education, income, gender, language, urban location, and region. In terms of use, 84 percent reported using the Internet for electronic mail to friends, family, or work associates – that is, for social and economic, but not necessarily political, purposes. Seventy-five percent of users reported using the Internet to search for information on goods and services. Of this group, the highest three categories of information sought were arts, entertainment, and sports (56 percent), travel (45 percent), and business (34 percent) – roughly 22 percent reported searching for local or community information. Fifty-five percent of all users reported using the medium to access news; 41 percent sought information on government programs or services; 34 percent played games; 30 percent used chat services; 23 percent did their banking online; and 16 percent subscribed to newsgroups or listservs. Recent data from the United States more or less replicate these use patterns. The dominant categories were: e-mail (82 percent); hobbies (57 percent); news (56 percent); entertainment (54 percent); shopping (52 percent); travel (46 percent); and gaming (33 percent).[97] Another US study conducted in 1998 showed that only 4 percent of Internet users reported having engaged in political discussions on-line.[98]

There is little in these numbers to indicate a widespread re-invigoration of the public sphere. The dialogic applications of this technology remain far from being universally accessible, and even among those who do have access to it, using the Internet for rational-critical political discourse or speaking the truth to power is not high on the list for the majority of everyday people. Confirming Habermas's observation that the posture of contemporary citizenship is primarily one of demand rather than of participation, it is typical that even those users who do engage the state via this medium do so primarily as clients (that is, as recipients of information and services) rather than as deliberative critics – a tendency that is encouraged by the presentation of "e-government" as digitally mediated service delivery.[99] This is not to say that no one uses the Internet as a medium for participatory, engaged citizenship activity: many do, but they are a small minority, and they tend to be the same people and groups who were politically active before the arrival of the Internet. As Pippa Norris has shown, rather than drawing more and new people into the politicized public sphere, digital media have simply provided a new and very useful tool for that minority which is already politicized to speak to itself, reinforcing the existing patterns of political engagement rather than mobilizing new forces.[100] Despite the massive quantities of politically relevant information made available in the digital sphere, even those individuals who are so inclined gravitate toward established commercial sources whose incentives lie somewhere other than in the concerted subjection of political authority to rational criticism and civic debate. As Norris concludes, even among the conventionally politicized users of the medium "the Web seems to have been used more often as a means to access traditional news rather than as a radical new source of unmediated information and communication."[101]

On the other hand, agents of the culture of consumption, entertainment, and diversion, which Habermas identifies as corrosive of the political public sphere, summarily dominate the proliferation of this medium. The supposed explosion of information availability and communication capacity proclaimed in the rhetoric of the "information society" has amounted, in fact, to an incredible concentration of ownership of digital content and carriage infrastructure – a dynamic of "convergence" that has been encouraged by the policy and regulatory regimes of North American governments.[102] As a result, virtually the same conglomerated capitalist enterprises that traditionally have dominated the mass media environment have rapidly colonized the digital frontier as well, which suggests that this medium may have a significant role to play as yet another "gate through which privileged private interests invade the public sphere," as Habermas characterizes the commercialized press.[103] Exploring this possibility in detail, Dwayne Winseck writes: "After spending several hundreds of billions of dollars to acquire content and networks, it was inevitable that multimedia goliaths would design mediaspaces that do more to defend their investments than to promote open and transparent communication systems."[104]

Under the auspices of an increasingly de-regulated market, dominated by large, vertically and horizontally integrated firms that exercise control across the fields of technology, carriage, and content, the prevailing dynamic of the digital sphere is best described as one of expanding reach and diminishing diversity/publicity. These actors employ a range of techniques that combine to compromise the publicity of the digital sphere, including network design and architecture that privileges certain types and sources of content over others; control over access and acceptable use; and sophisticated surveillance regimes. As Winseck observes, "in essence, gatekeeping functions have been hardwired into network architectures as part of the communications industries' strategy to cultivate and control markets ... These companies now have the unprecedented ability to regulate the Internet, endowed as they are with the technical capabilities and incentive to stifle threats to their own services."[105]

Under current conditions, it would seem that digital technologies resemble "steering media" for the manufacture and management of compliance more than they do a public sphere of genuine democratic discourse in which the legitimacy of power can be routinely tested. Indeed, the peculiar characteristics of digital media present unique and unprecedented opportunities for those who seek to manage and manipulate public opinion and behaviour instead of yielding to it. Popular discourse surrounding the digital democracy question tends to emphasize the information distribution capacity of digital media. It may be the case that the particular utility of these technologies lies in their capacity to gather and process massive quantities of detailed, complex behavioural and attitudinal information about individuals and groups. As scholars of privacy and surveillance have documented, this gathering occurs on an incessant and automated basis in a networked society, wherein an increasing array of everyday practices and transactions are mediated digitally.[106] The opportunities that this treasure trove of data presents to marketers are considerable, whether they are commercial operatives seeking to habituate consumers and engender brand loyalty, enterprise managers crafting self-disciplined employees in digitized workplaces, or political organizations customizing campaigns and managing voters.[107] In this instance, the public sphere is transformed from a site for rational-critical debate into a vast, self-generating data mine, and its distinctly political function recedes into increasingly sophisticated techniques of systems control.

## Conclusion

The formidable utility of digital technologies fuels hope that they will mediate a rejuvenated public sphere in which citizenship, and rational-critical communication free of domination, can flourish. However, the socio-economic conditions in which these technologies are situated, and under whose imperatives they are developing, suggest another outcome: a continuation of the trajectory of modern liberal capitalism in which the public sphere experienced by most people, most of the time, is neutered of political substance and short on meaningful citizenship opportunities. The prevailing spirit of the digital sphere is expressed well in this media critic's wry observation following the merger of media giants Time-Warner and America Online: "America Online has 27 million subscribers ... 'They spend an incredible 84 percent of their Internet time on AOL alone, which provides a regulated leisure and shopping environment dominated by in-house brands – from Time magazine to Madonna's latest album.'"[108] The question is whether the digital sphere is one that links individuals concretely and primarily as political beings engaged in the practice of citizenship. For a number of reasons – because our inhabitation of the digital sphere is largely economic; because the digital sphere tends to dissolve the concrete world of things, which relates citizens in common concern; because its predominant uses are not characterized by political deliberation; and because it mediates a colonization of the public sphere by powerful private interests whose priorities and practices undermine, rather than complement, democracy – the answer to this question is no.

Where then, if not in digital technology *per se*, might we properly locate a reasonable hope for democratic public life? In the first place, we might catch sight of it in the remarkable resilience of the *principle* of the public sphere, despite its material decomposition as a historical form. The principle of the public sphere – the exposure of political power before universally accessible, rational-critical debate amongst a public of private persons – remains indispensable to liberal and/or social democracy. As Habermas observes, "publicity continues to be an organizational principle of our political order. It is apparently more and other than a mere scrap of liberal ideology that a social democracy could discard without harm."[109] Charters of political rights and democratic freedoms, social welfare policies aimed enfranchising marginalized constituencies, the periodic staging of elections, the unflagging regularity of news programming and journalism, the televising of parliamentary proceedings, talk radio – all testify to the endurance of the *idea* of the public sphere in the democratic imagination. So too do the efforts of those who, in giving themselves over to the excellence of citizenship, insist on using whatever means are available to them to seek this principle's realization in fact, including those who use digital technologies, subversively, to engage in democratic citizenship. It is in the tenacity of their convictions, rather than the novelty of their instruments, that our hope for the public sphere ultimately ought to reside.

**Notes**

1 David Lyon, *Surveillance Society: Monitoring Everyday Life* (Buckingham, UK: Open University, 2001); Simson Garfinkel and Deborah Russell, *Database Nation: The Death of Privacy in the Twenty-First Century* (New York: O'Reilly and Associates, 2001); Jeffrey Rosen, *The Unwanted Gaze: The Destruction of Privacy in America* (New York: Random House, 2000); Reg Whitaker, *The End of Privacy: How Total Surveillance Is Becoming a Reality* (New York: New Press, 2000); and Colin Bennett and Rebecca Grant, eds., *Visions of Privacy: Policy Choices for the Digital Age* (Toronto: University of Toronto Press, 1998).

2 See recent issues of *Maclean's* (19 February 2001); *Atlantic Monthly* (March 2001); *Utne Reader* (March-April 2000); and *Harper's* (January 2000).

3 In the Canadian context, see the *Personal Information and Electronic Documents Act*, R.S.C. 2000 (2d Sess.).

4 See Toby Lester, "The Reinvention of Privacy," *Atlantic Monthly* (March 2001) 27-39.

5 Hannah Arendt, *The Human Condition* (Chicago: University of Chicago Press, 1958).

6 Jürgen Habermas, *The Structural Transformation of the Public Sphere: An Inquiry into a Category of Bourgeois Society*, translated by Thomas Burger (Cambridge, MA: MIT Press, 1991).

7 Arendt, *supra* note 5 at 7.

8 Aristotle, *Politics*, edited and translated by Ernest Barke (New York: Oxford University Press, 1962) at 5; Arendt, *supra* note 5 at 22-23.

9 Arendt, *supra* note 5 at 13.

10 *Ibid.*

11 *Ibid.* at 28.

12  *Ibid.* at 29.
13  As Arendt points out, in the Athenian context, to be free "meant neither to rule nor to be ruled" (*ibid.* at 32).
14  *Ibid.* at 26-27.
15  *Ibid.* at 180.
16  *Ibid.* at 58.
17  *Ibid.* at 198.
18  *Ibid.* at 52.
19  *Ibid.* at 38.
20  *Ibid.* at 58.
21  *Ibid.* at 176.
22  See Carole Pateman, "Feminist Critiques of the Public Private Dichotomy," in S.I. Benn and G.F. Gaus, eds., *Public and Private in Social Life* (New York: St. Martin's Press, 1983) 281-303; and Susan Moller Okin, *Women in Western Political Thought* (Princeton: Princeton University Press, 1978).
23  Arendt, *supra* note 5 at 37.
24  *Ibid.*
25  *Ibid.* at 59; 65.
26  *Ibid.* at 46.
27  *Ibid.* at 28.
28  *Ibid.* at 41.
29  *Ibid.* at 159-62.
30  Arendt notes modern philosophy's "exclusive concern with the self, as distinguished from the soul or person or man in general" as being symptomatic of this attribute of modern society (*ibid.* at 254).
31  *Ibid.* at 69. This modern concept of government receives its paradigmatic expression in Locke's admonition that "the great and *chief end*, therefore, of men's uniting into commonwealths and putting themselves under government, *is the preservation of their property*." John Locke, *Second Treatise of Government* (Indianapolis: Hackett, 1980) at 66.
32  *Ibid.* at 69.
33  Habermas, *Structural Transformation of the Public Sphere, supra* note 6.
34  *Ibid.* at 117.
35  *Ibid.* at 7.
36  *Ibid.* at 20. Recall that for Arendt, it is precisely at this point – when private economic interests escape the household and appear in public – that the public sphere loses its distinction, and the *polis* degenerates into a marketplace.
37  Habermas, *Structural Transformation of the Public Sphere, supra* note 6 at 74.
38  *Ibid.* at 27.
39  *Ibid.* at 25.
40  *Ibid.* at 83.
41  *Ibid.* at 85.
42  It is here that Habermas himself points out the ideological character of the bourgeois public: "The dissolution of feudal relations of domination in the medium of the public engaged in rational-critical debate did not amount to the purported dissolution of political domination in general but only to its perpetuation in different guise. The bourgeois constitutional state, along with the public sphere as the central principle of its organization, was mere ideology." His concern, however, is less with this particular contradiction than with "what the idea of the bourgeois public sphere promised" (*ibid.* at 125).
43  *Ibid.* at 90.
44  *Ibid.* at 219.
45  M. Guizot, quoted in Habermas, *ibid.* at 101.
46  *Ibid.* at 33.
47  *Ibid.* at 24.
48  *Ibid.* at 181.
49  *Ibid.* at 70-71.
50  *Ibid.* at 227.

51  *Ibid.* at 144.
52  *Ibid.* at 4.
53  *Ibid.* at 140.
54  Jürgen Habermas, *Theory of Communicative Action, Vol. 2: Lifeworld and System: A Critique of Functionalist Reason*, translated by T. McCarthy (Boston: Beacon Press, 1987) at 396.
55  *Ibid.* at chs. 6 and 8.
56  *Ibid.* at 319.
57  Habermas, *Structural Transformation of the Public Sphere*, *supra* note 6 at 175.
58  *Ibid.* at 192.
59  *Ibid.* at 105.
60  *Ibid.* at 185.
61  Habermas, *Theory of Communicative Action*, *supra* note 54 at 325.
62  Habermas, *Structural Transformation of the Public Sphere*, *supra* note 6 at 178.
63  *Ibid.* at 195.
64  Habermas, *Theory of Communicative Action*, *supra* note 54 at 346.
65  Habermas, *Structural Transformation of the Public Sphere*, *supra* note 6 at 288, note 49.
66  Habermas, *Theory of Communicative Action*, *supra* note 54 at 325 and 346.
67  Habermas, *Structural Transformation of the Public Sphere*, *supra* note 6 at 211.
68  Jürgen Habermas, "The Public Sphere: An Encyclopedia Article," in M.G. Durham and D.M. Kellner, eds., *Media and Cultural Studies* (Oxford: Blackwell, 2001) at 102.
69  For the genesis of this line of thought, see Max Horkheimer and Theodor Adorno, *The Dialectic of Enlightenment*, (New York: Continuum, 1995).
70  Habermas, *Theory of Communicative Action*, *supra* note 54 at 389-90.
71  *Ibid.* at 390.
72  For critiques of Habermas and Arendt on these, and related, terms, see Craig Calhoun and John McGowan, eds., *Hannah Arendt and the Meaning of Politics* (Minneapolis: University of Minnesota Press, 1997); Leah Bradshaw, *Acting and Thinking: The Political Thought of Hannah Arendt* (Toronto: University of Toronto Press, 1989); Dossa Shiraz, *The Public Realm and the Public Self: The Political Theory of Hannah Arendt* (Waterloo, ON: Wilfrid Laurier University Press, 1989); Craig Calhoun, ed., *Habermas and the Public Sphere* (Cambridge, MA: MIT Press, 1992); Nancy Fraser, "Rethinking the Public Sphere," *Justice Interruptus: Critical Reflections on the Postcolonial Condition* (New York: Routledge, 1997), 68-98.
73  On these matters, see three excellent contributions to this volume: Lisa Philipps, "There's Only One Worker: Toward the Legal Integration of Paid Employment and Unpaid Caregiving"; Damian Collins and Nicholas Blomley, "Private Needs and Public Space: Politics, Poverty, and Anti-Panhandling By-Laws in Canadian Cities"; Stepan Wood, "Green Revolution or Greenwash? Voluntary Environmental Standards, Public Law, and Private Authority in Canada."
74  Neil Postman, *Technopoly: The Surrender of Culture to Technology* (New York: Vintage, 1992) at 7.
75  Habermas, *Theory of Communicative Action*, *supra* note 54 at 390.
76  For accounts of a number of these practices, see Barry Hague and Brian Loader, eds., *Digital Democracy: Discourse and Decision-making in the Information Age* (London: Routledge, 1999) and Kevin Hill and John Hughes, *Cyberpolitics: Citizen Activism in the Age of the Internet* (London: Rowman and Littlefield, 1998).
77  Darin Barney, *Prometheus Wired: The Hope for Democracy in the Age of Network Technology* (Vancouver: UBC Press, 2000).
78  On consumption as shadow work, and its relationship to digital technology, see Heather Menzies, "Telework, Shadow Work: The Privatization of Work in the New Digital Economy" (1997) 53 Studies in Political Economy 103-23.
79  Arendt, *supra* note 5 at 52-53.
80  For a sampling of the work on virtual community, see Steve G. Jones, ed., *Cybersociety 2.0: Revisiting Computer-Mediated Communication and Community* (Newbury Park, CA: Sage, 1998); Marc A. Smith and Peter Kollock, eds., *Communities in Cyberspace* (New York: Routledge, 1999); and Howard Rheingold, *The Virtual Community: Homesteading on the Electronic Frontier* (New York: Addison-Wesley, 1993).

81  On this issue, see Stephen Doheny-Farina, *The Wired Neighbourhood* (New Haven, CT: Yale University Press, 1996).
82  Nicholas Negroponte, *Being Digital* (New York: Knopf, 1995) at 153.
83  Robert Putnam, *Bowling Alone: The Collapse and Revival of American Community* (New York: Simon and Schuster, 2000) at 177-79. For more on this theme, see Cass Sunstein, *Republic.com* (Princeton: Princeton University Press, 2001).
84  Michele Willson, "Community in the Abstract: A Political and Ethical Dilemma?" in David Bell and Barbara Kennedy, eds., *The Cybercultures Reader* (London: Routledge, 2000), 649-50.
85  David Holmes, "Virtual Identity: Communities of Broadcast, Communities of Interactivity," in David Holmes, ed., *Virtual Politics: Identity and Community in Cyberspace* (London: Sage, 1997), 38-39.
86  *Ibid.* at 39.
87  Arendt, *supra* note 5 at 41.
88  Arendt, *supra* note 5 at 152.
89  Todd Gitlin, "Public Sphere or Public Sphericules?" in Tamar Liebes and James Curran, eds., *Media, Ritual and Identity* (London: Routledge, 1998), 172.
90  *Ibid.* at 173.
91  *Ibid.* at 173.
92  Mark Poster, "Cyberdemocracy: Internet and the Public Sphere," in David Porter, ed., *Internet Culture* (New York: Routledge, 1997), 213.
93  *Ibid.* at 213. For a thorough account of these activities in this environment, see Sherry Turkle, *Life on the Screen: Identity in the Age of the Internet* (New York: Simon and Schuster, 1995).
94  Poster, *supra* note 92 at 213.
95  *Ibid.* at 213.
96  Heather Dryburgh, "Changing Our Ways: Why and How Canadians Use the Internet" (Ottawa: Statistics Canada, March 2001), catalogue no. 56F0006XIE. (Note: all the following data are taken form this source unless otherwise noted.)
97  UCLA Center for Communication Policy, "The UCLA Internet Report: Surveying the Digital Future" (Los Angeles, 2000) at 10, available at http://ccp.ucla.edu/pages/internet-report.asp> (accessed 15 December 2002).
98  Pew Center for the People and the Press, "1998 On-line Use Survey," as reported in Pippa Norris, "Who Surfs? New Technology, Old Voters and Virtual Democracy," in Elaine Ciulla Kamarck and Joseph Nye, Jr., eds., *Democracy.com? Governance in a Networked World* (Hollis, NH: Hollis Publishing, 1999), 81.
99  For this emphasis on service delivery, see the "Government On-Line" section of Industry Canada's, *Connecting Canadians* website at <http://connect.gc.ca/> (accessed 1 December 2002).
100  Norris, *supra* note 98 at 88.
101  *Ibid.* at 89.
102  On this dynamic in Canada, see Dwayne Winseck, "Lost in Cyberspace: Convergence, Consolidation and Power in the Canadian Mediascape," paper presented at the Canadian Communication Association Annual Conference, Quebec City, 2001, and Donald Gutstein, *E.con: How the Internet Undermines Democracy* (Toronto: Stoddart, 1999). In the US context, see Dan Schiller, *Digital Capitalism: Networking the Global Market System* (Cambridge, MA: MIT Press, 1999) and Robert McChesney, *Rich Media, Poor Democracy: Communication Politics in Dubious Times* (Urbana, IL: University of Illinois Press, 1999), ch. 3.
103  Habermas, *Structural Transformation of the Public Sphere, supra* note 6 at 185.
104  Winseck, *supra* note 102 at 15.
105  *Ibid.* at 12.
106  See the literature listed in *supra* note 1, especially Lyon, *Surveillance Society*.
107  On the use of digital technologies in managing commercial consumption, see Schiller, *supra* note 102 at ch. 3; Barney, *supra* note 77 at 163-87; 225-31; Whitaker, *supra* note 1 at ch. 6. On the use of digital technologies in political marketing, see R. Kenneth Carty, William Cross, and Lisa Young, *Rebuilding Canadian Party Politics* (Vancouver: UBC Press, 2000) at 200-10.

108 Norman Solomon, "Simulating Democracy Can Be a Virtual Breeze," *Media Beat, Fairness and Accuracy in Reporting* website (24 May 2001), <www.fair.org/media-beat> (1 June 2001). Strictly speaking, the word "leisure" in this sentence ought to be replaced with "recreation."
109 Habermas, *Structural Transformation of the Public Sphere, supra* note 6 at 4.

## Bibliography

Arendt, Hannah, *The Human Condition* (Chicago: University of Chicago Press, 1958).
Aristotle, *Politics,* Ernest Barker (trans.) (New York: Oxford University Press, 1962).
Barney, Darin, *Prometheus Wired: The Hope for Democracy in the Age of Network Technology* (Vancouver: UBC Press, 2001).
Bennett, Colin, and Rebecca Grant, eds., *Visions of Privacy: Policy Choices for the Digital Age* (Toronto: University of Toronto Press, 1998).
Bradshaw, Leah, *Acting and Thinking: The Political Thought of Hannah Arendt* (Toronto: University of Toronto Press, 1989).
Calhoun, Craig, ed., *Habermas and the Public Sphere* (Cambridge, MA: MIT Press, 1992).
Calhoun, Craig, and John McGowan, eds., *Hannah Arendt and the Meaning of Politics* (Minneapolis: University of Minnesota Press, 1997).
Carty, R. Kenneth, William Cross, and Lisa Young, *Rebuilding Canadian Party Politics* (Vancouver: UBC Press, 2000).
Doheny-Farina, Stephen, *The Wired Neighbourhood* (New Haven, CT: Yale University Press, 1996).
Dryburgh, Heather, *Changing Our Ways: Why and How Canadians Use the Internet* (Ottawa: Statistics Canada, 2001), Catalogue no. 56F0006XIE.
Fraser, Nancy, *Justice Interruptus: Reflections on the Postcolonial Condition* (New York: Routledge, 1997).
Garfinkel, Simson, and Deborah Russell, *Database Nation: The Death of Privacy in the Twenty-First Century* (New York: O'Reilly and Associates, 2001).
Gitlin, Todd, "Public Sphere or Public Sphericules?" in Tamar Liebes and James Curran, eds., *Media, Ritual and Identity* (London: Routledge, 1998), 168-74.
Gutstein, Donald, *E.con: How the Internet Undermines Democracy* (Toronto: Stoddart, 1999).
Habermas, Jürgen, "The Public Sphere: An Encyclopedia Article," in M.G. Durham and D.M. Kellner, eds., *Media and Cultural Studies* (Oxford: Blackwell, 2001), 102-7.
—, *The Structural Transformation of the Public Sphere: An Inquiry into a Category of Bourgeois Society*, Thomas Burger (trans.) (Cambridge, MA: MIT Press, 1991).
—, *Theory of Communicative Action*, Vol. 2, *Lifeworld and System*, Thomas McCarthy (trans.) (Boston: Beacon Press, 1987).
Hague, Barry, and Brian Loader, eds., *Digital Democracy: Discourse and Decision-Making in the Information Age* (London: Routledge, 1999).
Hill, Kevin, and John Hughes, *Cyberpolitics: Citizen Activism in the Age of the Internet* (London: Rowman and Littlefield, 1998).
Holmes, David, "Virtual Identity: Communities of Broadcast, Communities of Interactivity," in David Holmes, ed., *Virtual Politics: Identity and Community in Cyberspace* (London: Sage, 1997), 26-45.
Horkheimer, Max, and Theodor Adorno, *The Dialectic of Enlightenment* (New York: Continuum, 1995).
Jones, Steve G., ed., *Cybersociety 2.0: Revisiting Computer-Mediated Communication and Community* (Newbury Park, CA: Sage, 1998).
Lester, Toby, "The Reinvention of Privacy," *Atlantic Monthly* (March 2001), 27-39.
Locke, John, *Second Treatise of Government* (Indianapolis: Hackett, 1980).
Lyon, David, *Surveillance Society* (Buckingham, UK: Open University Press, 2001).
McChesney, Robert, *Rich Media, Poor Democracy: Communication Politics in Dubious Times* (Urbana, IL: University of Illinois Press, 1999).
Menzies, Heather, "Telework, Shadow Work: The Privatization of Work in the New Digital Economy" (1997) 53 Studies in Political Economy 103-23.
Negroponte, Nicholas, *Being Digital* (New York: Knopf, 1995).

Norris, Pippa, "Who Surfs? New Technology, Old Voters and Virtual Democracy," in Elaine Ciulla Kamarck and Joseph Nye, Jr., eds., *Democracy.com? Governance in a Networked World* (Hollis, NH: Hollis Publishing, 1999), 71-94.

Okin, Susan Moller, *Women in Western Political Thought* (Princeton: Princeton University Press, 1978).

Pateman, Carole, "Feminist Critiques of the Public Private Dichotomy," in S.I. Benn and G.F. Gaus, eds., *Public and Private in Social Life* (New York: St. Martin's Press, 1983), 281-303.

Poster, Mark, "Cyberdemocracy: Internet and the Public Sphere," in David Porter, ed., *Internet Culture* (New York: Routledge, 1997), 201-17.

Postman, Neil, *Technopoly: The Surrender of Culture to Technology* (New York: Vintage, 1992).

Putnam, Robert, *Bowling Alone: The Collapse and Revival of American Community* (New York: Simon and Schuster, 2000).

Rheingold, Howard, *The Virtual Community: Homesteading on the Electronic Frontier* (New York: Addison-Wesley, 1993).

Rosen, Jeffrey, *The Unwanted Gaze: The Destruction of Privacy in America* (New York: Random House, 2000).

Schiller, Dan, *Digital Capitalism: Networking the Global Market System* (Cambridge, MA: MIT Press, 1999).

Shiraz, Dossa, *The Public Realm and the Public Self: The Political Theory of Hannah Arendt* (Waterloo, ON: Wilfrid Laurier University Press, 1989).

Smith, Marc A., and Peter Kollock, eds., *Communities in Cyberspace* (New York: Routledge, 1999).

Solomon, Norman, "Simulating Democracy Can Be a Virtual Breeze. Media Beat, 24 May 2001," *Fairness and Accuracy in Reporting* website, <www.fair.org/media-beat> (1 June 2001).

Sunstein, Cass, *Republic.com* (Princeton: Princeton University Press, 2001).

Turkle, Sherry, *Life on the Screen: Identity in the Age of the Internet* (New York: Simon and Schuster, 1995).

UCLA Center for Communication Policy, "The UCLA Internet Report: Surveying the Digital Future" (Los Angeles, 2000), available at http://ccp.ucla.edu/pages/internet-report.asp> (accessed 15 December 2002).

Whitaker, Reg, *The End of Privacy: How Total Surveillance Is Becoming a Reality* (New York: New Press, 2000).

Winseck, Dwayne, "Lost in Cyberspace: Convergence, Consolidation and Power in the Canadian Mediascape," paper presented at the Canadian Communication Association Annual Conference, Quebec City, 2001.

Willson, Michele, "Community in the Abstract: A Political and Ethical Dilemma," in David Bell and Barbara Kennedy, eds., *The Cybercultures Reader* (London, Routledge, 2000), 644-58.

# 5
# Green Revolution or Greenwash? Voluntary Environmental Standards, Public Law, and Private Authority in Canada

*Stepan Wood*

This essay examines the transformation of the public–private divide in Canadian law and politics in the context of a little-known set of voluntary initiatives for corporate "greening," which are known as environmental management system (EMS) standards. These standards are developed and applied in the relative obscurity of corporate offices, management consulting firms, and standardization bodies (national and international organizations that write technical standards). They have received little attention from academics and almost none from the popular news media and non-governmental organizations (NGOs). The standardization bodies that develop them have gone almost entirely unnoticed in the recent wave of controversy and popular protest over globalization and free trade that has swept the major intergovernmental trade and financial institutions. Nonetheless, voluntary EMS initiatives have significant and largely unexplored implications for environmental quality, public health, and the definition of "public" and "private" in Canadian law and politics.

## Environmental Management Systems

An EMS is a system of management policies, procedures, structures, and practices that enables an organization to anticipate, identify, and manage the environmental impacts of its activities. The major elements of an EMS include: a written environmental *policy* setting out the organization's environmental vision and basic commitments; a *planning* process to evaluate the organization's environmental impacts, identify the applicable legal requirements, and set environmental objectives and targets; *implementation* of the EMS through roles, responsibilities, resources, training, communication, documentation, and operational controls; the *checking* of the organization's performance through regular monitoring, measurement, and audits along with *corrective action* to remedy any problems; and a regular *management review* to ensure the continuing suitability and effectiveness of the EMS. This ongoing cycle of planning, implementation, checking, corrective action, and review (which is also known as the "Plan-Do-Check-Act" or PDCA model) is meant to result in the continual improvement of the EMS and, ultimately, the organization's environmental performance.

While many other voluntary environmental initiatives set environmental performance goals for organizations to meet, EMSs leave it up to the organization to set its own environmental performance objectives in accordance with its needs and interests. Thus, an EMS is primarily procedural rather than performance oriented. The thinking behind an EMS is that improved management processes will lead to improved environmental outcomes.

EMSs emerged as a distinct management tool in the late 1980s in the wake of several prominent environmental disasters, including the chemical disaster in Bhopal, India. A growing number of industrial firms, many of them large multinational corporations, expanded and consolidated their existing environmental management tools (for example, environmental policies, environmental audits, public environmental reports, and pollution prevention programs) into systematic programs to manage the environmental impacts of their operations. Many of these EMSs were modelled after the "total quality management" systems that had recently swept the business world. By the early 1990s, many firms supported the development of uniform guidelines for EMSs to enable comparability and to create a level playing field for trade. Standardization bodies in several jurisdictions, buoyed by the meteoric rise of the ISO 9000 quality management standards, took up this challenge and began to develop voluntary EMS standards.

The most prominent EMS standardization initiative is the ISO 14000 series of global standards developed by the International Organization for Standardization (ISO). The ISO 14000 series consists of ISO 14001, which specifies requirements for an EMS that may be objectively audited;[1] ISO 14004, which is a more detailed and flexible guide to designing and implementing an EMS;[2] and around twenty other supporting standards related to EMS auditing, life-cycle analysis, ecolabelling, environmental performance evaluation, and other matters. The ISO is a global federation of around 140 national standardization bodies. The main work of the ISO and its member bodies is the development of technical standards by business for business. The ISO 14000 standards are expressly intended to be one of the global business community's major contributions to the global public policy goal of sustainable development and to inaugurate a new paradigm of environmental management that is applicable not only to business firms but to all organizations, from hospitals, to universities, to military bases, to government departments.

Having an EMS in place is only part of the story. Many organizations want to be able to demonstrate to relevant external audiences (for example, customers, competitors, trade associations, consumers, or regulators) that their EMS conforms to a recognized standard, thereby realizing reputational, competitive, or regulatory benefits or responding to customer demand. This is typically achieved by having the EMS audited and certified as conforming to the ISO 14001 standard by an accredited third-party registrar. Independent third-party certification has long been used to verify conformance to technical product safety or performance standards. In recent years, it has been extended to demonstrate conformance to a broader range of quality, environmental, labour, social, and other criteria. Examples include product ecolabelling programs,[3] sustainable forestry or fisheries management programs,[4] and environmental, quality, or occupational health and safety management system standards, including ISO 14001.

EMSs have become widespread in the private sector in the last ten years, particularly among multinational corporations and corporations operating in international markets. A growing number of multinational corporations require their suppliers to have ISO 14001 EMSs in place. EMS certification is fast becoming a requirement for doing business in a few industry sectors (for example, auto manufacturing), and the number of ISO 14001 certificates worldwide is growing rapidly.[5]

What little scholarship there is about EMS initiatives emphasizes their private and voluntary character. While some writers extol EMSs as evidence of a revolution in corporate environmental practices and an example of the promise of corporate self-regulation,[6] others see EMSs as an example of corporate "greenwash" and a pretense for governments to retreat from environmental regulation.[7] Running through these debates is the theme of the increasing power of private authority in public affairs.[8] This literature makes a contribution to our knowledge by demonstrating that these voluntary initiatives, far from being apolitical, reflect the political agendas and public order conceptions of particular social actors. It also contributes to the burgeoning debates about regulatory "reinvention"[9] and the role that voluntary corporate initiatives should play in public policy.[10]

This tendency to focus on the "privatization" of environmental policy tends, however, to underemphasize an important aspect of the politics of voluntary environmental initiatives, namely, the fact that public authorities and legal systems are deeply involved in the constitution and exercise of "private" authority to the point that it may no longer be useful to discuss these voluntary initiatives in terms of a public–private divide. By emphasizing the voluntary and private character of these environmental initiatives, the debates over EMS initiatives tend not to acknowledge the full extent of the entanglement of public authorities and voluntary initiatives.[11] Numerous writers have addressed certain aspects of this interaction,[12] but very few have attempted to examine it comprehensively.[13] This is also true to a lesser extent of the literature on voluntary environmental intiatives generally.[14] In fact, diverse public authorities around the world have begun to participate in, and influence, the development of voluntary EMS initiatives and incorporate them into their strategies and programs in an increasing variety of ways, including officially endorsing or encouraging private sector EMS implementation, conducting or disseminating research about EMSs, providing financial incentives for EMS implementation, relaxing regulatory requirements or criminal penalties for companies that implement voluntary EMS standards, making the implementation of voluntary EMS standards mandatory through legislation or court order, applying voluntary EMS standards to their own operations, developing or agreeing to international trade rules that may turn voluntary international standards into constraints on governments' regulatory options, and steering the development and use of voluntary EMS standards in particular directions.

It is at this interface between state and non-state regimes that the most interesting questions about EMS standards and other voluntary initiatives arise. Distinctions between public and private, state and non-state, mandatory and voluntary are not particularly helpful in understanding the significance of EMS standards. Rather, EMS standards demonstrate that the practices of government traverse the categories on which our understandings of law and politics are typically based. I investigate this interface by exploring the forms of public authorities' engagements with voluntary EMS standards in Canada and examining the "governmental" implications of this important experiment in "private" regulation. In the second part of this chapter, I describe the ways in which Canadian public authorities have engaged with voluntary EMS initiatives. In the third part, I explore the implications of these engagements for the (re)definition of the public–private divide in Canadian law and politics. I conclude with some suggestions about the possible role of law in facilitating or resisting these transformations.

### Public Authorities' Engagements with Voluntary EMS Initiatives in Canada

A variety of public authorities in Canada have begun to engage with EMSs and voluntary EMS standards in a range of interesting ways. I use the term "public authorities" broadly to denote the entire Canadian state apparatus, including government ministers, departments, agencies, bureaucrats, procurement personnel, regulators, committees, legislatures, prosecutors, courts, administrative tribunals, military facilities, local governments, and public utilities. Their engagements with EMS initiatives to date have fallen, I suggest, into five rough categories: steering, self-discipline, knowledge production, reward, and command. I also identify three other categories of engagement, which have not yet been employed by Canadian public authorities in relation to EMSs but which can be discerned in their engagements with other voluntary initiatives: benchmarking, challenging, and borrowing. Together these eight categories give an indication of the range of Canadian public authorities' engagements with "private" governance in the field of environmental protection.[15]

## Modes of Engagement

*Steering*
First, Canadian public authorities have sometimes engaged with voluntary initiatives such as EMSs and EMS standards in a mode that can be described as "steering," namely encouraging voluntary initiatives, inhibiting them, or steering their development, content, or use in a particular direction. At a certain level, all the modes of engagement that I identify could be described in this way. "Steering" might thus be viewed as an umbrella category covering most public authorities' interactions with voluntary initiatives. Nonetheless, Canadian public authorities have exhibited several types of conduct that are distinct enough from the other categories of engagement to be considered separate. The primary driver for these engagements is, as Pollution Probe observes, that "notwithstanding their voluntary nature, standards are properly regarded by policy makers as an instrument of governance."[16]

Although "steering" often involves active, intentional efforts to mold conduct, it can also be passive or even inadvertent. First, it may include surveillance or intelligence gathering. Government officials may participate in standards development, for instance, as much to observe and stay abreast of industry developments as to push standards in any particular direction.[17] In this case, "steering" consists in patrolling a particular conception of the appropriate boundary between government and "private" spheres. Second, public authorities may inadvertently send signals that influence voluntary initiatives. For instance, governments may, on one hand, publicly encourage firms to use EMSs and environmental certification initiatives but, on the other, maintain regulatory frameworks, such as forest tenure laws or environmental audit disclosure rules, that inadvertently inhibit such use.[18]

In any event, public authorities in Canada have engaged in "steering" voluntary EMS initiatives in at least five ways: by pronouncing official policies on EMSs, by formally constituting and funding standardization bodies, by participating in the development of voluntary EMS standards, by providing strategic policy leadership for standardization activities, and by regulating the development, content, or use of voluntary initiatives.

*"Talking the Talk": Official Policy Pronouncements*   First, some public authorities in Canada and elsewhere have formulated and pronounced official policies on the private sector use of voluntary EMS initiatives. Such pronouncements, which range from off-the-cuff remarks to detailed policy statements, can have important legitimation or delegitimation effects for

voluntary initiatives.[19] Their content varies from enthusiastic (but often vague) endorsement, to active promotion, to the enunciation of conditions or goals for public authorities' involvement or support, to the enumeration of concerns, to active resistance (although this last initiative is very rare in the case of EMS). In Canada, official pronouncements have tended toward endorsement and promotion – "talking the talk" of EMS as part of a broader agenda of regulatory flexibility. Very few Canadian government authorities have initiated serious consultations or issued careful policy pronouncements about how, why, or in what conditions they will endorse voluntary EMS initiatives, but this inaction is changing as some federal and provincial authorities have begun earnest policy development efforts regarding EMS.[20]

*Constitution and Funding of Standardization Bodies*   Second, the federal government is involved in the establishment and operation of voluntary standards-setting bodies in Canada. Although this does not involve the overt direction of standardization activities, it is an interesting but overlooked dimension of interaction between governments and voluntary standardization. Standards-setting bodies in most countries have complicated relationships with the state apparatus. The Standards Council of Canada, which is Canada's principal voluntary standardization organ, and its national ISO member body, is a "quasi-non-governmental organization."[21] It is a federal crown corporation, established by statute in 1970. It reports to parliament through Industry Canada and receives federal government funding.[22] Its statutory mandate is to promote efficient and effective voluntary standardization in Canada by, *inter alia*, promoting public–private sector cooperation.[23] Thus, its constitutive instrument emphasizes the hybrid public–private character of standardization.[24]

*Participation in Standards Development*   Third, Canadian government officials have participated directly in the development of EMS standards in Canada and the ISO since the beginning of EMS standardization in the early 1990s, by sitting on national standards committees and by serving as Canadian delegates to ISO meetings.[25] Indeed, government officials participate in most voluntary standards development in Canada.[26] Canadian standards committees operate on a consensus basis and employ a "balanced matrix" to ensure that their membership reflects a rough balance among standards users (industry), service/professional representatives (including consultants, auditors, and registrars), government officials, and "general interest" members (a grab-bag of consumer, environmental, and labour representatives, academics, and so on).[27] Government officials often cite the balanced membership and consensual process of Canadian standards committees and the ISO itself as key reasons to endorse voluntary EMS standards,[28] but the impression of balanced consensus may be misleading. Industry and consultants usually make up a large majority of the committees, and, thus, the Canadian Standards Association (CSA) often has difficulty maintaining the "balanced matrix" of its environmental standards committees,[29] and the ISO has been criticized repeatedly for its dominance by big industry from advanced industrial countries.

*Strategic Policy Leadership* Fourth, many governments see strategic leadership of national and international standardization activities as a priority for ensuring international competitiveness of their home industry. It was only in March 2000, however, that the Canadian federal government launched the Canadian Standards Strategy, which serves to "provide direction and leadership on how to use standardization to best advance the social and economic well-being of Canadians in a global economy."[30] The strategy promotes the use of standards as complements to regulation, calls for fuller representation of the broadening range of "standardization stakeholders," and acknowledges that fiscal restraint and global trade are driving public authorities' increasing reliance on voluntary standards to achieve public policy goals.[31]

*Regulation of Voluntary Initiatives* Finally, public authorities may regulate the development, use, or content of voluntary environmental initiatives. Canadian public authorities have generally taken a "hands off" approach to the development and use of voluntary initiatives,[32] including EMSs. Nonetheless, various forms of state regulation may affect the development and use of EMS initiatives directly or indirectly, including:

- competition law, which addresses the possible anti-competitive effects of competitors coming together to devise rules for themselves;
- misleading advertising laws, which may apply when a firm violates the requirements of a voluntary standard to which it subscribes (for example, ISO 14001) yet represents itself as conforming;
- international trade law, in particular, the Agreement on Technical Barriers to Trade (TBT Agreement), which requires member states, including Canada, to do everything reasonable to ensure that voluntary standards-setting bodies in their jurisdiction adhere to the Code of Good Practice for the Preparation, Adoption and Application of Standards, which essentially applies the TBT Agreement's trade disciplines to voluntary standardization (that is, where international standards exist on a subject, domestic standardization bodies should use them as the basis for their own standards);[33]
- the presence or absence of clear ground rules for the development and use of voluntary initiatives, such as the requirements of public participation in the development or implementation of voluntary initiatives or

the public disclosure of information on participants' performance (to date, Canadian governments have not enacted such rules); and
- the presence or absence of a credible "regulatory backstop" in the form of monitoring and enforcing existing environmental laws and demonstrating a will to step in with regulatory instruments should the voluntary initiatives fail to achieve public policy objectives.[34]

### Self-Discipline

The second major way that Canadian public authorities have engaged with voluntary EMS initiatives can best be described as self-discipline.[35] It is possible to distinguish two forms of self-discipline: (1) when public authorities "walk the walk" by implementing EMSs in their own operations, and (2) when public authorities ratify international agreements that turn voluntary standards into potential constraints on their authority.

*"Walking the Walk": Implementing EMSs in Government Operations*   Canadian public authorities at all levels of government have begun to develop and implement their own EMSs, some on their own initiative and others as a result of pressure from central government authorities. At the federal level, most major departments and several agencies now have EMSs, although they vary substantially in scope, detail, and the degree of implementation. The federal auditor general and the commissioner of the environment and sustainable development (CESD) began to encourage federal organizations to implement EMSs in the mid-1990s. Facing mostly desultory responses, they soon turned to prodding and shaming, referring to EMSs as "essential" for government operations and publicly exposing the foot dragging that was happening in several departments.[36] The CESD and Environment Canada play central roles in assisting federal government bodies to develop and implement EMSs and appear to consider EMSs mandatory, at least for the twenty-five major federal departments and agencies that must file sustainable development strategies.[37]

Some provincial and territorial ministries have also begun to implement EMSs, and a substantial and growing number of Canadian municipalities have implemented EMSs either for their entire operations or for subordinate bodies such as water or waste management units. Central provincial government authorities have generally done little to coordinate, encourage, assist, or push these developments. Several interesting issues arise from these self-applications of EMSs in the public sector, including:

- Reasons for implementing EMSs: Although Canadian public authorities list many reasons for implementing EMSs, one looms large – to set an example for the private sector.[38] In reality, however, the leading edge of

EMS design and implementation is found in forward-thinking corporations, consulting firms, and standardization bodies, along with innovative public–private consortia outside Canada.[39] Far from leading by example, many Canadian public authorities are simply scrambling to keep up with the private sector.[40]

- Endorsement of ISO standards: Most Canadian public authorities' EMSs are modelled on ISO 14004 or (less often) ISO 14001. The federal government has expressly endorsed ISO 14004 as a guide for public sector EMSs.
- Verification and oversight: Verification of the implementation and performance of public sector EMSs in Canada is haphazard and incomplete. Most government organizations disclose basic information about their EMSs, and some report publicly on their EMS performance. The auditor general and the CESD monitor the federal government's implementation of EMSs (there is typically no such oversight in the provinces). While some Canadian public authorities have obtained third-party certification for certain individual facilities' EMSs, most have avoided certification largely because of the expense involved.
- Variety of settings: Finally, Canadian public authorities have implemented EMSs in a wide variety of organizational settings, from entire government departments to individual branches, agencies, operating units, facilities, or even single buildings. They have been applied in a range of fields including environmental regulation, food inspection, transportation, electricity generation, water and waste management, military supply, forestry operations, and other resource activities.

*Voluntary Standards as Self-Imposed Constraints on Public Authority* Canada is a party to certain international trade agreements that may transform voluntary international standards developed by obscure, often industry-dominated standardization bodies, such as the ISO, into potential constraints on Canadian governments' freedom to set their own legal standards for health, safety, and the environment. Under the 1994 TBT Agreement, member states must base their domestic "technical regulations" (that is, environmental and other regulations governing products or their related processes or production methods) on existing voluntary standards developed by international standardization bodies such as the ISO unless the standards would be "an ineffective or inappropriate means for the fulfilment of the legitimate objectives pursued, for instance because of fundamental climatic or geographical factors or fundamental technological problems."[41] Under these rules, regulations that are based on existing international standards are presumed not to create an illegal obstacle to trade, but regulations that deviate from international standards may be, and have been, challenged as trade barriers.[42]

Although the full measure of these trade disciplines has yet to be taken, they clearly have potential implications for public authorities' engagements with voluntary environmental initiatives. When public authorities begin to promulgate mandatory regulations on matters covered by voluntary standards, such as when Nova Scotia and New Brunswick made ISO 14000-based EMSs mandatory in the gas pipeline industry,[43] those standards may limit governments' authority to design their own regulations.[44] Ironically, therefore, EMS standards, which are almost universally identified with regulatory flexibility, may ultimately impose a constraint on such flexibility.

*Knowledge Production*
The third mode of engagement has as its defining feature the generation and dissemination of knowledge about voluntary initiatives. Canadian public authorities have engaged in such knowledge production by conducting or sponsoring research and education regarding the design, implementation, verification, or effects of EMSs. With respect to research, numerous federal and provincial government departments have funded or carried out modest pilot projects, case studies, and surveys of the design, implementation, or performance of EMSs in particular firms or jurisdictions, but none have come close to the research programs on EMS that have been sponsored by various governments and public–private consortia in the United States and Europe.[45] Canadian governments have also supported EMS research by sponsoring research conferences on voluntary initiatives, publishing collections of research papers, and hosting electronic research discussion fora.[46] With respect to education, Canadian public authorities have propagated knowledge and expertise regarding EMSs through two principal modalities: training and publicity. Training ranges from basic primer courses for business people to advanced training for experts such as EMS auditors. More commonly, Canadian public authorities have responded to the emergence of voluntary EMS standards by simply publicizing information about EMSs, typically through passive means such as government websites. Such publicity is usually aimed at industry but sometimes at consumers as well. It usually encourages the use of EMSs and conveys information about EMS standards and the design, implementation, certification, advantages, or sector-specific applications of EMSs. It seldom enunciates public authorities' reservations or concerns since these are typically addressed in other contexts.[47]

These activities are closely related to official policy development and pronouncement[48] – research is a crucial input in policy development and education is an important channel for generating support for preferred policies among relevant constituencies. Governments often sponsor or conduct research and education programs as elements of carefully orchestrated policy projects and incorporate the fruits of non-state research and creativity into their own policy-making, effectively moving some policy development costs outside of government budgets.[49] In any event, these engagements with voluntary initiatives are usually integrated more or less into the public authorities' broader political agendas, particularly those springing from platforms of fiscal restraint, government downsizing, regulatory reinvention, free enterprise, and global competitiveness.

*Reward*

One of the most prominent themes in discussions of voluntary initiatives is the idea that voluntary initiatives can be the basis for a new relationship between regulators and industry – a relationship that emphasizes flexibility, efficiency, partnership, and market incentives rather than the perceived rigidity and inefficiency of conventional "command and control" regulation. In this light, public authorities in various countries, including Canada, have begun to incorporate voluntary EMS initiatives into their regulatory strategies by offering concrete rewards for voluntary EMS implementation. These rewards typically take three forms: (1) regulatory relief or forbearance (that is, the relaxation of existing regulatory requirements or forbearance from introducing new ones), (2) financial incentives, and (3) "green procurement" policies.

*Regulatory Relief and Forbearance*　First, governments in several jurisdictions have begun to establish programs that relax existing regulatory requirements (such as permits, reports, inspections, or technology requirements) for firms that implement EMSs.[50] In 2001, Alberta became the first Canadian jurisdiction to launch an official program offering regulatory relief to firms that have EMSs in place.[51] Alberta Environment's Leaders Environmental Approval Document (LEAD) program, which is currently in a pilot phase, requires participating facilities to implement a very rudimentary EMS,[52] maintain a clean compliance record, demonstrate past environmental performance that exceeds legal requirements, commit to future environmental performance goals and measures that exceed legal requirements and that are based on continuous improvement and pollution prevention, implement meaningful public consultation, and report annually on performance. In return, facilities will receive modest regulatory incentives, such as pre-approval for minor process and equipment changes, facility-wide performance targets ("bubbles"), performance- rather than technology-based requirements, and expedited permitting procedures, along with various forms of public recognition. Ontario is likely soon to follow with its own program, and other Canadian governments may be considering such programs as well.[53] In addition to these general regulatory exemption programs, some Canadian public authorities have experimented to a small degree with incorporating EMSs or EMS-related initiatives into government-industry negotiated agreements, but it is unclear to what extent such agreements have involved the relaxation of existing regulations or a forbearance from introducing new rules.[54]

In addition, firms that have EMSs may be rewarded with leniency in enforcement after a regulatory violation is discovered. Environmental enforcement policies in some jurisdictions extend some leniency in the exercise of enforcement discretion to firms with EMSs. However, this is not the case in Canada. Although many environmental policy-makers and permitting authorities in Canada encourage firms to implement EMSs, Canadian environmental enforcement policies appear to give little or no weight to voluntary EMSs.[55] Upon conviction, courts may consider the implementation of a voluntary EMS as a mitigating factor in sentencing for environmental regulatory offences, although I am unaware of any instances of this happening.[56]

*Financial Incentives*   While numerous foreign governments have offered grants, tax credits, preferential access to government loans, and other financial incentives for private sector EMS implementation or certification, Canadian public authorities, to date, have not made much use of these tools.[57]

*Green Government Procurement*   Governments are among the largest purchasers of goods and services in a jurisdiction, and their purchasing policies can have a substantial impact on business. Many governments, including the Canadian federal government, have encouraged suppliers to implement EMSs or obtain third-party certification of their EMSs, but only a handful, none of which are Canadian, have made this implementation a formal purchasing preference or requirement.[58] Although green procurement policies may reward firms that adhere to voluntary initiatives, they can also have a coercive aspect. EMSs may ultimately be transformed into a *de facto* requirement for doing business if enough public and private sector buyers make EMS implementation or certification a purchasing requirement.[59]

*Command*
Both industry and government usually resist proposals to make voluntary initiatives mandatory. It is very uncommon for public authorities to issue legally binding commands requiring firms to implement EMSs or demonstrate their conformance to an EMS standard. On the rare occasion that such commands have been issued in Canada, it has been with the affected firms' or industry's support, either because they found the alternatives even worse, they were already planning to implement or obtain certification of an EMS, or they stood to benefit directly from the arrangement.

First, in a handful of cases, Canadian judges have used creative sentencing powers[60] to order an environmental offender to implement an ISO 14001-based EMS or to obtain ISO 14001 certification.[61] In every case, the defendant has either proposed or agreed to the order, often because it was considering implementing or certifying an EMS anyway and could therefore expect lower fines and fewer charges in exchange. Prosecutors and judges support such orders because they believe ISO certification will enhance future compliance. Moreover, it is easy to verify and is obtained at the defendant's expense.[62] Second, Nova Scotia and New Brunswick were among the first jurisdictions in the world to make EMS implementation mandatory for all firms in a particular industry sector.[63] Both provinces have enacted regulations requiring gas pipeline operators to implement ISO 14000-based EMSs.[64] These developments were part of a move toward greater self-regulation in the sector. The governments supported mandatory ISO 14000 implementation as a credible external benchmark that would make self-regulation acceptable, while industry positively preferred ISO 14000 to government regulation.[65] Finally, Alberta's LEAD program will make implementation and maintenance of an EMS a licence term and specify the minimum elements of the EMS in the licence itself. This decision appears to be the first instance in Canada in which regulators will require EMS implementation or certification as a term of an operating permit or administrative order.[66]

Industry's willingness to have these EMS standards turned into binding legal requirements may also reflect the special role that voluntary standards developed by formal standardization bodies, such as the CSA and the ISO, play in government regulation. Governments have a long tradition of incorporating voluntary technical standards (for example, for building materials, construction, plumbing, fire safety, engineering, food safety, medical devices, and so on) into mandatory regulations.[67]

In addition to these "public law" methods, the terms of a voluntary EMS initiative may be made mandatory through private litigation. A firm may agree to adhere to an EMS standard or other voluntary initiative in an agreement with regulators, a commercial supply contract, or trade association membership agreement.[68] Such a voluntary undertaking may be converted into a legally binding command when a party to the agreement seeks judicial enforcement of the agreement.[69] Some commentators believe that these private law enforcement tools hold the key to successful regulation of corporate behaviour through voluntary codes.[70]

*Other Engagements*
Finally, three other modes of engagement can be discerned in Canadian public authorities' interactions with voluntary initiatives other than EMSs. These engagements may at some point be employed in relation to EMS initiatives.

*Benchmarking* Canadian courts often use widely accepted voluntary standards and other evidence of industry custom as benchmarks[71] for determining whether a defendant exercised "reasonable care" in a tort case[72] or "due diligence" to avoid committing a regulatory offence.[73] Several commentators and government officials have suggested that implementation of an ISO EMS constitutes "due diligence."[74] Although no Canadian court has yet to use voluntary EMS standards as a benchmark for liability, the prospect is increasingly likely and deserves critical attention because:

- it is doubtful that an ISO 14001 EMS satisfies the requirements of reasonable care. While it enables an organization to implement systematically its own environmental goals and prevent unplanned pollution incidents, it does not require the organization to achieve any particular level of environmental performance or legal compliance – its focus is on ensuring *conformance to the standard* rather than avoiding breach of legal duties of care;
- the use of EMS standards as benchmarks for liability may give voluntary industry-developed initiatives a power that they could not achieve on their own, by effectively imposing the terms of such initiatives on organizations that neither used the initiative nor participated in its development;[75] and
- the prospect of such judicial benchmarking may place other state actors in a dilemma, as Kernaghan Webb points out. If government officials fail to participate in the development of voluntary initiatives, "there is a risk that the standards produced will be considered reasonable by judges ... even though they may be viewed as inadequate by government"; but if government officials do participate in the development of voluntary initiatives in an effort to influence their content, it may be difficult for prosecutors to argue later that the initiative does not constitute "due diligence" even though the government's views may not have been reflected in the initiative as adopted.[76]

*Challenge*   Another mode of engagement with voluntary initiatives that has been pursued by some public authorities in the environmental arena is to challenge firms to pledge to implement voluntary environmental measures and report their results publicly. This is often used as an alternative to introducing new regulatory measures. In Canada, it has been used to address such issues as greenhouse gas emissions and releases of toxic substances, but no government has yet developed a challenge program involving the industry adoption of EMSs.

*Borrowing*   Finally, public authorities can incorporate voluntary initiatives developed by non-governmental bodies into legal instruments without making their observance mandatory. For instance, statutes, regulations, operating permits, or agreements with regulated entities might specify a voluntary standard as a default basis for issuing approvals; make exceedance of a voluntary standard the trigger for documentation, reporting, or remediation duties; adopt a voluntary standard's definition of a term; or authorize the use of a voluntary standard for testing, inspecting, or measuring a regulated entity's operations, equipment, or products. Although this has not been done with EMS standards, one could imagine regulations, for example, authorizing the use of ISO environmental auditing standards or specifying ISO 14001 certification as a basis for "deemed" approval of particular kinds of activities.

## Implications for the Public–Private Divide

For the most part, these interactions among public authorities and voluntary non-state initiatives occur in a quiet corner of environmental politics populated mainly by technical experts – indeed, in a space that many participants do not even perceive as political. Nonetheless, the participants are involved, wittingly or unwittingly, in the definition and redefinition of the scope and concerns of politics and law in the field of the environment. It would not be accurate to view these developments as evidence of a "relentless augmentation of the powers of a centralizing, controlling and regulating state" that has increasingly colonized the "lifeworld."[77] It would be absurd to suggest that Canadian public authorities' engagements with voluntary environmental initiatives evidence a takeover of society and the market by the agents and machinery of the state. Nor, on the other hand, does the evidence reveal a takeover of public policy-making by industry. Rather, what emerges is a range of heterogeneous, shifting links among a variety of public and private authorities, through which these authorities pursue their goals not so much by domination and control as by exercising subtle and unpredictable influences upon the interests, beliefs, and choices of free individuals. These links rely upon a range of experts and associated bodies of knowledge perceived to be relatively autonomous from both politics and the market (for example, accounting, engineering, standardization, and law); and they involve alliances and tensions not just between public and private authorities but also among a multiplicity of public authorities themselves (for example, government ministers, environmental commissioners, legislators, regulators, inspectors, prosecutors, judges, and government purchasing personnel).

This hybridization of law and market, state and non-state, suggests the need for an alternative characterization of "government" that moves beyond the metaphor of a public–private divide to encompass the entire complex of ideals, goals, rationales, techniques, procedures, and programs by which a diversity of state and non-state authorities seek to shape human conduct to their desired ends. This alternative conception of government prompts us, first, to examine law and politics at the level of the mundane techniques by which various authorities seek to effectuate their governmental ambitions. Viewed this way, EMSs and EMS standards instantiate a broader tendency in contemporary practices of government in the advanced industrial democracies to "depoliticize" certain issues and problems by positioning them either as technical matters to be resolved by the application of neutral expertise or as private matters to be resolved by market forces. The EMS example also signals a shift in political rationales, a redrawing of the appropriate aims and forms of "governance," of the boundaries of politics, law, and market, and of the distribution of tasks between different authorities. Finally, it is possible to make some tentative suggestions as to the role law might play in facilitating or resisting these transformations.

### Beyond the Public–Private Divide:
### An Alternative Conception of Government

One of the questions posed by the organizers of this symposium was whether the metaphor of a public–private divide is still appropriate. The problem with using such language to analyze contemporary practices of ordering and directing social relations, as Nikolas Rose and Peter Miller point out, is that "the political vocabulary structured by oppositions between state and civil society, public and private, government and market, coercion and consent, sovereignty and autonomy and the like, does not adequately characterize the diverse ways in which rule is exercised in advanced liberal democracies."[78]

What is needed is an alternative way of thinking about government, which avoids the limitations of these dichotomies. There is nothing new in this suggestion, of course. These dichotomies have been questioned repeatedly by successive waves of criticism in legal studies, from legal realism, to feminist legal theory, to critical legal studies, to legal pluralism. Exploding, fragmenting, or contextualizing categories of state, sovereignty, public, private, and so on have been regular features of criticism and innovation in the social sciences and law throughout the last century – so much so, that proclaiming the "death of the state" has become part of the ritual of renewal in discipline after discipline.[79] Scholars have repeatedly attempted to sever the "king's head" in social and legal thought, yet the next generation of critics always seems to find it back on the sovereign's shoulders.[80]

The fact that these conventional categories remain central to the theories and practices of government after all this critical attention is a puzzle in itself. We might gain analytical leverage over this puzzle if we focus on the *problematics of government* instead of over-valuing the problem of the *state*.[81] The example of EMSs and EMS standards demonstrates that the regulation of environment-economy interactions is accomplished by an array of public and private authorities and institutions, including standardization bodies, EMS auditors and certifiers, consultants, corporate managers, customers, regulatory agencies, legislatures, government inspectors, courts, and (to a lesser extent) labour unions, consumers, and public interest NGOs. It is the practices and projects of this array of state and non-state authorities that "make possible the continual definition and redefinition of what is within the competence of the state and what is not, the public versus the private, and so on."[82] In this context, the familiar feminist claim that "the personal is political," modified to read "the private is public," may be more appropriate than the metaphor of a public–private divide to characterize the implications of voluntary EMS standards.

Disrupting the public–private dichotomy, however, does not mean denying its continuing relevance. Rather, it calls for a broader conception of government, which enables us to uncover and examine the ways in which conventional divisions between state, society, law, market, public, and private are used to position certain concerns within and others outside the domains of politics, law, or the state. This uncovering may in turn allow us to reclaim excluded concerns for contestation or examine how such exclusion or inclusion tracks or reproduces social relations of power and inequality.

In this broader conception, "government" can be understood as the entire collection of goals, rationales, plans, procedures, and programs by which a diversity of state and non-state authorities seek more or less systematically to shape the conduct of individuals, organizations (including firms), and populations to their desired ends.[83] Michel Foucault coined the term "governmentality" to describe the techniques and justifications by which government, in this sense, is effectuated.[84] Governmentality can be analyzed in terms of political rationalities and governmental technologies. Political rationalities are "the changing discursive fields within which the exercise of power is conceptualized, the moral justifications for particular ways of exercising power by diverse authorities, notions of the appropriate forms, objects and limits of politics, and conceptions of the proper distribution of such tasks among secular, spiritual, military and familial sectors."[85] Governmental technologies are "the complex of mundane programmes, calculations, techniques, apparatuses, documents and procedures through which authorities seek to embody and give effect to governmental ambitions."[86]

Expertise plays a key role in governmentality. In the field of environmental management, expertise in the form of the specialized knowledges and vocabularies of environmental management consultants, standardization experts, auditors, and certifiers provides a link between the governmental objectives of public and private authorities and the minutiae of daily life in factories, offices, markets, and homes. Making this link is crucial because neither complete knowledge nor total control of the conduct of individuals, groups, firms, or populations is possible. Liberal forms of government rely on "action at a distance," recognizing a reserved domain for individual, autonomous action and moulding the conception and exercise of this capacity for action without destroying its autonomy.[87] Expertise makes it possible to "reconcile the principle that the domain of the political must be restricted with the recognition of the vital political implications of formally private activities."[88] Experts forge a link between authorities and subjects of rule, while preserving the autonomy of a "private" sphere, by translating the governmental concerns of authorities and the daily worries of individuals and groups into specialized technical vocabularies that claim the power of truth and objectivity and offer techniques to manage better, live healthier, and align individual choices with governmental ends.[89]

A few socio-legal scholars have examined law from a governmentality perspective,[90] and, more recently, a small number of environmental studies scholars have begun to apply governmentality analysis to environmental politics.[91] In the next two sections, I explore what it might mean to apply governmentality analysis to the interface between environmental law and voluntary corporate initiatives.

### EMSs as Governmental Technologies

EMSs and EMS standardization can be viewed as technologies for governing human-environment interactions – collections of standard procedures, routines, techniques, and documents through which the aspiration to manage the environmental impacts of an organization's activities, products, and services is rendered operable. It is through these sorts of detailed, repetitive, mundane mechanisms –such as assessing the environmental impacts of an organization's activities; setting environmental objectives and targets; developing and applying environmental performance indicators; assigning organizational roles and responsibilities; establishing and documenting operational procedures and controls; training employees; measuring and monitoring the organization's performance; testing and calibrating measurement equipment; calculating, computing, and analyzing data; maintaining and managing records; and auditing and reviewing the management system – that the governmental ambitions and schemes of public and private authorities are instantiated.

What is revealed by viewing voluntary EMS initiatives in this light? EMSs treat the problem of environmental degradation as a question of managerial technique, to be resolved by the application of neutral technical expertise in light of the judgments of commercial actors in the market place. Conflicts about public health, environmental quality, competitiveness, corporate accountability, and dominance among competing firms or trading blocs are acted out as if they were merely technical matters.[92] The result, as we shall see, is the depoliticization of a set of important environmental, public health, and economic issues.

The development, standardization, and implementation of EMSs are driven and dominated by industry. Within the EMS standardization community and among most public authorities, this is generally acknowledged as being appropriate – industry is the primary user of the standards and should play the major role in developing and implementing them.[93] EMS standards are primarily a form of corporate self-regulation, and, as such, it is no surprise that their development is dominated by business firms (especially multinational corporations) and associated professionals and that their content reflects the needs and interests of increasingly mobile capital in a global economy.[94] It is also no surprise that EMSs address a number of issues with vital political implications. These issues include:

- the acceptable environmental impacts of business: EMSs address this issue by establishing processes within each organization to identify the significant environmental impacts of its activities, products, and services and set, implement, monitor, and measure its own environmental objectives and targets;
- the improvement of environmental performance: EMSs leave it to each organization to decide whether, how, and at what rate to improve its environmental performance;[95]
- the question of how to manage the risk of disaster: EMSs consider the risk of environmental disaster as a matter for proper emergency planning rather than as a reason to question the continued use of certain activities or substances;
- the role of public consultation and accountability in environmental management: most EMSs treat public environmental reporting and the views of local communities, the public, and NGOs as matters for "stakeholder management," which are to be used by the organization to the extent that it considers necessary or desirable to maintain its viability or competitiveness;[96]
- the relationship between voluntary initiatives and state regulatory systems: EMSs erect a distinct barrier between themselves and state regulatory systems, positioning the latter as a special element of the EMS's external environment that generates obligations and expenses for the organization and possesses exclusive authority and responsibility to determine societal environmental goals and impose corresponding legal requirements. The EMS addresses this external regulatory system through a policy commitment to legal compliance and a set of processes that treat legal requirements much like other performance parameters,[97] but the incompleteness of the arbitrage between legal systems and the EMS is underlined by the fact that organizations, which have been convicted of environmental regulatory violations, have still been certified as conforming to ISO 14001; and
- verification of environmental claims and performance: EMSs treat the question of verification of an organization's environmental performance or their adherence to particular standards as matters for objective, neutral

determination by independent commercial experts who operate with specialized professional training, tools, and vocabularies, provide verification services for profit, and treat the information on which verification is based as confidential so that the only information disclosed publicly is whether the organization has conformed or not conformed with an EMS standard.

On the one hand, standardization bodies and other EMS proponents frequently acknowledge these political stakes at least implicitly (for example, by characterizing voluntary EMS standards as a contribution to public policy goals, such as sustainable development, by admitting that the development and use of EMS standards implicate important public interests, or by calling for broader "stakeholder" participation in standards development and corporate environmental management). On the other hand, the same actors regularly remind each other and anyone else that EMSs (and standards generally) are primarily useful tools developed by business, for business, pointedly declining to characterize the involvement or conflicting interests of industry participants as "political."[98]

What is most interesting for our present purposes is that the choice to employ the techniques of management systems and standardization appears to predispose the resolution of this ambivalence about the political stakes of corporate environmental management. The techniques and procedures of standardization and EMSs deactivate these political stakes by transforming them into technical matters to be resolved by the application of professional expertise, according to apparently neutral technical criteria, while simultaneously turning them into matters of consumer or commercial preference to be resolved by the exercise of autonomous choice in market transactions. EMSs constitute environmental protection as an apolitical matter to be administered through bureaucratic organizations. While they can, in theory, be adapted to organizations of all types and sizes, EMSs are modelled on the management hierarchies and processes of large business organizations. They emphasize routine, procedure, paperwork, formality, and technical expertise. They rely largely on private-market dynamics to signal the need for, and success of, these technical procedures and decisions, through the preferences and demands of customers, suppliers, or ultimate consumers. The EMS is quintessentially a technology of the large bureaucratic organization.[99]

Standardization, for its part, transforms conflicts over market dominance, trade barriers, international competitiveness, health, safety, and environmental protection into technical decisions for experts, and it submits the determination of the appropriateness of the resulting standards to the market through firms' decisions to purchase and implement the standards and market participants' demand for certified products or firms.[100] Standardization has been called "the housework of capitalism;" like housework, it is "detailed, mundane, repetitive, and never completed," and it is "both essential and unrecognized in the constitution and reproduction of economic and class relationships."[101] It is "usually considered a 'MEGO' ('my eyes glaze over') subject" in most corporate boardrooms.[102]

EMSs and EMS standards are a significant form of governmental technology precisely *because* they make one's "eyes glaze over" – that is, they mute the struggles over the distribution of risks, harms, jobs, and profits, which are inherent in environmental politics. By transforming debates over justice, poverty, racism, ecological integrity, animal rights, the intrinsic value of nature, and so on into matters of managerial expertise and market preference, these technologies both enable relations of inequality and repression to be perpetuated and disguise their own role in that perpetuation.

In these respects, EMSs and standardization instantiate a broader tendency in contemporary liberal practices of government to depoliticize certain political stakes by positioning them either as "technical" matters to be resolved by the application of neutral expertise or "private" matters to be resolved by market forces.[103] The tendency to "technicalize" is commonly associated with welfare state liberalism (for example, the creation of social insurance schemes), while the "privatization" tendency is commonly associated with free-market neoliberalism. EMSs, interestingly, embody both tendencies, perhaps reflecting some of the complexity and ambivalence in the encounter between welfarist and neoliberal mentalities in contemporary government.

In general, Canadian public authorities have allowed or encouraged this (re)drawing, without attempting to push the content or the use of EMSs in any particular direction. Their engagements (for example, implementing their own EMSs as examples for industry, encouraging or requiring firms to implement EMSs, and beginning to offer crudely crafted regulatory relief programs to firms with EMSs) have been relatively credulous and unreflective in comparison to those of American and European public authorities. One might criticize these engagements as an abdication of governmental authority to regulate corporate practices, but this point begs the question of how different state regulation is from private self-regulation. Among the possible differences are the following. First, official regulations are not developed by regulated entities themselves but by government officials with ultimate accountability to an electorate. This separation between regulators and the regulated in standard-setting is often criticized as being illusory, however, due to a heavy reliance on industry for information, an increasing "customer service" orientation toward regulated industry in some governments, intense negotiation with industry over pollution standards, and the risk of regulatory "capture" of government agencies by industry. Second, state regulatory systems usually have public consultation processes that do not depend on the regulated entity's discretion (for instance, notice and comment, environmental assessment, and judicial review), yet these are often perceived to be underused and ineffective. Third, there is Garret Hardin's famous question, "who will watch the watchers?"[104] Most governments have established formal, public mechanisms to monitor the behaviour of regulatory agencies, from government watchdog agencies to citizen suits and judicial review, whereas monitoring of EMS auditors and certifiers is generally non-public and achieved mainly through accreditation processes that are supervised by standardization bodies themselves or even more obscure institutions.[105] Moreover, since auditors and certifiers rely on their clients for income, there is some risk of "regulatory capture" by the client companies. While this danger is real, the risk of regulatory capture also exists in regulatory agencies, particularly given the recent tendency of many environmental agencies and their political masters to reinvent industry as clients to be served rather than as polluters to be controlled.

More importantly, the technologies of contemporary state environmental regulation embody, to a significant extent, the same managerialist tendencies as EMSs to obscure the stakes, struggles, and repressions of environmental politics, relying heavily on technical expertise, detailed, mundane, repetitive techniques of measurement, monitoring, calculation, assessment, inspection, and so on, and relying increasingly on private-market dynamics. While EMSs are a particularly clear example of these tendencies, state environmental regulation shares the same characteristics to a significant degree.

Viewed as governmental technologies, then, EMSs and standardization render environmental management a matter of technical expertise, an organizational routine, and market preference, contributing to the expulsion of a set of environmental and economic issues from the political domain.[106] Not all voluntary corporate initiatives share these characteristics, but this case nonetheless draws attention to the benefits of examining the problems of "government" at the level of mundane mechanisms of rule. Such an examination can enable one to expose the redrawings of the public–private divide and reclaim environmental management as an arena for political contestation.

### EMSs and the Shifting Rationales of Governance

The organizers of this symposium asked participants to consider the extent to which the blurring of the public–private divide signals a shift in the rationales of governance.[107] The case of an EMS provides evidence of such a shift of political rationalities, not just in the area of corporate environmental management but also in governance generally. Political rationalities provide the discursive "software" through which governmental technologies operate and produce effects.[108] The political rationality of EMSs – that is, the discursive field within which the forms and goals of governance, the proper boundaries of state and market, and the roles of public and private authorities are conceptualized and justified – reinforces the tendency of EMSs and standardization, described earlier, to depoliticize environmental management.

The political rationality of EMSs consists of a set of ideas, claims, justifications, themes, and story-lines about environmental management that are developed and maintained by a transnational coalition of corporate managers, industry groups, management consultants, trade publications, standardization professionals, public authorities, academics, and others. These actors are united not by a common goal or strategy (indeed, many of them have never met, let alone agreed on goals or strategies) but rather by their employment of a particular set of claims and story-lines about the challenge of environmental degradation and the appropriate tools and actors to address it.[109]

First, the discourse of an EMS reflects a distinctly "managerialist" view of the challenge of environmental degradation. Improving management practices, in particular, by adopting an organization-wide management system based on the "total quality management" concept, is the best way to improve the environmental performance of organizations and their products.[110] This implies a particular conception of the environmental crisis. While acknowledging that industrial society has produced severe environmental degradation, the managerialist conception does not view this crisis as a fundamental challenge to existing institutions and practices of industrial society. Rather, major environmental disasters of recent memory are interpreted primarily as management process failures, the environmental crisis is seen as being under control and gradually improving, and well-planned and properly implemented management systems are seen as the key to managing the adverse environmental impacts of business.[111] The environmental crisis is something to be managed through the application of managerial skill, objective technical expertise, organizational routine, and individual motivation.

Second, this managerialist approach is portrayed as both effecting, and depending for its own effectiveness upon, a transformation of corporate culture. The main potential of an EMS is often identified as its capacity to change organizational culture by integrating environmental protection into all activities and decisions of the enterprise.[112] This cultural transformation is accompanied by an ethic of individual responsibility for environmental protection, from the chief executive officer to the lowliest employee. An EMS "gathers all your employees and managers into a system of shared and enlightened awareness and personal responsibility for your organization's environmental performance," relying on training, competence, and motivation of individual employees rather than on blind obedience to regulations or corporate directives and the punishment of errors.[113]

Third, one of the most striking attributes of the discourse of EMSs, which is shared by most contemporary voluntary environmental initiatives, is its reinvention of environmental protection as "good business" rather than an unfortunate cost. The discourse presents both aggressive and defensive business rationales for EMSs. On the one hand, EMSs create "win-win" opportunities to improve environmental performance and increase shareholder value by enhancing corporate image, improving customer relations, realizing cost savings (for example, via energy conservation or waste recycling), and promoting innovation (for instance, product and process improvements).[114] On the other hand, EMSs are portrayed as defensive tools to maintain and increase competitiveness, especially in the face of globalization and trade liberalization.[115]

Fourth, EMSs and EMS standards are portrayed as a basis for a constructive new relationship with regulators and the public, which is based on cooperation and partnership rather than on coercion and mistrust.[116] The traditional "command and control" mode of regulation is acknowledged to have produced many successes, but it is seen as having reached its limit. EMSs are presented as a market-driven, voluntary, flexible, efficient, and effective alternative or supplement to sclerotic, inefficient, costly, rigid, nearsighted, backlogged, overtaxed, sometimes adversarial, and ineffective regulatory systems.[117] Private-market dynamics, in the form of supply-chain pressures, consumer demand, and trade association requirements, are positioned as constructive alternatives to messy political deliberations and inflexible, inefficient legal systems.[118] In turn, the citizen, who was formerly dependent on welfare state paternalism, is reinvented as the autonomous, self-helping consumer, exercising individual environmental responsibility through consumer choice.

All of these claims and story-lines are linked by an overarching goal and moral justification – that EMSs and EMS standards will contribute to the realization of sustainable development.[119] This claim is common in the discourses of corporate greening and is shared not just with most corporate environmental initiatives but also with almost all environmental policy initiatives in the last decade.

Finally, the discourse locates EMSs in a non-political arena. While acknowledging the political effects of EMSs and EMS standards (for example, their contribution to sustainable development, international trade, or state regulatory policy), the discourse of an EMS positions corporations, standards bodies, and EMSs as operating outside politics, in contrast to such "politically oriented bodies" as environmental NGOs, political parties, and public authorities.[120] The political rationality of an EMS thus redefines the legitimate concerns of the state in a manner that carves out a substantial chunk of environmental politics for organizations such as business firms to resolve on their own through technocratic management and private-market signals. It vests the elaboration and application of important norms of conduct and the delivery of certain environmental public goods in large NGOs, such as multinational corporations, standardization bodies, consulting firms, auditors, and certifiers. It presents a particular conception of the appropriate roles of the firm, market, employee, citizen, and state in managing environmental risks and harms and justifies these arrangements for the exercise of power in terms of good business sense, proper management processes, individual employee responsibility, the potential for autonomous consumer choice, the limits of the regulatory state, and the ultimate pursuit of sustainable development.

This redrawing of the domain and forms of government is closely linked to two broader political discourses: ecological modernization and smart regulation. Ecological modernization has emerged, since the late 1970s, as the dominant way of conceptualizing environmental problems in the advanced industrial democracies.[121] Ecological modernization understands environmental harm to be a systematic product of the modern industrial "risk" society, but one that can be addressed through technocratic management. In this vision, the environmental crisis no longer represents a fundamental threat to industrial society, as it did in the 1970s, but rather as an opportunity for its further development. Environmental protection and industrial development are compatible "win-win" propositions. The pursuit of sustainable development, which is one of the key moral justifications of EMSs, is intimately linked with ecological modernization by virtue of its emphasis on the integration of environmental considerations into all business and governmental decision-making, the consideration of, and communication with, a broad range of stakeholders, and the susceptibility of environmental crisis to rational management. The political rationality of EMSs thus coincides very closely with the discourse of ecological modernization.

Another prominent discourse in contemporary environmental politics, which is closely related to, and perhaps subsumed in, ecological modernization, is the discourse of "smart" or "responsive" regulation.[122] This discourse acknowledges the accomplishments of "command and control" regulation but argues that it has reached the limits of its cost-effectiveness and technical capacity, due to cost, inefficiency, inflexibility, and regulators' resource and information constraints. On the other hand, this discourse also rejects neoliberalism, with its radical scepticism about the capacities of the state to govern for the best and its enthusiasm for free markets, property rights, and deregulation. It argues that most "regulation" is already in the hands of actors other than the state and uses this insight to propose a new conception of the regulatory process that transcends sterile regulation-deregulation and market-state dichotomies. It proposes new regulatory strategies that combine state, market, private and public actors, and forms of regulation and enlists non-state resources and mechanisms, such as self-regulation, EMSs, ecolabelling schemes, environmental reporting, and industry-community agreements, in furtherance of the notion of "governing at a distance."[123] Some variants of this discourse draw upon private sector management discourses to promote competition and marketization in government functions, a "client service" orientation in public administration (regulated entities as clients, state as service provider), individual autonomy (individuals as self-helping, autonomous, co-responsible entrepreneurs), and managerialism (conceptualization of life in entrepreneurial terms; use of managerial techniques).[124] This discourse of regulatory reinvention meshes well with the discourse of EMSs and provides the broader rationale for most of the engagements I have observed between Canadian public authorities and EMS initiatives.

This examination of the political rationalities of EMS suggests two things. First, that the deactivation of political conflict seen in the discourses of EMSs and standardization will be one of the key political challenges in the era of "smart regulation." The political rationalities of EMS constitute the realm of EMSs as a private, voluntary order in dichotomous, sometimes antagonistic, relation to the messy, inefficient, public realm of law and politics and simultaneously obscure the process by which this division between public and private realms is created, by representing EMSs as always already private, voluntary, and non-political.[125] The interpretation of environmental crisis as a "win-win" proposition, an opportunity for entrepreneurial thinking, and a matter for expert, technocratic management "at a distance" reinforces this tendency to mute the political struggles and distributive stakes of environmental management.

Second, it seems likely that "steering" may emerge as the most prominent form of engagement of public authorities with private authority in the field of environmental governance. The increasing emphasis on "action at a distance" in the current mentalities of government points to a conception of the state as helmsman, selectively steering the development and use of regulatory strategies and tools by others through participation in the creation of voluntary programs, funding of non-state policy development institutions such as standardization bodies, providing high-level strategic direction for non-state policy-making, pronouncing official positions on voluntary initiatives, and regulating the ground rules, boundaries, and limits of non-state governance by manipulating competition, securities, corporate and consumer protection law, public participation rules, and regulatory "backstops." One might also expect "reward" and "self-discipline" to figure prominently in state strategies as public authorities attempt to steer environmental self-government by offering regulatory incentives and setting examples through the self-application of voluntary disciplines.

**What Role for Law?**
I conclude with some tentative suggestions about the role for law in the transformation of the public–private divide in Canadian politics. My research into

EMSs and EMS standards reveals two important characteristics of contemporary government. First, government (understood as being all of the more or less systematic attempts to direct human conduct to appropriate ends) is widely distributed among a myriad of public and private authorities in a hybridized public–private space. Second, in any given problem space, the unequal distribution of governmental authority tends to produce and reproduce social relations of power and inequality. Two general conclusions follow from these observations: that some form of "smart regulation," relying on a mix of state and non-state actors and regulatory tools, is appropriate to deal with the distributed character of government, but that, in addition, a key challenge in the design and exercise of such government will be to resist the tendency to "depoliticize" through the move to neutral technical expertise and private-market transactions. Opening space for such resistance requires, first of all, attention to the political stakes that EMSs and EMS standards tend to submerge. This involves asserting the politics of "merely technical" choices,[126] such as the decision to delegate authority to technical experts or the private market and the construction of the citizen as autonomous consumer and self-helping entrepreneur. It also calls for more concrete exploration of the distributive consequences of corporate environmental management decisions than I have attempted in this essay, along with a more detailed examination of how the rationalities and technologies of environmental management produce and obscure such consequences.

Law and legal practitioners can play numerous roles in the politics of voluntary EMS standards – in some cases, facilitating and shaping the expansion of "private" non-regulatory initiatives, in others, resisting it, and still in others, playing little or no role. While strategies and techniques deployed in legal relations can probably have a significant impact on the transformation of the public–private divide, in the case of EMS standards, this potential has so far gone largely unrealized in Canada. Although Canadian regulators, legislators, and courts have employed most of the modes of engagement that I describe in the second part of this essay, it is fair to say that their responses to voluntary EMS initiatives have been minimal and incoherent.

The important question for present purposes is whether and how law can be used to resist the depoliticization of environmental management – that is, to insist on the political stakes of environmental management decisions and create space to work toward greater justice, equality, human health, and ecological integrity? At a minimum, law might be deployed as a "border guard" to define and protect certain "public" stakes of EMSs. EMSs can be a very useful tool for organizations internally as well as in their relations with business partners and market participants, but many (including ISO 14001-based EMSs) provide inadequate guarantees of public consultation and accountability, environmental performance, and legal compliance to merit giving them any particular weight in non-market relations with governments and the public. Legal tools and strategies should be designed, at a minimum, to insist on these basic public stakes when rewarding or relying on them in state regulatory instruments (for instance, by requiring more than the minimal "basic EMS" defined in Alberta's new LEAD program, requiring public consultation and transparency in the setting, monitoring, and review of environmental performance, and rewarding only firms that consistently exceed compliance with legal requirements, including the improvement of performance on non-regulated parameters). Basic corporate governance rules, requiring the maximization of shareholder value, might be revisited to expand the range of "stakeholders" whose interests managers are permitted (or required) to take into account. Moreover, legal actors such as prosecutors and courts should be urged to take a firmly sceptical attitude toward EMSs and EMS standards and inform themselves fully of their characteristics before incorporating them in orders or using them as a standard for liability.

More ambitiously, governments, lawyers, and citizens might use law as part of a broader political strategy to influence the redefinition of public and private in the context of environmental management. The role of law and legal practitioners in this strategy could be to claim and defend a broad space for democratic experimentation in the face of the homogenizing tendencies of global trade liberalization (as evidenced, for instance, in the TBT Agreement) and government "reinvention." Just how this might be done is a question for further research.

### Acknowledgments
I am grateful to Michael Fortier (LL.B./M.E.S., York University, 2001); Anastasia Lintner (LL.B, Osgoode Hall Law School, 2002); and Michelle Fernando (LL.B/M.E.S., York University, 2002) for capable research assistance. I thank participants in the 2001 Legal Dimensions session at Laval University, Quebec, and the symposium on Environmental Law and Stewardship for a Sustainable Society at the University at Buffalo School of Law for feedback on earlier drafts. The research on which this chapter is based was current as of late 2001.

### Notes
1 *ISO 14001: 1996, Environmental Management Systems – Specification* with *Guidance for Use* (Geneva: International Organization for Standardization [hereinafter ISO], 1996).
2 *ISO 14004: 1996, Environmental Management Systems – General Guidelines on Principles, Systems and Supporting Techniques* (Geneva: ISO, 1996). Both ISO 14001 and 14004 are currently being revised within the ISO, with publication of second generation standards expected to be released in 2003.
3 Ecolabelling programs may apply across a range of products, such as Canada's Environmental Choice program, or they may be product-specific, such as ecolabels for bananas, coffee, or forest products.
4 The most prominent programs are the Forest Stewardship Council's program for certifying sustainable forest management operations and the Marine Stewardship Council's program for certifying sustainable fisheries management operations.
5 The number of ISO 14001 registrations worldwide reached approximately 30,000 by July 2001. For data on registrations, see Gergely Tóth, "The ISO 14001 Speedometer," available

at <http://www.inem.org/htdocs/iso/speedometer/speedometer-4_2001.html> (accessed 30 October 2001).

6 See, for example, Joseph Cascio, "Introduction," in Joseph Cascio, ed., *The ISO 14000 Handbook* (Milwaukee: ASQ Quality Press, 1996), 1 at 1: "The ISO 14000 standards hold out the promise to revolutionize environmental protection as we have known it in the past quarter century"; Ruth Hillary, ed., *Environmental Management Systems and Cleaner Production* (Chichester, UK: John Wiley and Sons, 1997); Amy Pesapane Lally, "ISO 14000 and Environmental Cost Accounting: The Gateway to the Global Market" (1998) 29 Law and Pol'y Int'l Bus. 501. For other examples, see note 12 in this essay.

7 See, for example, Riva Krut and Harris Gleckman, *ISO 14001: A Missed Opportunity for Sustainable Global Industrial Development* (London: Earthscan, 1998); Saeed Parto, "Aiming Low," in Robert Gibson, ed. *Voluntary Initiatives: The New Politics of Corporate Greening* (Peterborough, ON: Broadview, 1999), 182. For other examples, see note 12 later in this essay.

8 See, for example, A. Claire Cutler, Virginia Haufler, and Tony Porter, eds., *Private Authority and International Affairs* (Albany: State University of New York Press, 1999); and Virginia Haufler, *A Public Role for the Private Sector: Industry Self-Regulation in a Global Economy* (Washington, DC: Carnegie Endowment for International Peace, 2001).

9 See, for example, Cass Sunstein, "Paradoxes of the Regulatory State" (1990) 57 U. Chi. L. Rev. 407; Cass Sunstein, *After the Rights Revolution: Reconceiving the Regulatory State* (Cambridge, MA: Harvard University Press, 1990); D. Osborne and T. Gaebler, *Reinventing Government* (Boston: Addison-Wesley, 1992); Ian Ayres and John Braithwaite, *Responsive Regulation* (New York: Oxford University Press, 1992); and Neil Gunningham and Peter Grabosky, *Smart Regulation* (Oxford: Clarendon, 1998).

10 See, for example, Gunningham and Grabosky, *supra* note 9; Gibson, *supra* note 7; Carlo Carraro and François Lévêque, eds., *Voluntary Approaches in Environmental Policy* (Dordrecht: Kluwer, 1999).

11 Compare with Liora Salter, *Mandated Science: Science and Scientists in the Making of Standards* (Dordrecht: Kluwer, 1988) at 31-32 and 178-80 (arguing that the debate over regulation versus deregulation neglects the reality of standards, which are neither fully public nor fully private and always involve some degree of coordination between public and private sectors).

12 See, for example, Naomi Roht-Arriaza, "Shifting the Point of Regulation: The International Organization for Standardization and Global Lawmaking on Trade and the Environment" (1995) 22 Ecology L.Q. 479-539; Scott Butner, "ISO 14000 – Policy and Regulatory Implications for State Agencies," paper presented at the National Pollution Prevention Roundtable Annual Meeting, 10 April 1996, available at <http://www.seattle.battelle.org/p2online/iso-regs.htm> (accessed 21 June 2001); Anthony Reiley, "The New Paradigm: ISO 14000 and Its Place in Regulatory Reform" (1997) 22 J. Corp. L. 535; Henry Balikov and Patrick Cavanaugh, "The Overselling of Government 'Reinvention': How Government Expectations of EPA's Project XL and ISO 14000 May Prove Counter-Productive" (Spring-Summer 1997) Albany Law Environmental Outlook 23; Naomi Roht-Arriaza, "Developing Countries, Regional Organizations, and the ISO 14001 Environmental Management Standard" (1997) 9 Geo. Int'l Envtl. L. Rev. 583; Douglas Taylor, "Is ISO 14001 Standardization in Tune with Sustainable Development?" (1998) 13 J. Envtl. L. and Litigation 509; Douglas Taylor, "ISO 14000 and Environmental Regulation" (1999) 9 J. Envtl. L. and Practice 1; Paula C. Murray, "Inching Toward Regulatory Reform – ISO 14000: Much Ado about Nothing or a Reinvention Tool?" (1999) 37 Am. Bus. L.J. 35; Keith Pezzoli, "Environmental Management Systems and Regulatory Innovation" (2000) 36 Cal. W.L. Rev. 335; Pollution Probe, *The Future Role of Environmental Standards* (Ottawa: Pollution Probe, 2000); Paulette Stenzel, "Can the ISO 14000 Series Environmental Management Standards Provide a Viable Alternative to Government Regulation?" (2000) 37 Am. Bus. L.J. 237; Jason Morrison et al., *Managing a Better Environment: Opportunities and Obstacles for ISO 14001 in Public Policy and Commerce* (Oakland, CA: Pacific Institute, 2000), available at <http://www.pacinst.org> (accessed 30 July 2001); Roy W. Shin and Yu-Che Chen, "Seizing Global Opportunities for Accomplishing Agencies' Missions: The Case of ISO 14000" (2000) 24 Public Administration Quarterly 69-94; Dianne Saxe, "ISO 14001/14004 and Compliance in Canada," paper prepared for the Canadian

Standards Association, 20 December 2000 (copy on file with author); Cary Coglianese and Jennifer Nash, eds., *Regulating from the Inside: Can Environmental Management Systems Achieve Policy Goals?* (Washington, DC: Resources for the Future, 2001).

13   A notable exception is Errol Meidinger's work on the interaction between the US legal system and environmental certification systems, including EMS standards. See, for example, Errol Meidinger, "Environmental Certification Programs and U.S. Environmental Law: Closer Than You May Think" (2001) 31 Environmental Law Reporter 10162.

14   The literature on voluntary environmental initiatives generally lacks systematic inquiry into how non-state regulatory systems interact with each other and with other forms of regulation, or how state actors can engage with voluntary initiatives in an integrated public–private regulatory strategy. Notable exceptions include Ronald B. Mitchell, *Intentional Oil Pollution at Sea* (Cambridge, MA: MIT Press, 1994); Gunningham and Grabosky, *supra* note 9; Kernaghan Webb, "Voluntary Initiatives and the Law," in Gibson, *supra* note 7 at 32; Kernaghan Webb and Andrew Morrison, "Voluntary Approaches, the Environment and the Law: A Canadian Perspective," in Carraro and Lévêque, *supra* note 10 at 229.

15   Two caveats are in order. First, these eight categories of engagement overlap substantially. A single program or action may involve several modes of engagement simultaneously. Second, the list of categories is tentative and open-ended, subject to variation with changing information and the character and purposes of analysis. Its main purpose is not to set down a definitive typology but to expose the extent and variety of interactions among public and private authorities in the field of environmental management.

16   Pollution Probe, *supra* note 12 at 41.

17   In Liora Salter's view, this is also true of industry participants: intelligence gathering about competitors and informal coordination are often more important to industry participants than the content of particular standards. Liora Salter, "The Housework of Capitalism: Standardization in the Communications and Information Technology Sectors" (1993-94) 23 International Journal of Political Economy 105 at 116.

18   A recent report by the BC government, for example, found that the province's forest tenure system, in which government determines forestry planning requirements, harvest rates, and environmental protection standards, made it difficult for forestry companies to demonstrate the long-term commitment to sustainable management planning for a defined geographic forest area required for certification under the leading sustainable forestry management programs. British Columbia Ministry of Forests, *Implementing Forest Certification in British Columbia: Issues and Options — Report Summary* (March 2001), available at <http://www.for.gov.bc.ca/het/certification/researchproject.htm> (accessed 7 August 2001).

19   Such legitimation effects depend largely on the credibility of official pronouncements among relevant audiences, with off-hand, vague endorsements typically having much less effect on the use of voluntary initiatives by industry or consumers than deliberate pronouncements by well-informed officials who are capable of distinguishing genuine innovations from mere "business as usual" advances. See Carlo Carraro and François Lévêque, "Introduction: The Rationale and Potential of Voluntary Approaches," in Carraro and Lévêque, *supra* note 10 at 9-10.

20   Some federal government departments (for example, Environment Canada) and government officials in several provinces (for example, Alberta, British Columbia, Nova Scotia, and Ontario) have expressly encouraged private sector use of EMSs, often in very general terms in public remarks, websites, or pamphlets. Some have issued discussion papers or established modest government-industry partnerships around EMS implementation, but most of these efforts have been ad hoc and uncoordinated. More recently, federal officials participated in the development of a joint Canada-Mexico-US policy statement on EMSs. See North American Commission for Environmental Cooperation [hereinafter CEC], *Improving Environmental Performance and Compliance: 10 Elements of Effective Environmental Management Systems* (Montreal: CEC, 2000), available at <http://www.cec.org> (accessed 31 January 2003) (cautiously supporting use of EMSs to achieve public policy goals, endorsing structure and approach of leading EMS standards such as ISO 14001, setting out ten elements that voluntary EMSs should have to satisfy and enunciating governments' concerns about environmental performance, pollution prevention, public accountability, and legal

compliance). Alberta and Ontario have begun to elaborate policies on the incorporation of an EMS into their regulatory frameworks. See the section entitled "Reward" later in this essay. Still, considering that EMSs have been in wide use for more than a decade, the paucity of considered policy statements is surprising.

21 Leon Gordenker and Thomas G. Weiss, "Pluralising Global Governance: Analytical Approaches and Dimensions" (1995) 16 Third World Quarterly 357; compare with Salter, *Mandated Science, supra* note 11 at 179.

22 *Standards Council of Canada Act*, R.S.C. 1985, c. S-16, as am. S.C. 1987, c. 1, S.C. 1996, c. 24. The Standards Council of Canada oversees Canada's National Standards System, an informal federation of more than 270 independent organizations. It delegates the actual writing of standards to accredited standards development bodies, such as the Canadian Standards Association [hereinafter CSA], a private not-for-profit corporation. For an excellent overview of standardization in Canada, see Canadian Institute for Environmental Law and Policy [hereinafter CIELAP], *CSA Environmental Standards Writing: Barriers to Environmental Non-Governmental Organizations Involvement* (Toronto: CIELAP, May 1997). Like the Standards Council of Canada, the majority of ISO national member bodies are state-owned, but the ISO member bodies in most advanced industrial democracies other than Canada are private not-for-profit organizations formally independent of the state.

23 *Standards Council of Canada Act, supra* note 22 at s. 4(1).

24 Salter's work on health, safety, and communication standards provides a detailed insight into this public–private hybridization inherent in standardization bodies. See, for example, Salter, *Mandated Science, supra* note 11, and Salter, "The Housework of Capitalism, *supra* note 17.

25 Federal government officials have been the most active, a few playing prominent roles in the development of the ISO 14000 standards. Provincial officials have also participated on a limited scale, and municipal officials have begun to participate in Canadian EMS standards committees.

26 In addition to participating in many non-governmental standards committees, governments have their own standards development organs. For example, one of the four standards development organizations accredited by the Standards Council of Canada, the Canadian General Standards Board [hereinafter CGSB], is a federal government organization within Public Works and Government Services Canada. Although the CGSB does not develop EMS standards, it provides EMS auditing and registration services to public and private sector clients.

27 See CSA, *Guideline B: Procedures for Establishing and Maintaining Standards Steering Committees*, 2nd edition (Toronto: CSA, 1989, revised 1990), reprinted in CIELAP, *supra* note 22 at Appendix C.

28 See, for example, Commissioner of the Environment and Sustainable Development [hereinafter CESD], *Report of the Commissioner of the Environment and Sustainable Development 1999* (Ottawa: Queen's Printer, 1999), available at <http://www.oag-bvg.gc.ca/domino/reports.nsf/html/c9menu_e.html> (accessed 1 April 2001).

29 See CIELAP, *supra* note 22.

30 See Standards Council of Canada, *Canadian Standards Strategy and Implementation Proposals* (Ottawa: Standards Council of Canada, March 2000), available at <http://www.scc.ca/> (accessed 31 January 2003). The strategy was the product of a stakeholder consultation process led by the Standards Council of Canada and Industry Canada.

31 The strategy is expressly based on two assumptions: that (1) standards are becoming a pillar of the new global trade system, and (2) fiscal restraint means that industry and government are struggling to do more with less, and standards can offer effective, less costly ways to achieve the objectives of reducing costs, eliminating regulatory burdens, and protecting the public interest. *Ibid.*

32 See, for example, Webb, *supra* note 14.

33 See Agreement on Technical Barriers to Trade, 1994, reprinted in GATT Secretariat, *The Results of the Uruguay Round of Multilateral Trade Negotiations: The Legal Texts, Uruguay Round (1987-1994)* (Geneva: GATT Secretariat, 1994), arts. 3.1, 4.1, and Annex 3 [hereinafter TBT Agreement]. The TBT Agreement is also available at <http://www.wto.org/english/docs_e/

legal_e/legal_e.htm> (accessed 31 January 2003). See also the heading "Self-Discipline" later in this essay.

34   See, generally, Webb, *supra* note 14; and John Moffet and François Bregha, "Non-Regulatory Environmental Measures," in Gibson, *supra* note 7 at 15.

35   This category coincides roughly with Bruce Doern et al.'s "regulatory regime III," the state's regulation of itself. G. Bruce Doern et al., "Canadian Regulatory Institutions: Converging and Colliding Regimes," in G. Bruce Doern et al., eds., *Changing the Rules: Canadian Regulatory Regimes and Institutions* (Toronto: University of Toronto Press, 1999), 3.

36   See, for example, CESD, *supra* note 28.

37   The CESD has said that he expects to see "accelerated development" of EMSs in the current round of sustainable development strategies. CESD, "Moving Up the Learning Curve: The Second Generation of Sustainable Development Strategies" (undated), available at <http://www.oag-bvg.gc.ca/domino/cesd_cedd.nsf/html/c9dec_e.html> (accessed 1 May 2001). Environment Canada has produced an EMS Self-Assessment Guide for federal organizations and has said that individual federal departments and agencies "are to develop and implement formal environmental management systems." Environment Canada, *Directions on Greening Government Operations* (undated), available at <http://www.sdinfo.gc.ca/SDinfo/ENG/docs/ggo/default.cfm> (accessed 30 April 2001). Nonetheless, EMSs have not expressly been made legally mandatory for federal organizations in Canada, in contrast to the United States where all federal facilities must implement EMSs by 2005. See *Greening the Government through Leadership in Environmental Management*, Executive Order no. 13148, 65 Fed. Reg. 24593 (21 April 2000). The new *Canadian Environmental Protection Act* authorizes regulations respecting the establishment of environmental management systems for federal government operations, but none have yet been promulgated. *Canadian Environmental Protection Act, 1999*, S.C. 1999, c. 33, s. 209(1)(a) [hereinafter *CEPA 1999*].

38   As Agriculture and Agri-Food Canada expresses it, the federal government, as the single largest organization in Canada and the largest employer, purchaser, and landlord, can set an excellent example for Canada by implementing EMSs. Agriculture and Agri-Food Canada, *Agriculture in Harmony with Nature II: AAFC's Sustainable Development Strategy 2001-2004*, Publication 2074/E (Ottawa: Public Works and Government Services Canada, 2001) at 43, available at <http://www.agr.ca/policy/environment/eb/public_html/pdfs/sds/SDSII_en.pdf> (accessed 24 April 2001).

39   See, for example, the Sigma Project in the United Kingdom, "Sustainability – Integrated Guidelines for Management," available at <http://www.projectsigma.com> (accessed 31 January 2003), and the Multi-State Working Group on Environmental Management Systems in the United States, available at <http://www.dep.state.pa.us/dep/deputate/pollprev/mswg/mswg.htm> (accessed 31 January 2003).

40   See, for example, CESD, "Moving Up the Learning Curve," *supra* note 37; Auditor General of Canada, *Report of the Auditor General of Canada to the House of Commons* (Ottawa: Office of the Auditor General of Canada, October 1995), ch. 11, Environmental Management Systems: A Principle-based Approach," available at <http://www.oag-bvg.gc.ca/domino/reports.nsf/html/9511ce.html> (accessed 1 May 2001) (observing that federal organizations are far behind the private sector in EMS implementation).

41   TBT Agreement, *supra* note 33 at art. 2.4. It is not clear whether regulations relating to EMSs would come within the definition of "technical regulations."

42   Indeed, Canada has been among the most aggressive states in enforcing these disciplines against its trading partners, for instance, successfully challenging the European Communities' ban on hormone-fed beef as an unjustified deviation from international food safety standards. See *EC - Measures Affecting Meat and Meat Products (Hormones)*, Report of the Appellate Body, WTO Doc. WT/DS26/AB/R, WT/DS48/AB/R (adopted 13 February 1998). More recently, however, the WTO Appellate Body rejected Canada's challenge to a French ban on chrysotile asbestos, holding that the ban was a "technical regulation" within the meaning of the TBT Agreement but holding (for the first time in the history of the General Agreement on Tariffs and Trade [hereinafter GATT], that it was justified under the public health exception of Article XX of the GATT. See *EC - Measures Affecting Asbestos and Asbestos-Containing Products*, Report of the Appellate Body, WTO Doc. WT/DS135/AB/R (12 March 2001).

43  See note 64 later in this essay as well as the text connected with it.
44  See, generally, David Hunter, James Salzman, and Durwood Zaelke, *International Environmental Law and Policy* (New York: Foundation Press, 1998) at 1407.
45  Probably the most ambitious empirical study of EMS implementation and performance is the ISO 14001 Pilots project sponsored by the US Environmental Protection Agency [hereinafter EPA] and conducted by researchers from the Environmental Law Institute and the University of North Carolina. Information on the project can be found online at <http://www.eli.org/isopilots.htm>.
46  As to the latter, Industry Canada hosts the Voluntary Codes Research Forum, a leading arena for informal exchange of information about research into voluntary corporate codes, generally with frequent attention to standardization and EMS-related issues. The forum consists of a website and a listserv facilitated by Kernaghan Webb, Senior Legal Policy Advisor and Chief of Research, Canadian Office of Consumer Affairs, Industry Canada. The forum can be found online at <http://strategis.ic.gc.ca/SSG/ca00973e.html>.
47  See the discussion of official policy pronouncements under the heading "Steering" earlier in this essay.
48  *Ibid.*
49  See, for example, Kal Raustiala, "The 'Participatory Revolution' in International Environmental Law" (1997) 21 Harvard Envtl L. Rev. 537.
50  These programs also often provide other kinds of incentives, including subsidies, technical assistance, and reputational benefits (for example, official government recognition, eligibility for awards, and the privilege to display logos or other indicia of participation). The most prominent examples are probably the US EPA's National Environmental Performance Track and the Netherlands' framework licence system.
51  See Alberta Environment, *LEAD Program Guide – A Guide to Alberta Environment's Leaders Environmental Approval Document (LEAD) Program: Pilot Phase* (April 2001), available at <http://www.gov.ab.ca/env/protenf/publications/LEADProgramGuideApr01.pdf> (accessed 17 July 2001).
52  In contrast to most EMS-based regulatory relief programs, which either require a mature, third-party certified EMS or an EMS that goes significantly beyond the requirements of ISO 14001, the Leaders Environmental Approval Document [hereinafter LEAD] program requires only a loosely defined "basic" EMS that need not be fully developed, need not have all the elements of an ISO 14001 EMS, and need not be verified by an independent third party. Alberta Environment is, however, considering a "tiered" program in which upper tier participants must have an ISO 14001-equivalent, independently audited EMS. *Ibid.*
53  Ontario is seriously considering regulatory incentives for EMS implementation in its Co-operative Agreements program, which is currently under development. As to other governments, it is possible, for instance, that Environment Canada could couple EMSs with regulatory incentives in pollution prevention plans authorized under the new *CEPA*. *CEPA 1999, supra* note 37 at s. 56.
54  See, for example, Ontario Ministry of the Environment, Environmental Partnerships Branch, *Progress Report 2001: Ontario Initiatives in Pollution Prevention* (Toronto: Queen's Printer, 2001); Draft Memorandum of Understanding between the Governments of Canada, Ontario and Alberta and the Canadian Chemical Producers' Association on Environmental Protection through Action under CCPA Responsible Care, which is available at <http://www.ec.gc.ca/nopp/chemical/ccpa/indexe.htm> (accessed 30 October 2001).
55  Environment Canada's new Compliance and Enforcement Policy, for instance, makes no mention of EMSs at all, although it does recognize the "power and effectiveness of environmental audits as a management tool" and encourages their use. Environment Canada, *Compliance and Enforcement Policy for the Canadian Environmental Protection Act, 1999* (Ottawa: Environment Canada, 2001), available at <http://www.ec.gc.ca/enforce/homepage/cepa/CEPA99_final_eng.pdf.pdf> (accessed 4 July 2001).
56  For example, the new *CEPA* is the first legislation in Canada to expressly authorize a sentencing court to take the presence of an EMS into account as a mitigating factor in sentencing. *CEPA 1999, supra* note 37 at s. 287(c).
57  Between 1994 and 2000, the province of Nova Scotia offered a corporate income tax credit to assist Nova Scotia companies with the costs of achieving ISO 9000 or 14001 certification.

The credit was 25 percent of eligible expenditures, which included audits, registrar fees, training, and documentation. Very few companies claimed this tax credit for ISO 14001 certification expenses, reportedly because the provincial government failed adequately to bring it to the industries' attention (personal communication).

58 No Canadian government appears to have made EMSs a formal procurement considera-tion or requirement, although the federal government encourages government buyers to purchase from firms that are ISO 14001 certified. Public Works and Government Services Canada, "ISO 14001 – A New Tool for Buying Green," <http://contractscanada.gc.ca/sl/en/iso14-e.htm> (20 March 2001). Some government entities in Japan and Switzerland report-edly give formal preference to suppliers with EMSs. Laura E. Berón, "ISO 14000 and Trade Implications: Facts and Trends," paper presented at the Seminar on Trade, Environment and the ISO 14000 Series, ninth Annual Meeting of the ISO/TC 207, Kuala Lumpur, Malay-sia, 4 July 2001 (copy on file with author). The US EPA is considering preferential govern-ment procurement treatment of products manufactured at facilities participating in the Performance Track program. US EPA, *Summary of EPA's Performance Track Proposal* (9 March 2000) (copy on file with author). The US Departments of Defense and Energy reportedly require first- and second-level suppliers to be ISO 14001 certified. Stenzel, *supra* note 12 at 270.

59 Although this situation is still a long way off, the trend toward requiring EMSs can be expected to continue in private sector procurement (see *supra* note 5 and accompanying text) and spread to public sector purchasing as well.

60 See, for example, *Environmental Protection and Enhancement Act*, S.A. 1992, c. E-13.3, s. 220(1); *Environmental Protection Act*, R.S.O. 1990, c. E.19, s. 190. The *CEPA* expressly authorizes a sentencing court to direct an offender to "implement an environmental management sys-tem that meets a recognized Canadian or international standard," but no orders appear to have been made under this new provision. *CEPA 1999, supra* note 37 at s. 291(1). Although Ontario pioneered creative sentencing in Canada, the Harris Conservative government has ordered provincial prosecutors not to use it. Saxe, *supra* note 12 at 29. Two pillars of neoliberal politics appear to be in tension. On the one hand, an agenda of flexible regulation in which voluntary initiatives are encouraged and proposed regulations are subject to cost-benefit analysis and, on the other hand, an agenda of "zero tolerance" laws and tougher penalties that seldom seem to be subjected to the same cost-benefit disciplines.

61 *R. v. Prospec Chemicals Ltd.* (1996), 19 C.E.L.R. (N.S.) 178 (Alta. Prov. Ct.) (ordering a chemi-cal company that was already a member of the chemical industry's voluntary Responsible Care program to implement a third-party certified ISO 14001 EMS); *R. v. Van Waters and Rogers Ltd.* (1998), 220 A.R. 315 (Prov. Ct.) (ordering a chemical company to undergo inde-pendent environmental compliance and ISO 14001 EMS audits, upgrade its EMS manual and operational controls, establish procedures for ongoing evaluation of conformance to ISO 14001, and present an EMS workshop to industry peers, but not ordering ISO 14001 certification); *R. v. Calgary (City)* (2000), 272 A.R. 161, 35 C.E.L.R. (N.S.) 253 (Prov. Ct.) (ordering city to obtain ISO 14001 certification for two of its water treatment plants by 2003 and declaring that an ISO 14001 EMS was "far in excess of what the present law and regulations require of a municipality"). Saxe discusses these cases and also mentions a fourth unreported decision, *R. v. Prototype Circuits Inc.* (ordering circuit board manufacturer to establish an EMS leading to ISO 14000 certification). Saxe, *supra* note 12. Finally, in another case, the court ordered the federal government to fund a tribal council's develop-ment of an EMS: *R. v. Canada (Minister of Indian Affairs)*, [2000] O.J. 5076 (Ont. S.C.J.) (Quicklaw) (ordering Department of Indian Affairs to pay $200,000 to support tribal coun-cil's development of a pollution prevention and environmental management system pro-gram for fuel storage tanks).

62 Saxe, *supra* note 12 at 26.

63 Governments in Brazil, the Caribbean, Zimbabwe, and elsewhere have reportedly consid-ered or enacted legislation requiring all firms in sectors such as forestry or cruise shipping to implement EMSs, and some developing countries have reportedly considered requiring all firms to implement EMSs as an easy fix for inadequate or under-enforced environmen-tal regulation. See, for example, Meidinger, *supra* note 13 at 10166; Saxe, *supra* note 12 at

30; and Stenzel, *supra* note 12 at 276. The European Union recently considered, but rejected, the idea of making its voluntary EMS initiative, the Eco-Management and Audit Scheme, mandatory.

64  See *Pipeline Regulations*, N.S. Reg. 66/98, s. 19(1) (requiring pipeline companies to establish an EMS to the ISO 14000 standard or equivalent); *Gas Pipeline Regulation,* N.B. Reg. 99-61, s. 46 (requiring all gas distributors to develop and implement an EMS); and *Gas Distribution and Marketers' Filing Regulation* N.B. Reg. 99-60, s. 7(12) (requiring all gas distributors applying for a permit for a gas pipeline that will affect a "sensitive feature" to develop an EMS that meets the requirements of ISO 14000 or a similar standard). Neither province requires companies to have their EMSs certified by a third party.

65  Saxe, *supra* note 12 at 38.

66  See Alberta Environment, *supra* note 51 at 7, and Appendix B. In addition, at least one licensing authority has expressly relied on a regulated entity's plans to obtain ISO 14001 certification as a basis for issuing an environmental approval. *Re Material Resource Recovery SRBP Inc.,* Doc. no. EP-97-04 (Ont. Envtl. Assessment Bd., 21 January 1998) (approving hazardous waste facility partly in reliance on applicant's plan to apply for ISO 14001 certification). The decision is discussed in Saxe, *supra* note 12 at 30.

67  See Salter, *Mandated Science, supra* note 11 at 25. The CSA estimates that approximately one-third of its standards have been referred to in provincial and federal laws. CSA, "Association Activities," in *ISO 14001: 1996, supra* note 1 (back matter). Saxe reports that the term "CSA" is mentioned 233 times in Ontario statutes and regulations alone, 170 of these mentions being in building code regulations. Saxe, *supra* note 12 at 37. See also Robert W. Hamilton, "The Role of Nongovernmental Standards in the Development of Mandatory Federal Standards Affecting Safety or Health" (1978) 56 Tex. L. Rev. 1329, for an account of the use of voluntary standards in the development of US health and safety regulations.

68  For example, the Canadian Electrical Association has announced that all of its members must have an ISO 14001 or equivalent EMS in place by a certain date; the US-based International Council of Cruise Lines recently announced that it will make EMS implementation a mandatory membership condition in an effort to preempt tougher government regulation and reduce adverse attention to chronic marine pollution; the Canadian Chemical Producers' Association requires its members to implement the Responsible Care program; and numerous other industry associations in Canada and around the world require their members either to subscribe or verifiably demonstrate conformance to various environmental principles or codes of conduct. Courts have held that industry associations may use contract-based actions to discipline members for failure to meet agreed-upon voluntary standards. Webb, *supra* note 14 at 38. Adherence to voluntary initiatives could also be made a term of insurance or finance contracts, although I know of no such contracts involving an EMS.

69  Webb, *supra* note 14; and Meidinger, *supra* note 13.

70  See, for example, Webb, *supra* note 14 at 38-39. Webb has also made this argument in postings to the Voluntary Codes Research Forum listserv (see *supra* note 46). In addition to contract law, voluntary initiatives may also be enforced through property or trust law in certain circumstances. See Meidinger, *supra* note 13.

71  The term "benchmarking" is often used to describe a technique used by organizations to study "best practices" in other organizations or industries in order to assess and improve their own practices. I do not use the term in this sense but in the sense of an external adjudicator judging an organization's conduct against a chosen standard of care.

72  See, for example, Webb, *supra* note 14; Meidinger, *supra* note 13; and Saxe, *supra* note 12. In tort actions, voluntary initiatives may be used to determine "reasonable use" of land in a nuisance action or, more commonly, "reasonable care" in a negligence action. See, for example, *Visp Constr.* v. *Scepter Mfg.* (1991), 45 Constr. L. Rep. 170 (Ont. Gen. Div.) (defendant in product liability action not negligent because its manufacturing process conformed to voluntary CSA standard, CSA standard was reasonable notwithstanding that CSA was made up largely of manufacturers' representatives and that higher standards allegedly existed, and defendant took reasonable care to assure its product met the CSA standard particularly by maintaining CSA certification of its products and manufacturing process).

73  In Canada, a defendant will not be found guilty of a strict liability offence, which includes most environmental regulatory offences, if the person establishes that he or she exercised "due diligence" – that is, did everything reasonable in the circumstances to avoid committing the offence. See *R.* v. *Sault Ste. Marie*, [1978] 2 S.C.R. 1299, 85 D.L.R. (3d) 161, 40 C.C.C. (2d) 353; and Elaine L. Hughes, "The Reasonable Care Defences" (1992) 2 J. Envtl. L. and Practice 214. Due diligence is essentially equivalent to the civil negligence standard. In both civil and regulatory cases, conformance to industry custom is usually strong evidence of reasonableness unless the custom itself is unreasonable or the defendant's particular circumstances require more.

74  See, for example, Saxe, *supra* note 12 at 21; Taylor, "ISO 14000 and Environmental Regulation," *supra* note 12 at 20; Taylor, "Is ISO 14001 Standardization in Tune with Sustainable Development?" *supra* note 12 at 530-31; CESD, *supra* note 28 at para. 1.45 (declaring ISO 14001 to be the standard of due diligence). In fact, demonstrating "due diligence" and thereby avoiding regulatory liability appears to be one of the leading motivations for public sector organizations to implement EMSs, as Canadian public authorities face more frequent environmental prosecutions and increasingly severe penalties if convicted.

75  Webb, *supra* note 14 at 32 and 40.

76  *Ibid.* at 35-36.

77  Nikolas Rose, *Powers of Freedom* (Cambridge: Cambridge University Press, 1999) at 18.

78  Nikolas Rose and Peter Miller, "Political Power beyond the State: Problematics of Government" (1992) 43 British Journal of Sociology 173 at 174.

79  Compare with David Kennedy, "Thinking against the Box: When Renewal Repeats" (2000) 32 N.Y.U. J. Int'l L. and Pol. 335 (describing similar dynamics of intellectual renewal in the field of international law).

80  See Michel Foucault, *The History of Sexuality*, vol. 1: *Introduction* (London: Allen Lane, 1978) 88-89 (remarking that two centuries after the political revolutions that overthrew the absolutist monarchies of Europe, in the field of political thought, we have not yet cut off the king's head).

81  Rose and Miller, *supra* note 78 at 174-75.

82  Michel Foucault, "Governmentality," in Graham Burchell, Colin Gordon, and Peter Miller, eds., *The Foucault Effect* (Chicago: Chicago University Press, 1991), 87 at 103.

83  In this conception, government includes the government of the state, the government of others and the government of oneself. See generally Foucault, "Governmentality," *supra* note 82; Burchell, Gordon, and Miller, *supra* note 82; Rose and Miller, *supra* note 78; Rose, *supra* note 77; Mitchell Dean, *Governmentality: Power and Rule in Modern Society* (London: Sage, 1999); and Paul Rutherford, "The Entry of Life into History," in Éric Darier, ed., *Discourses of the Environment* (Oxford: Blackwell, 1999), 37.

84  Foucault, "Governmentality," *supra* note 82.

85  Rose and Miller, *supra* note 78 at 175.

86  *Ibid.*

87  This idea of "action at a distance" has been used quite effectively by some proponents of "regulatory reinvention." See, for example, Gunningham and Grabosky, *supra* note 9 at 10 and 123-25; Peter N. Grabosky, "Using Non-Governmental Resources to Foster Regulatory Compliance" (1995) 8 Governance 527.

88  Rose and Miller, *supra* note 78 at 187.

89  The power of expertise has been recognized in numerous other contexts, from the crucial role of experts in policy networks (see, for example, M.M. Atkinson and W.D. Coleman, "Policy Networks, Policy Communities, and the Problems of Governance," in L. Dobuzinskis, M. Howlett, and D. Laycock, eds., *Policy Studies in Canada: The State of the Art* [Toronto: University of Toronto Press, 1996] at 193) to the influence of "epistemic communities" in international environmental politics (see, for example, Peter M. Haas, *Saving the Mediterranean* (New York: Columbia University Press, 1990); and the Special Issue on Epistemic Communities and International Policy Coordination (1992) 46 International Organization 1).

90  See, for example, Nikolas Rose and Mariana Valverde, "Governed By Law?" (1998) 7 Social and Legal Studies 541; Alan Hunt and G. Wickham, *Foucault and Law: Towards a Sociology of*

*Law as Governance* (London: Pluto, 1994); and Alan Hunt, *Explorations in Law and Society: Toward a Constitutive Theory of Law* (New York: Routledge, 1993).

91 See, for example, Darier, *supra* note 83.

92 Compare with Salter, "Housework of Capitalism," *supra* note 17 at 106 (commenting on standardization generally).

93 Compare with *ibid.* at 109-10.

94 Compare with Cutler, Haufler, and Porter, *supra* note 8 (identifying and analyzing inter-firm regulation as one of the principal expressions of private authority in international affairs).

95 While "continual improvement" is usually understood in the environmental policy community as meaning continual improvement of environmental performance, ISO 14001 and 14004 define it as the "process of enhancing the environmental management system to achieve improvements in overall environmental performance" and emphasize that the rate and extent of improvement in environmental performance are up to the organization to determine and will not necessarily follow simply from the establishment and operation of an EMS. See, for example, ISO 14001, *supra* note 1 at clauses 3.1 and A.1.

96 For an account of the "stakeholder management" approach to corporate social responsibility and a proposal for an alternative "rights"-based approach, see Richard Boele, Heike Fabig, and David Wheeler, "Shell, Nigeria and the Ogoni: A Study in Unsustainable Development? Part II – Corporate Social Responsibility and 'Stakeholder Management' versus a Rights-Based Approach to Sustainable Development" (2001) 9(3) Sustainable Development 121-35.

97 For example, ISO 14001 and 14004 provide frameworks for identifying and documenting applicable legal requirements, setting objectives and targets for them, monitoring, measuring, and reviewing their achievement, and taking corrective action when non-compliance is discovered.

98 Compare with Salter, "Housework of Capitalism," *supra* note 17 at 113 (commenting on standardization generally). As Salter explains, this tendency does not reflect a desire to disguise the dominant role played by industry in standardization, but simply to deny that this role is political.

99 This fact may help explain the growing use of EMSs by government departments and might justify the inference that the EMS is a mechanism by which multinational corporations and other large private organizations, such as standardization bodies, are redrawing the lines between public and private in informal alliances with large public organizations.

100 See, for example, ISO, *ISO's Long-Range Strategies 1999-2001: Raising Standards for the World* (Geneva: ISO, 1998). A summary of this document, entitled "ISO in the New Century," is available at <http://www.iso.ch/iso/en/prods-services/otherpubs/pdf/longrang.pdf> (accessed 30 October 2001) ("ISO develops only those standards that are required by the market. This work is carried out by experts on loan from the industrial, technical, and business sectors, which have asked for the standards and which subsequently put them to use").

101 Salter, "Housework of Capitalism," *supra* note 17 at 107.

102 Christopher Sheldon, "Introduction," in Christopher Sheldon, ed., *ISO 14001 and Beyond* (Sheffield, UK: Greenleaf, 1997), 11 at 11.

103 See, generally, Rose and Miller, *supra* note 78 at 196-201.

104 Garret Hardin, "The Tragedy of the Commons" 162 Science (13 December 1968) 1243 at 1245-46 (*"Quis custodiet ipsos custodes?"*).

105 Accreditation refers to the designation of individuals or organizations as accredited to certify an organization or product's conformance to a voluntary standard. Accreditation of ISO 14001 certifiers is done by standards bodies themselves, and while there have been rumours about the inferior quality of some certifiers, particularly in the developing world, this is usually left to the market to sort out. There is very little oversight either of accreditation or accredited certifiers. Some coordination of accreditation is achieved through organizations such as the International Accreditation Forum and the International Social and Environmental Accreditation and Labelling Alliance. For more information on the latter, see Errol Meidinger, "Emerging Trans-Sectoral Regulatory Structures in Global Civil

Society: The Case of ISEAL (International Social and Environmental Accreditation and La-belling Alliance)," paper presented at the joint meetings of Law and Society Association and Research Committee for the Sociology of Law, 4-7 July 2001, Budapest, Hungary, <http://law.buffalo.edu/homepage/eemeid/scholarship/ISEAL.pdf> (1 August 2001).

106  The success of this expulsion is reflected in the fact that despite their major implications for environmental quality, public health, international competitiveness, and regulatory autonomy, voluntary EMS initiatives have received little attention from academics, almost none from news media and grassroots organizations, and have only recently begun to attract serious attention from public authorities.

107  To those familiar with international law or international relations, the very move to the term "governance" signals a multiple shift in political rationalities: a rejection of ineffec-tive, formal, inflexible, hierarchical organizations in favour of pragmatic, effective, infor-mal, organic, flexible "regimes" and networks and a move from inefficient, corrupt, centralized public administration to efficient, honest, liberal-democratic, rule-of-law, free-market, World-Bank-friendly "good governance." Exploring the implications of this move is beyond the scope of this essay.

108  Compare with Maarten Hajer, *The Politics of Environmental Discourse* (Oxford: Clarendon, 1995) at 60.

109  Compare with *ibid.* at 12-13, 58-68; and Dorte Salskov-Iversen, Hans Krause Hansen, and Sven Bislev, "Governmentality, Globalization and Local Practice: Transformations of a Hegemonic Discourse" (2000) 25 Alternatives: Social Transformation and Humane Gov-ernance 183.

110  See, for example, ISO Technical Committee 207 [hereinafter ISO/TC 207], "About ISO/TC 207" (undated), available at <http://www.tc207.org/abouttc207/aboutTC207_main.html>; Cary Coglianese and Jennifer Nash, "Environmental Management Systems and the New Policy Agenda," in Coglianese and Nash, *Regulating from the Inside, supra* note 12, 1 at 11.

111  See, for example, Sheldon, "Introduction," *supra* note 102 at 12; Joseph Cascio, "The ISO 14001 Standard," in Cascio, *supra* note 6, 24 at 25.

112  See, for example, Coglianese and Nash, *supra* note 110 at 12; Joseph Cascio, "Introduc-tion," *supra* note 6 at 4; John D. Wolfe, "CSA's Environmental Management Program and Its Relationship to Other National and International Environmental Management Systems Initiatives," in Canadian Institute, *Environmental Management Systems: Preparing for the New Reality* (Toronto: Canadian Institute, 1992).

113  Cascio, "The ISO 14001 Standard," *supra* note 6 at 24-25.

114  See, for example, Coglianese and Nash, *supra* note 110 at 11; Oswald A. Dodds, "An Insight into the Development and Implementation of the International Environmental Manage-ment System ISO 14001," in Hillary, *supra* note 6, 27; Dick Hortensius and Mark Barthel, "An Introduction to the ISO 14000 Series," in Sheldon, *supra* note 102, 19; Gabriele Crognale, "Environmental Management at a Crossroads: Time for a Radical Breakthrough," in Gabriele Crognale, ed., *Environmental Management Strategies: The Twenty-First Century Perspective* (Upper Saddle River, NJ: Prentice Hall PTR, 1999) 2 at 2.

115  See, for example, John Wolfe, "Drivers for International Integrated Environmental Man-agement," in Hillary, *supra* note 6, 15.

116  See, for example, Hortensius and Barthel, *supra* note 114 at 32.

117  See, for example, Reiley, *supra* note 12; Murray, *supra* note 12; Pezzoli, *supra* note 12; Stenzel, *supra* note 12; Lally, *supra* note 6; Crognale, *supra* note 114; Cascio, "Introduction," *supra* note 6; Coglianese and Nash, *supra* note 110 at 7-9.

118  See, for example, Sheldon, "Introduction," *supra* note 102 at 14.

119  See, for example, ISO/TC 207, *supra* note 110; Crognale, *supra* note 114 at 6; Cascio, "Intro-duction," *supra* note 6 at 4. The ISO's work on EMS standards, for instance, was explicitly initiated as one of the global business community's main contributions to sustainable development in the context of the 1992 Rio Earth Summit. ISO/TC 207, *supra* note 110; Hortensius and Barthel, *supra* note 114.

120  See, for example, Cascio, "Background and Development of ISO 14000 Series," in Cascio, *ISO 14000 Handbook, supra* note 6, 4 at 10.

121  See, generally, Hajer, *supra* note 108.

122 See, generally, Gunningham and Grabosky, *supra* note 9 at 5-19; Ayres and Braithwaite, *supra* note 9; and Osborne and Gaebler, *supra* note 9.
123 Gunningham and Grabosky, *supra* note 9 at 10-13.
124 Salskov-Iversen *et al., supra* note 109.
125 Miguel De Larrinaga makes a similar argument regarding the discourse surrounding Shell's involvement in Nigeria. Miguel de Larrinaga, "(Re)Politicizing the Discourse: Globalization Is a S(h)ell Game," (2000) 25 Alternatives: Social Transformation and Humane Governance 145.
126 Compare Duncan Kennedy, "The Political Stakes in 'Merely Technical' Issues of Contract Law" (unpublished paper, 17 September 2000) (copy on file with author).

## Bibliography

### Jurisprudence
*Measures Affecting Asbestos and Asbestos-Containing Products*, Report of the Appellate Body, WTO Doc. WT/DS135/AB/R (12 March 2001).
*Measures Affecting Meat and Meat Products (Hormones)*, Report of the Appellate Body, WTO Doc. WT/DS26/AB/R, WT/DS48/AB/R (adopted 13 February 1998).
*R. v. Calgary (City)* (2000), 272 A.R. 161, 35 C.E.L.R. (N.S.) 253 (Prov. Ct.).
*R. v. Canada (Minister of Indian Affairs)*, [2000] O.J. No. 5076 (Ont. S.C.J.) (Quicklaw).
*R. v. Prospec Chemicals Ltd.* (1996), 19 C.E.L.R. (N.S.) 178 (Alta. Prov. Ct.).
*R. v. Sault Ste. Marie*, [1978] 2 S.C.R. 1299, 85 D.L.R. (3d) 161, 40 C.C.C. (2d) 353.
*R. v. Van Waters and Rogers Ltd.* (1998), 220 A.R. 315 (Prov. Ct.).
*Re Material Resource Recovery SRBP Inc.*, No. EP-97-04 (Ont. Envtl. Assessment Bd., 21 Jan. 1998).
*Visp Constr. v. Scepter Mfg.* (1991), 45 Constr. L. Rep. 170 (Ont. Gen. Div.).

### Legislation
*Canadian Environmental Protection Act,* 1999, S.C. 1999, c. 33.
*Environmental Protection Act*, R.S.O. 1990, c. E.19.
*Environmental Protection and Enhancement Act*, S.A. 1992, c. E-13.3.
*Gas Pipeline Regulation*, N.B. Reg. 99-61.
*Gas Distribution and Marketers' Filing Regulation,* N.B. Reg. 99-60.
*Pipeline Regulations*, N.S. Reg. 66/98.
*Standards Council of Canada Act*, R.S.C. 1985, c. S-16.

### Government Documents

*Canada*
Agriculture and Agri-Food Canada, *Agriculture in Harmony with Nature II: AAFC's Sustainable Development Strategy 2001-2004*, Publication 2074/E (Ottawa: Public Works and Government Services Canada, 2001), available at <http://www.agr.ca/policy/environment/eb/public_html/pdfs/sds/SDSII_en.pdf> (accessed 24 April 2001).
Alberta Environment, *LEAD Program Guide: A Guide to Alberta Environment's Leaders Environmental Approval Document (LEAD) Program: Pilot Phase* (April 2001), available at <http://www.gov.ab.ca/env/protenf/publications/LEADProgramGuideApr01.pdf> (accessed 17 July 2001).
Auditor General of Canada, *Report of the Auditor General of Canada to the House of Commons* (October 1995), available at <http://www.oag-bvg.gc.ca/domino/reports.nsf/html/9511ce.html> (accessed 1 May 2001).
British Columbia Ministry of Forests, Implementing Forest Certification in British Columbia: Issues and Options – Report Summary (March 2001), available at <http://www.for.gov.bc.ca/het/certification/researchproject.htm> (accessed 7 August 2001).
Commissioner of the Environment and Sustainable Development, *Report of the Commissioner of the Environment and Sustainable Development 1999* (Ottawa: Queen's Printer, 1999).
Commissioner of the Environment and Sustainable Development, "Moving Up the Learning Curve: The Second Generation of Sustainable Development Strategies," available at

<http://www.oag-bvg.gc.ca/domino/cesd_cedd.nsf/html/c9dec_e.html> (accessed 1 May 2001).

Environment Canada, *Compliance and Enforcement Policy for the Canadian Environmental Protection Act, 1999* (Ottawa: Environment Canada, 2001), available at <http://www.ec.gc. ca/enforce/homepage/cepa/CEPA99_final_eng.pdf> (accessed 4 July 2001).

Environment Canada, *Directions on Greening Government Operations* (undated), available at <http://www.sdinfo.gc.ca/SDinfo/ENG/docs/ggo/default.cfm> (accessed 30 April 2001).

Government of Canada et al., Draft Memorandum of Understanding between the Governments of Canada, Ontario and Alberta and the Canadian Chemical Producers' Association on Environmental Protection through Action under CCPA Responsible Care, available at <http://www.ec.gc.ca/nopp/chemical/ccpa/indexe.htm> (accessed 30 October 2001).

Ontario Ministry of the Environment, Environmental Partnerships Branch, *Progress Report 2001: Ontario Initiatives in Pollution Prevention* (Toronto: Queen's Printer, 2001), available at <http://www.ene.gov.on.ca/envision/techdocs/355101e.pdf>.

Public Works and Government Services Canada, "ISO 14001: A New Tool for Buying Green," available at <http://contractscanada.gc.ca/sl/en/iso14-e.htm> (20 March 2001).

Standards Council of Canada, *Canadian Standards Strategy and Implementation Proposals* (March 2000), available at <http://www.scc.ca>.

*United States*
*Greening the Government through Leadership in Environmental Management*, Executive Order no. 13148, 65 Fed. Reg. 24593 (21 April 2000).

United States Environmental Protection Agency, *Summary of EPA's Performance Track Proposal* (9 March 2000).

**International Documents**
Agreement on Technical Barriers to Trade, 1994, reprinted in GATT Secretariat, *The Results of the Uruguay Round of Multilateral Trade Negotiations: The Legal Texts, Uruguay Round (1987-1994)* (Geneva: GATT Secretariat, 1994).

ISO, *ISO 14001:1996, Environmental Management Systems: Specification with Guidance for Use* (Geneva: ISO, 1996).

ISO, *ISO 14004:1996, Environmental management systems: General Guidelines on Principles, Systems and Supporting Techniques* (Geneva: ISO, 1996).

ISO, *ISO's Long-Range Strategies 1999-2001: Raising Standards for the World* (Geneva: ISO, 1998).

ISO Technical Committee 207 (ISO/TC 207), "About ISO/TC 207" (undated), available at <http://www.tc207.org/abouttc207/aboutTC207_main.html> (accessed 31 January 2003).

North American Commission for Environmental Cooperation, *Improving Environmental Performance and Compliance: 10 Elements of Effective Environmental Management Systems* (Montreal: CEC, 2000).

**Books and Articles**
Ayres, Ian, and John Braithwaite, *Responsive Regulation* (New York: Oxford, 1992).

Balikov, Henry, and Patrick Cavanaugh, "The Overselling of Government 'Reinvention': How Government Expectations of EPA's Project XL and ISO 14000 May Prove Counter-Productive" (Spring-Summer 1997) Albany L. Envtl. Outlook 23.

Berón, Laura E., "ISO 14000 and Trade Implications: Facts and Trends," paper presented at the Seminar on Trade, Environment and the ISO 14000 Series, ninth Annual Meeting of the ISO/TC 207, Kuala Lumpur, Malaysia, 4 July 2001.

Boele, Richard, Heike Fabig, and David Wheeler, "Shell, Nigeria and the Ogoni: A Study in Unsustainable Development? Part II – Corporate Social Responsibility and 'Stakeholder Management' versus a Rights Based Approach to Sustainable Development" (2001) 9(3) Sustainable Development 121.

Braithwaite, John, and Peter Drahos, *Global Business Regulation* (Cambridge, UK: Cambridge University Press, 2000).

Burchell, Graham, Colin Gordon, and Peter Miller, eds., *The Foucault Effect* (Chicago: University of Chicago Press, 1991).

Butner, Scott, "ISO 14000 – Policy and Regulatory Implications for State Agencies," paper presented at the National Pollution Prevention Roundtable Annual Meeting (10 April 1996), available at <http://www.seattle.battelle.org/p2online/iso-regs.htm> (accessed 21 June 2001).

Canadian Institute for Environmental Law and Policy, *CSA Environmental Standards Writing: Barriers to Environmental Non-Governmental Organizations Involvement* (Toronto: CIELAP, 1997).

Carraro, Carlo, and François Lévêque, eds., *Voluntary Approaches in Environmental Policy* (Dordrecht: Kluwer, 1999).

Cascio, Joseph, ed., *The ISO 14000 Handbook* (Milwaukee: ASQ Quality Press, 1996).

Coglianese, Cary, and Jennifer Nash, eds., *Regulating from the Inside: Can Environmental Management Systems Achieve Policy Goals?* (Washington, DC: Resources for the Future, 2001).

Crognale, Gabriele, "Environmental Management at a Crossroads: Time for a Radical Breakthrough," in Gabriele Crognale, ed., *Environmental Management Strategies: The 21st Century Perspective* (Upper Saddle River, NJ: Prentice Hall PTR, 1999), 2.

Cutler, A. Claire, Virginia Haufler, and Tony Porter, eds., *Private Authority and International Affairs* (Albany: State University of New York Press, 1999).

Darier, Éric, ed., *Discourses of the Environment* (Oxford: Blackwell, 1999).

Dean, Mitchell, *Governmentality: Power and Rule in Modern Society* (London: Sage, 1999).

Dodds, Oswald A., "An Insight into the Development and Implementation of the International Environmental Management System ISO 14001," in Ruth Hillary, ed., *Environmental Management Systems and Cleaner Production* (Chichester, UK: John Wiley and Sons, 1997), 27.

Doern, G. Bruce et al., "Canadian Regulatory Institutions: Converging and Colliding Regimes," in G. Bruce Doern et al., eds., *Changing the Rules: Canadian Regulatory Regimes and Institutions* (Toronto: University of Toronto Press, 1999), 3.

Foucault, Michel, "Governmentality," in Graham Burchell, Colin Gordon, and Peter Miller, eds., *The Foucault Effect* (Chicago: Chicago University Press, 1991), 87.

—, *The History of Sexuality,* vol. 1: *Introduction* (London: Allen Lane, 1978).

Gibson, Robert, ed., *Voluntary Initiatives: The New Politics of Corporate Greening* (Peterborough, ON: Broadview, 1999).

Gordenker, Leon, and Thomas G. Weiss, "Pluralising Global Governance: Analytical Approaches and Dimensions" (1995) 16 Third World Q. 357.

Grabosky, Peter N., "Using Non-Governmental Resources to Foster Regulatory Compliance" (1995) 8 Governance 527.

Gunningham, Neil, and Peter Grabosky, *Smart Regulation* (Oxford: Clarendon, 1998).

Haas, Peter M., *Saving the Mediterranean* (New York: Columbia University Press, 1990).

Hajer, Maarten, *The Politics of Environmental Discourse* (Oxford: Clarendon, 1995).

Hamilton, Robert W., "The Role of Nongovernmental Standards in the Development of Mandatory Federal Standards Affecting Safety or Health" (1978) 56 Tex. L. Rev. 1329.

Hardin, Garret, "The Tragedy of the Commons" (13 December 1968) 162 Science 1243.

Haufler, Virginia, *A Public Role for the Private Sector: Industry Self-Regulation in a Global Economy* (Washington, DC: Carnegie Endowment for International Peace, 2001).

Hillary, Ruth, ed., *Environmental Management Systems and Cleaner Production* (Chichester, UK: John Wiley and Sons, 1997).

Hortensius, Dick, and Mark Barthel, "An Introduction to the ISO 14000 Series," in Christopher Sheldon, ed., *ISO 14001 and Beyond* (Sheffield, UK: Greenleaf, 1997), 19.

Hughes, Elaine L., "The Reasonable Care Defences" (1992) 2 J. Envtl. L. and Practice 214.

Hunt, Alan, *Explorations in Law and Society: Toward a Constitutive Theory of Law* (New York: Routledge, 1993).

—, and G. Wickham, *Foucault and Law: Towards a Sociology of Law as Governance* (London: Pluto, 1994).

Hunter, David, James Salzman, and Durwood Zaelke, *International Environmental Law and Policy* (New York: Foundation Press, 1998).

*International Organization*, Special Issue on Epistemic Communities and International Policy Coordination (1992) 46 Int'l Org. 1.

Kennedy, David, "Thinking against the Box: When Renewal Repeats" (2000) 32 N.Y.U. J. Int'l L. and Pol. 335.

Kennedy, Duncan, "The Political Stakes in 'Merely Technical' Issues of Contract Law" (unpublished paper, 17 September 2000).

Krut, Riva, and Harris Gleckman, *ISO 14001: A Missed Opportunity for Sustainable Global Industrial Development* (London: Earthscan, 1998).

Lally, Amy Pesapane, "ISO 14000 and Environmental Cost Accounting: The Gateway to the Global Market" (1998) 29 Law and Pol'y Int'l Bus. 501.

Larrinaga, Miguel de, "(Re)Politicizing the Discourse: Globalization Is a S(h)ell Game" (2000) 25 Alternatives: Social Transformation and Humane Governance 145.

Meidinger, Errol, "Emerging Trans-Sectoral Regulatory Structures in Global Civil Society: The Case of ISEAL (International Social and Environmental Accreditation and Labelling Alliance)," paper presented at the joint meetings of Law and Society Association and Research Committee for the Sociology of Law, 4-7 July 2001, Budapest, Hungary, available at <http://law.buffalo.edu/homepage/eemeid/scholarship/ISEAL.pdf> (accessed 1 August 2001).

—, "Environmental Certification Programs and U.S. Environmental Law: Closer Than You May Think" (2001) 31 Envtl L. Rptr. 10162.

Mitchell, Ronald B., *Intentional Oil Pollution At Sea* (Cambridge, MA: MIT Press, 1994).

Moffet, John, and François Bregha, "Non-Regulatory Environmental Measures," in Robert Gibson, ed., *Voluntary Initiatives: The New Politics of Corporate Greening* (Peterborough, ON: Broadview, 1999),15.

Morrison, Jason et al., *Managing a Better Environment: Opportunities and Obstacles for ISO 14001 in Public Policy and Commerce* (Oakland, CA: Pacific Institute, 2000), available at <http://www.pacinst.org> (accessed 30 July 2001).

Murray, Paula C., "Inching Toward Regulatory Reform – ISO 14000: Much Ado about Nothing or a Reinvention Tool?" (1999) 37 Am. Bus. L.J. 35.

Osborne, D., and T. Gaebler, *Reinventing Government* (Boston: Addison-Wesley, 1992).

Parto, Saeed, "Aiming Low," in Robert Gibson, ed. *Voluntary Initiatives: The New Politics of Corporate Greening* (Peterborough, ON.: Broadview, 1999), 182.

Pezzoli, Keith,"Environmental Management Systems (EMSs) and Regulatory Innovation" (2000) 36 Cal. W. L. Rev. 335.

Pollution Probe, *The Future Role of Environmental Standards* (Ottawa: Pollution Probe, 2000).

Raustiala, Kal, "The 'Participatory Revolution' in International Environmental Law" (1997) 21 Harvard Envtl. L. Rev. 537.

Reiley, Anthony, "The New Paradigm: ISO 14000 and Its Place in Regulatory Reform" (1997) 22 J. Corp. L. 535.

Roht-Arriaza, Naomi, "Developing Countries, Regional Organizations, and the ISO 14001 Environmental Management Standard" (1997) 9 Geo. Int'l Envtl. L. Rev. 583.

—, "Shifting the Point of Regulation: The International Organization for Standardization and Global Lawmaking on Trade and the Environment" (1995) 22 Ecology L.Q. 479.

Rose, Nikolas, *Powers of Freedom* (Cambridge: Cambridge University Press, 1999).

—, and Peter Miller, "Political Power beyond the State: Problematics of Government" (1992) 43 British Journal of Sociology 173.

—, and Mariana Valverde, "Governed By Law?" (1998) 7 Social and Legal Studies 541.

Rutherford, Paul, "The Entry of Life into History," in Éric Darier, ed., *Discourses of the Environment* (Oxford: Blackwell, 1999), 37.

Salskov-Iversen, Dorte, Hans Krause Hansen, and Sven Bislev, "Governmentality, Globalization and Local Practice: Transformations of a Hegemonic Discourse" (2000) 25 Alternatives: Social Transformation and Humane Governance 183.

Salter, Liora, *Mandated Science: Science and Scientists in the Making of Standards* (Dordrecht: Kluwer, 1988).

—, "The Housework of Capitalism: Standardization in the Communications and Information Technology Sectors" (1993-94) 23 International Journal of Political Economy 105.

Saxe, Dianne, "ISO 14001/14004 and Compliance in Canada," paper prepared for the Canadian Standards Association, 20 December 2000 (copy on file with author).

Sheldon, Christopher, ed., *ISO 14001 and Beyond* (Sheffield, UK: Greenleaf, 1997).

Shin, Roy W., and Yu-Che Chen, "Seizing Global Opportunities for Accomplishing Agencies' Missions: The Case of ISO 14000" (2000) 24 Public Administration Quarterly 69.

Stenzel, Paulette, "Can the ISO 14000 Series Environmental Management Standards Provide a Viable Alternative to Government Regulation?" (2000) 37 Am. Bus. L.J. 237.

Sunstein, Cass, "Paradoxes of the Regulatory State" (1990) 57 U. Chi. L. Rev. 407.

—, *After the Rights Revolution: Reconceiving the Regulatory State* (Cambridge, MA: Harvard University Press, 1990).

Taylor, Douglas, "Is ISO 14001 Standardization in Tune with Sustainable Development?" (1998) 13 J. Envtl. L. and Litigation 509.

—, "ISO 14000 and Environmental Regulation" (1999) 9 J. Envtl. L. and Practice 1.

Tóth, Gergely, "The ISO 14001 Speedometer," available at <http://www.inem.org/htdocs/iso/speedometer/speedometer-4_2001.html> (accessed 30 October 2001).

Webb, Kernaghan, "Voluntary Initiatives and the Law," in Robert Gibson, ed., *Voluntary Initiatives: The New Politics of Corporate Greening* (Peterborough, ON: Broadview, 1999), 32.

—, and Andrew Morrison, "Voluntary Approaches, the Environment and the Law: A Canadian Perspective," in Carlo Carraro and François Lévêque, eds., *Voluntary Approaches in Environmental Policy* (Dordrecht: Kluwer, 1999), 229.

Wolfe, John D., "CSA's Environmental Management Program and Its Relationship to Other National and International Environmental Management Systems Initiatives," in Canadian Institute, *Environmental Management Systems: Preparing for the New Reality* (Toronto: Canadian Institute, 1992).

—, "Drivers for International Integrated Environmental Management," in Ruth Hillary, ed., *Environmental Management Systems and Cleaner Production* (Chichester, UK: John Wiley and Sons, 1997), 15.

# 6

# The Emergence of Parallel Identity-Based Associations in Collective Bargaining Relations

*Christian Brunelle*

A love of democracy is a love of equality.

— Montesquieu

If we are to judge by the statistics compiled over the last twenty years, union membership is declining almost everywhere in the industrialized world.[1] The decrease in numbers of union members is especially alarming in the United States and can also be observed, although to a lesser extent, in Quebec[2] and in the other provinces of Canada.[3] Although there is no general agreement as to the precise causes of this phenomenon, economic reasons spring most immediately to mind. Following the example of salaried workers, unions too have to deal with a labour market where job losses, whether in the form of unemployment or claims for social welfare, are a serious concern.

At a time of market globalization, where the neoliberal approach seems to have become dominant, the prosperity of companies is measured less in terms of the jobs they create and more in terms of the number of jobs they eliminate in the name of rationalization as dictated by the competition and the shareholders! In fact, the economic logic supporting the recognition of collective bargaining relationships in our current labour laws seems to be breaking down.[4] Reduced to its simplest terms, this logic assumes that profits lead to investment; that investment makes it possible to increase production; that increased production encourages job creation; that jobs generate salaries; that the paying of salaries helps to increase consumption; and, ultimately, that this consumption leads to new profits.[5] As a result of investments in technology, production can now increase both quantitatively and qualitatively without any corresponding job creation. Moreover, these technological changes even enable an employer to reduce the number of employees without in any way affecting production.[6] These phenomena, which are linked to the globalization of the economy and technological innovation, have had a particularly harsh impact on the manufacturing sector,[7] which is the traditional bastion of the union movement.[8] At the same time, we have for a while been witnessing a gradual movement of employment away from the goods sector toward the services sector.[9] This movement is not likely to make the job of union organizations any easier since the people who work in the tertiary sector are often more reluctant to join unions.[10]

However, this movement of jobs toward the services sector has been accompanied by an increase in the precarious nature of employment. It is losing its character of permanence, its full-time nature, and is taking on so-called "atypical" forms (part-time work, freelance work, on-call work, casual work, self-employment, and others).[11] The union movement has experienced serious problems in its attempts to rally this "variegated" workforce to its cause.[12] To compound the problem, many of the jobs that have been freshly created by the "new economy" are in small- and medium-sized businesses.[13] Once again, unions seeking to recruit new members in these companies of more modest size[14] will certainly experience resistance.

The new rules of the game in the international economy, devised by individuals and corporations whose sole motive is profit, leave little room for labour organizations to manoeuvre. Moreover, while the rate of union membership is declining because of economic phenomena largely beyond the control of the unions,[15] there is another social and demographic factor that helps to explain the decline in union membership: the increasing diversification of the workforce.[16] The arrival of large numbers of women and of various minorities in the workforce is irreversibly changing its make-up. Women employees today are just as numerous as men.[17] Furthermore, workers who are distinguished from the "majority" by their colour, race, ethnic origin, age, religion, language, disability, or sexual orientation are more present and visible than ever before in both government institutions and private enterprise. When linked to the decline in the birth rate that has been observed in Canada,[18] including Quebec,[19] this tendency toward "cosmopolitanism" in the workforce can only grow. Unions have scarcely begun to measure the magnitude of the changes that this emerging reality will force upon them.[20]

Indeed, unions – of which members typically work full time[21] and are white, male,[22] Catholics or Protestants, middle-aged, married,[23] heads of families, and heterosexual[24] – seem to have experienced a number of problems in meeting the needs of employees who are part of the new-style workforce.[25] In the gradual diversification of the workforce, there is potential for both destruction and renewal of the union movement, depending on the extent to which it is able to adapt.

In Quebec, a relatively new phenomenon attests to the unique difficulties of labour unions in adjusting to the increase in demands for equality in those workplaces where the workforce is increasingly heterogeneous. In fact, employees who are dissatisfied with the union certified to represent them are creating – on the sidelines, away from the established union structures recognized by law – separate associations with a mission to defend the rights of those workers in the workplace.

This study aims to provide a better understanding of this phenomenon and to measure its potential long-term impact on the vitality of the union movement in the context of the debate on the private or public nature of unions. To this end, it is important to begin by briefly describing the dominant characteristics of these "parallel" associations, their approaches, and the motives of those individuals who helped bring these organizations into being. Second, we need to identify the shortcomings in the existing system of union-management relations, which are highlighted by the emergence of these associations. Finally, we also need to question the nature of the thinking that is necessary within the union movement in order for it to be better able to reconcile the exercise of collective rights and the inexorable growth of individual rights in today's world. The thesis that is advocated here is that unions need to change to better reflect the diversity of workers, and they are being forced to do so because of the emergence of parallel identity-based associations that challenge publicly the nature of a private contract – that is, the collective agreement. To respond to the possible threat that is creating these parallel identity-based associations, the unions need to define themselves more as public forums than as private organizations.

### Emergence of Parallel Identity-Based Associations

The emergence of parallel identity-based associations in Quebec is generally the result of the steps taken by the provincial government to reform public spending. As part of the extensive Summit on the Economy and Employment, which was held in Montreal in October 1996, unions and management agreed to cooperate with the government in order to achieve the goal of a "zero deficit." The "sacrifices" demanded of the unions took the form of wage concessions in later collective bargaining. Since the unions were concerned not to alienate the support of the generally older workers who justified their presence in the workplace, some of them agreed to have the younger workers bear a larger part of the burden by agreeing to various conditions, which are more appropriately called "orphan" clauses.[26] The process, which was condemned by some employees as a fundamental breach of intergenerational equity,[27] provoked a reaction that was unprecedented in collective bargaining relations. Indeed, in a reaction to the apparent indifference of their union representatives in the face of what they felt was an injustice against young people, these workers established their own associations to defend their interests.

It was against this backdrop that the Association de défense des jeunes enseignants du Québec (ADJEQ)[28] and the Groupe d'action pour l'équité et l'égalité salariale du Service de police de la Communauté urbaine de Montréal (SPCUM) (GAPES)[29] were created. The ADJEQ challenged a freeze on wage increases negotiated by the Fédération des syndicats de l'enseignement of the Centrale des syndicats du Québec (formerly the Centrale de l'enseignement du Québec) and the Quebec Treasury Board because this freeze disproportionately affected the youngest teachers in comparison with their older colleagues.[30] For a young teacher at the start of his or her career, the total salary loss over the time of a normal career could amount to some $15,000. The GAPES, for its part, attacked the decision of the Fraternité des policiers et policières de la Communauté urbaine de Montréal (now called the Fraternité des policiers et policières de Montréal) to sign a collective agreement under which any police officer hired after 1 January 1997 had to climb an extra rung that was added to the very bottom of the salary scale. This process meant that new police officers lost more than $46,500 in gross salary over a six-year period.[31]

Another group, the Association des jeunes de la fonction publique du Québec (AJFP),[32] criticized the unions certified to represent its members for the lack of attention they paid to the increasingly precarious nature of employment for young people. The obligation imposed on any employee to have worked for at least twelve consecutive months in the same job in the same government department during the last fifteen months in order to be eligible to apply for a "reserved" competition was the target of the attacks by AJFP in this instance.[33] Another development that also elicited expressions of disapproval from the AJFP was the decision of the Quebec Treasury Board to no longer recognize a certain number of years of education as an "experience credit,"[34] thereby impeding the increases in young workers' salaries. In more general terms, criticism was expressed in response to the underrepresentation of workers under thirty-five years of age in the Quebec public service[35] and in response to the lack of effort by the existing unions to attempt to do something to rectify this situation.

While the differences that can exist between these various associations in terms of their internal management or their demands should not be denied, it is certainly possible to find certain features that they all share. First, they are on the sidelines of the union movement and could even be said to have been a reaction to that movement.[36] In fact, the relations between the workers who were members of these associations and their colleagues who have remained faithful to the duly-certified unions are apparently rather lukewarm if not positively hostile.[37] Second, these associations have grown up around a personal characteristic, namely age, which appears to be a stronger identifying factor than the simple community of economic interests that, as a rule, sustains the traditional solidarity of labour unions. Third, these associations break away from the classic forms in which dissent was expressed in union organizations. Whereas dissent has almost always been expressed in private closed circles at union meetings or in "raiding" periods, these new associations, for their part, took to public forums in order to make their dissatisfaction and demands better known. For example, all of them created sites on the Internet that they use to disseminate on a large scale and at low cost any information that they consider relevant. This means of communication also enabled them to recruit members in complete anonymity and to collect complaints or valuable information from the workers. These workers could express themselves all the more freely since the computer permits confidences as well as providing them with a certain guarantee of confidentiality.[38] Finally, these associations do not hesitate to make use of public forums by relying on standard methods of communication, such as newspapers, or more formal methods, such as appearances before committees of various legislative bodies.[39] Fourth, these associations have all filed a complaint of discrimination on the basis of age with the Quebec Commission des droits de la personne et des droits de la jeunesse, in the hope that it would eventually ask the Tribunal des droits de la personne du Québec[40] to strike out the provisions of the collective agreements that were alleged to have a discriminatory effect on their members.[41]

It might be assumed that these parallel identity-based associations reflect a phenomenon that is marginal in the final analysis. The fact remains, however, that they attract to their ranks a substantial number of members, especially considering that the recruiting technique they use is essentially word of mouth. Thus, it is claimed that almost 4,000 young teachers have already joined the ADJEQ. The example of GAPES is just as revealing. The Fraternité des policiers et policières de Montréal represents approximately 4,100 police officers. Of these individuals, 2,000 perform duties relating to investigations, and the remaining 2,100, who are generally less experienced, are assigned to patrolling duties. The GAPES has more than 725 members, which is one-third of these officers on patrol. The AJFP, for its part, is alleged to have close to 350 members.

### Shortcomings of Union Democracy

How can we explain the emergence of parallel identity-based associations in workplaces where a mechanism for representing employees already exists in the form of the union? Does their emergence possibly offer a sign that union democracy has become dysfunctional? An analogy has often been drawn between legislatures and unions.[42] A member of the legislature is elected in accordance with the absolute majority rule, as is the union, so that they both have a collective mandate. A member of a legislature represents all the voters in his or her riding whereas the union enjoys a monopoly in representing all the members of the certified bargaining unit. Moreover, all the elected representatives do not have to obey the instructions of the people who have elected them any more than the unions do.[43]

However, that is as far as the comparison can be stretched. While parliamentary democracy formally allows for expressions of dissent through the representatives of the official Opposition,[44] the collective bargaining system does not provide a similar opportunity for the defence of minority interests.[45] The rule of the majority applies with full force to them.[46]

In short, whether a worker reveres or scorns the elected union, whether this worker shares or opposes its policies, whether he or she respects or despises its leaders, he or she will nevertheless be required by law to hand over to the union his or her freedom to negotiate the conditions that will govern employment.[47] This being the case, "once representation is established, it will be provided regardless of the individual preferences of the employees ... regardless of their individual wishes."[48] Furthermore, "in such a system [in which there is a monopoly on representation], minorities do not have a say in the matter other than within the union structure ... opposition to the union has little chance of survival and even less of development in such an institutional straightjacket."[49]

This is precisely why the courts have imposed a duty on unions to provide fair representation for all employees who are in employment that is covered by the union's certification. It is interesting to note in this regard that the imposition of this duty by the courts was the product of a US court proceeding in which black employees who were injured by the decisions of the union in which a majority of the members were white wished to be admitted to defend their own interests. Rather than approve a fragmentation of unions on the basis of race, the courts chose to favour group cohesion by requiring the unions to refrain from acting in bad faith arbitrarily or in a discriminatory manner against any employee.[50]

Out of a concern to preserve labour organizations' room to manoeuvre,[51] the courts have given a very limited interpretation to the duty to provide fair representation. Essentially, it is the reasons given by the union that are examined by the judges.[52] The analysis usually focuses on the benevolence of the union's intentions[53] and on the rationality of the objectives that it seeks to attain without regard for the prejudicial effects that the measures taken to achieve those objectives may have.[54] In short, the union's conduct will be found to be beyond reproach if it exercises its discretion in complete good faith and for a laudable object,[55] even though some employees suffer inconvenience or are exposed to prejudice as a result of the decision made. In a sense, the union is ensured a certain measure of privacy in the way it deals with its members.

This interpretation testifies to a certain concern not to make the institution of the union unduly "fragile." If we understand it in this light, it fits perfectly into the logic of collective bargaining relations, according to which the restoration of a certain balance between the employer and employees can be achieved only if the parties take united joint action that is truly collective: "There are no means by which a worker can defend his or her most vital interests in isolation against the authority of the employer; only collective, episodic – a strike – or continuous – the union – action can rebalance for the benefit of the employees a dialogue that, when engaged in at the individual level, is reduced to an expression by the employer, armed with its economic power, of its wishes."[56]

In short, it is identical, undifferentiated, standardized, and majestically unified employees, who are prepared to deny their individuality in the face of the interests of the community, that, in a sense, act as a model for the legislature.[57] In order to enjoy the constant support of most of these "universal" employees[58] and the monopoly of representation that only this majority can give it, the union movement must be able to determine the common interests that they share and that specifically make it possible to maintain this majority support. With the gradual diversification of the labour force, this task is constantly increasing in complexity.[59]

Indeed, while it is true that in the homogenous and rather integrationist societies of the past, the ideology that required the individual to completely subsume him or herself in the group and to abdicate his or her desires in the name of the common good made a major impact on the working masses,[60] very little trace of that attraction remains today.[61] By an extraordinary flip of the scales, our societies are now resolutely focused on the assertion of the individual and his or her freedom and personal independence.[62] It is in this situation that the growing diversity of the labour force may become particularly threatening for the union movement. Free of all structured opposition and aware of the fact that it cannot please everyone,[63] the union may be tempted to exercise its monopoly of representation in light of the interests of the majority alone,[64] without really showing any concern for minority interests.[65]

When understood in this way, the only limit on the monopoly is the level of awareness shown among the union leaders. If this awareness is too "elastic" and blindly obeys the dictates of the largest number, employees who feel neglected may well turn toward another organization that is better able to defend their rights.[66] The fact that the union loses its influence and attraction in this situation is inevitable: "The greater demographic diversity of the labour force, the larger number of forms of employment, the assertion of new professional loyalties, the emergence of new forms of direct participation by employees, the assertion of individual projects and rights, especially under the influence of instruments setting out the fundamental rights of the person, the tendency toward diversification of collective identities and the resultant questioning of traditional homogenous union practices, are some of the factors that militate against the absolute exclusivity of union representation."[67]

There has always been a certain expression of dissent or discontent in unions. Generally, however, dissatisfied employees have attempted to make their colleagues aware of their issues and to change direction "from within," using the existing structures in *private*.[68] The creation of status of women committees in some unions was the first step in initiatives of this kind.[69] In the past, the rise of feminist independent unions by female employees dissatisfied with the way their claims were handled by major unions has also contributed to the emergence of these committees.[70] However, the organizations established by the young teachers, the young police officers, and the young public servants in Quebec can be distinguished from this type of committee in that they were a reaction and an expression of opposition to the existing unions. The threat that they pose to the union movement is more troublesome in this respect.

## The Necessary Awareness of Diversity

As holders of a monopoly on representation, the unions very soon had to adjudicate among the claims – which were often very diverse – of employees who were in the process of bargaining for a collective agreement with the employer. Without claiming that it was an easy task for them, let us say that there was a time when it used to be much easier because of the homogeneity that characterized the labour force. Without obtaining the unanimous consent of the employees, union leaders nevertheless succeeded in obtaining, generally without too much trouble, a majority consensus on the values and claims to be promoted in the course of negotiations with the employer. This was particularly true when the collective bargaining focused on a limited range of subjects, such as wage increases and reductions in hours of work as a result of extended vacations and holidays. The gradual broadening of the negotiations to other subjects, including the contractual framework that does not offer the same benefits for all, made it much more difficult to achieve this consensus.

Once it was concluded, a collective agreement became the "law of the parties"[71] – the company's internal value system[72] – and, as such, it created "the illusion of a social consensus."[73] The rights that it enshrined benefited all employees, but the obligations that it contained were also imposed on all. However reluctant the employees were to endorse the concessions made at the bargaining table, those who were in the minority had no option but to live with the choices made by their colleagues.[74] In fact, this system, which still applies today, was designed at a time when equality was synonymous above all with identical treatment. For employees who belonged to minority groups, the model to be followed primarily involved swallowing their differences and blending in with the majority in the hope of being better accepted by them.

Following the enactment of various human rights charters and acts, the courts slowly moved away from this concept of so-called formal equality in favour of one that was clearly more inclusive, referred to as substantive equality.[75] Today, in fact, judges agree that "equality ... does not necessarily connote identical treatment; in fact, different treatment may be called for in certain cases to promote equality."[76] More than ever, equality must be "anchored in the facts"[77] and be manifested in the *results*.[78] This change, which is viewed by minority groups as the expected end to a "long history of injustices, subordination and fear," is accompanied in some instances by a "fervent and widespread demand to be different":[79] "The discourse of the dominated then [takes] on a more radical content and a more demanding tone. Leaving the reformist undertakings, which are often purely legal in nature, there is a desire to change the structures that is more likely to be reflected in this discourse. In a word, the axis around which the liberation movement turns will gradually cease to be integration into the dominant model and will instead become the discovery of a difference."[80]

Just as the collective bargaining system postulates that the community of interests among workers transcends their differences[81] and that all employees have essentially the same values and needs,[82] any demand based on "difference" often seems suspect in the eyes of some union leaders. They see in it a threat to the authority of the union and to the minimum degree of solidarity that must prevail among its members in order to give strength to its actions.[83] However, given the inexorable diversification of the labour force in our pluralist societies, it is far from certain that this attitude, which is marked by a desire to level out differences or to suppress dissent, will ensure the viability of the union movement over the long term.[84] In effect, the diversity of the labour force is the source of many demands, often very diverse, among employees. A more heterogeneous labour force introduces new values into the workplace,[85] and with this, the danger that the workplace can become a marked source of discrimination grows at the same rate that the range of interests to be protected and the tensions that can necessarily arise in this situation expand.[86]

The emergence of parallel identity-based associations in unionized workplaces is an alarm signal for the union movement. Rather than arguing that they are "infallible" or turning a deaf ear to the demands that they receive from minority groups, it would be in the unions' interest to weigh the merits of these demands, make their members more aware of the problems thus identified, and attempt to find a compromise that is not dictated solely by the wishes of the majority. It is interesting to note that the process of challenging publicly the terms of the private collective agreement should force the unions to adopt new understandings of equality that have been defined outside of the union world. In a sense, it would provide the unions with the possibility of acting as a public forum rather than as a private club.

To borrow from Plato, who is still the lead singer in the historic concert for democracy, union leaders must be for their members what the guardians were supposed to be for the polity that Plato, a disciple of Socrates, wished to create. Instead of flirting with the crowd in order to please it, it is up to the union leaders to act in the presumed superior interests of all members in such a way that they all feel profit and loss with the same joy and the same suffering.[87] The fact that the collective agreement negotiated by the holder of a monopoly begins by defending the interests of those individuals who have secured the agreement is a quirk of unions that seems to be perpetuated by the current system of collective bargaining relationships.[88] Confined at the outset to the ranks of "negligible" employees because of their less obvious presence in the workplace, women and minorities very quickly became aware of the existence of this "artificial solidarity."[89] The union movement and its leaders must now review their idea of democracy and raise it above the law of the greatest number because "the concept of democracy is broader than the notion of majority rule."[90] As Christopher Schenk comments:

> Leadership will involve articulating a democratically arrived at vision, setting goals, and directing their strategic implementation. These will of necessity be decided upon within the framework of continued debate and pluralism – a pluralism inclusive of both different perspectives and multiple identities. The need to both respect people of various identities as feminists, environmentalists, or members of a particular ethnic community and, concomitantly, to create the necessary unity to defend their needs and aspirations as workers, is still ahead. This will involve some new leadership skills ... Such change is as difficult as it is possible.[91]

## Conclusion

The establishment of parallel identity-based associations designed to promote the rights of employees whose demands are not being met by the union certified to represent them is a relatively new phenomenon in collective bargaining relations. For the time being, it appears to be directly linked to the problem of so-called "orphan" clauses and can be found primarily in the public sector (such as in government departments, police forces, and school boards). However, while discrimination on the basis of age has led to the emergence of these associations, discrimination on the basis of any other personal characteristic included in the human rights legislation (for example, race, sex, disability, and sexual orientation) could just as easily result in the same process among the employees who are subject to such discrimination, whether they work in the public or the private sector. Will we witness the rise of a "new collectivism,"[92] a portent of a "fragmentation of identity,"[93] in which the union becomes something to be avoided by a growing number of employees[94] who feel that it is incapable of raising them to a level of equality that reflects their deepest aspirations?[95]

It is too early to judge. All things considered, it is still possible that this is a marginal and even ephemeral phenomenon. A lack of stable and adequate financial resources and the fact that these associations do not enjoy the benefits conferred by labour legislation on unions make their survival much more difficult in the long term. The fact remains, however, that their emergence is very significant and that the union movement would be wrong to ignore it. In fact, the birth of these organizations clearly reflects the growing complexity of labour relations in our pluralist societies and the difficulties involved in any attempt to reconcile collective rights and individual rights. In their own way, these associations also reflect a certain amount of dissatisfaction with the way in which union democracy operates in some work environments. Rather than seeing in this new phenomenon "the rise of irresponsible individualism that would replace union democracy with specific interest groups and resort to litigation,"[96] the union movement should display openness, engage in dialogue,[97] and, more generally, begin the think seriously about the very concept of democracy – and the underlying notion of equality – which is fundamental to human rights. In fact, it is considerably more important to preserve the public forum that the union can provide for democratic debate than it is to attempt to "privatize" the emerging dissent by reducing those who express it to the level of "permanent minorities."

Hitherto, unions have misjudged the importance and the unique complexity[98] of the task ahead of them if they wish to maintain their presence in the diversified workplaces of tomorrow. The highly collective logic that has always governed their actions and informed their concept of democracy must be combined with a new vision that not only makes room for individual rights but also recognizes their paramountcy under human rights legislation.[99] It is only under these conditions that employees of all kinds and all ranks will trust the unions. On the other hand, if the diversity of the labour force is not taken into account by the union movement, there is a serious risk that disputes that will weaken the movement in the long term will simply multiply.[100]

### Acknowledgment
A longer version of this essay appeared in French under the title "L'émergence des associations parallèles dans les rapports collectifs de travail" (2002) 57 (2) Relations industrielles/Industrial Relations at 282-308.

### Notes
1  Ernest B. Akyeampong, "Aperçu statistique du mouvement syndical ouvrier" (1997) 9(4) L'emploi et le revenu en perspective at 50 and 60 (Table 6).
2  Gouvernement du Québec, "La présence syndicale au Québec: bilan de l'année 2001," in *Travail-actualité/Statistique-travail* (Québec: Ministère du Travail, Direction de la recherche

et de l'évaluation, 2002), available at <http://www.travail.gouv.qc.ca/quoi_de_neuf/actualite/actualite.html>.

3   Gregor Murray, "Les transformations de la représentation collective au Québec," in Jean Bernier et al., eds., *L'incessante évolution des formes d'emploi et la redoutable stagnation des lois du travail* (Québec, Presses de l'Université Laval, 2001), 57 at 60-64.

4   Pierre Paquet, "Déclin et mutation des relations de travail fordiennes" (1993) 17(1) Possibles, 85 at 92-93, refers specifically to a deregulation of the "virtuous circle" of growth.

5   David Abraham, "Individual Economy and Collective Empowerment in Labor Law: Union Membership Resignations and Strikebreaking in the New Economy" (1988) 63 N.Y.U. L. Rev. 1268 at 1287.

6   Laurent Laplante, *La personne immédiate*, coll. La ligne du risque (Montréal: L'Hexagone, 1998) at 140-41.

7   Rachel Geman, "Safeguarding Employee Rights in a Post-Union World: A New Conception of Employee Communities" (1997) 30 Colum. J.L. and Soc. Probs. 369 at 374.

8   Carla Lipsig-Mumme, "Unions Struggle with New Work Order" (1995) 16(8) Political Options 1 at 3.

9   Gregor Murray and Pierre Verge, *La représentation syndicale: visage juridique actuel et futur* (Québec: Presses de l'Université Laval, 1999) at 107.

10  Christian Lévesque, Gregor Murray, and Stéphane Lequeux, "Transformations sociales et identités syndicales: l'institution syndicale à l'épreuve de la différenciation sociale contemporaine" (1998) 30(2) Sociologie et sociétés 131 at 134.

11  Anne Bourhis and Thierry Wils, "L'éclatement de l'emploi traditionnel: les défis posés par la diversité des emplois typiques et atypiques" (2001) 56 (1) Relations industrielles/Industrial Relations 66; Lucie France Dagenais, *Travail éclaté: protection sociale et égalité*, coll. Études et documents de recherche sur les droits et libertés, Vol. 7 (Cowansville, QC: Les Éditions Yvon Blais, 1998) at 8 *et seq.*; Fernand Morin and Jean-Yves Brière, *Le droit de l'emploi au Québec* (Montréal: Wilson and Lafleur, 1998) at Titre VI

12  Mona-Josée Gagnon, *Le syndicalisme: état des lieux et enjeux*, coll. Diagnostic, Vol. 17 (Québec: Institut québécois de recherche sur la culture, 1994) at 34. Concerning the nature of these problems, see Guylaine Vallée, "Pluralité des statuts de travail et protection des droits de la personne: quel rôle pour le droit du travail?" (1999) 54 (2) Relations industrielles/Industrial Relations 277 at 296 *et seq.*

13  Harry Arthurs and Robert Kreklewich, "Law, Legal Institutions, and the Legal Profession in the New Economy" (1996) 34 Osgoode Hall L.J. 1 at 14.

14  Judy Fudge and Harry Glasbeek, "The Legacy of PC 1003" (1995) 3 C.L.E.L.J. 357 at 391-93.

15  Jean Charest, "Le mouvement syndical," in Robert Boily, ed., *L'Année politique au Québec 1997-1998* (Montréal: Presses de l'Université de Montréal, 1999), 149.

16  Abraham, *supra* note 5 at 1293 and 1318; Charles B. Crever, *Can Unions Survive? The Rejuvenation of the American Labor Movement* (New York: New York University Press, 1993) at 37-40.

17  Edward B. Harvey and John H. Blakely, *Information Systems for Managing Workplace Diversity* (North York: CCH Canadian, 1996) at 3, para. 1010.

18  Diane Bellemare, Lise Poulin-Simon, and Diane-Gabrielle Tremblay, *Le paradoxe de l'âgisme dans une société vieillissante: enjeux politiques et défis de gestion* (Montréal: Édition Saint-Martin, 1998) at 9-10; Warren E. Kalbach, "The Demographic Transformation of Canada's Work Force," in Audrey Wipper, ed., *Work: The Sociology of Work in Canada* (Ottawa: Carleton University Press, 1994), 489.

19  Marc Termote, "Les défis démographiques du Québec" (1998) 22(3 and 4) Possibles 35 at 36.

20  Whereas 10.5 percent of union organizations feel that "the growing percentage of women and members of minorities" is "very important" as one of the many factors that may explain the changes marking the environment in which they exist, 44.2 percent of them felt that this factor was "fairly important." Surprisingly, 45.3 percent of the unions felt that this factor was quite simply "not important." Pradeep Kumar, Gregor Murray, and Sylvain Schetagne, "L'adaptation au changement: les priorités des syndicats dans les années 1990," in Government of Canada, Department of Human Resources Development, Workplace Information Directorate, *Directory of Labour Organizations in Canada 1998* (Ottawa: Canada Communication Group – Publishing, 1998), 45 (Table 4) [translation].

21   Murray and Verge, *supra* note 9 at 125-26.

22   Gillian Creese, "Gendering Collective Bargaining: From Men's Rights to Women's Issues" (1996) 33 Canadian Review of Sociology and Anthropology/Revue canadienne de sociologie et d'anthropologie 437 at 454; Gillian Lester, "Toward the Feminisation of Collective Bargaining Law" (1991) 36 McGill L.J. 1181 at 1205.

23   Molly S. McUsic and Michael Selmi, "Postmodern Unions: Identity Politics in the Workplace" (1997) 82 Iowa L. Rev. 1339 at 1343-44.

24   Judy Fudge, "Rights on the Labour Law Ladder: Using Gender to Challenge Hierarchy" (1996) 60 Sask. L. Rev. 237 at 252.

25   Isik U. Zeytinoglu and Jacinta K. Muteshi, " Gender, Race and Class Dimensions of Non-standard Work" (2000) 55 (1) Relations industrielles/Industrial Relations 133.

26   Commission des droits de la personne et des droits de la jeunesse, *L'équité entre générations et les clauses "orphelins": des droits à défendre*, Actes du Forum droits et libertés (Montréal: Commission des droits de la personne et des droits de la jeunesse, 1999); Michel Coutu, "Les clauses dites 'orphelins' et la notion de discrimination dans la *Charte des droits et libertés de la personne*" (2000) 55 (2) Relations industrielles/Industrial Relations 308.

27   Normand Morin, "Quand le 'Nous syndical' est plus important qu'un droit fondamental," *[Québec] Le Soleil* (6 August 1998) at B-7.

28   For more information on the Association de défense des jeunes enseignants du Québec [hereinafter ADJEQ], consult the following website: <http//:www.adjeq.qc.ca>.

29   For more information on the Groupe d'action pour l'équité et l'égalité salariale du Service de police de la Communauté urbaine de Montréal [hereinafter GAPES], consult the following website: <http//:www.gapes.org>.

30   Gilbert Leduc, "Les jeunes profs sévères pour la CEQ," *[Québec] Le Soleil* (11 June 1998) at A-12.

31   Patrick Lavallée et al., "Les jeunes policiers de la CUM dénoncent leur syndicat," *[Montreal] Le Devoir* (3 November 2000) at A-7.

32   For more information on the Association des jeunes de la fonction publique du Québec [hereinafter AJFP], consult the following website: <http//:www.ajfp.qc.ca>.

33   Sophie Auger-Giroux, "Une relève en ruine" (2001) 25(1) Proforma: Bulletin de liaison des avocates et avocats de la section de Québec, Jeune Barreau de Québec 3 and 7.

34   Gouvernement du Québec, Conseil du trésor, Directive concernant l'attribution des taux de traitement ou taux de salaire et des bonis à certains fonctionnaires, Dir. no. C.T. 194419, 14 March 2000, replacing Directive concernant les normes de détermination du taux de traitement de certains fonctionnaires, Dir. no. C.T. 184095, 9 November 1993.

35   Éric Bédard, *Le pont entre les générations* (Montréal: Les éditions des intouchables, 1998) at 62-63; Gilbert Leduc, "Les groupes de jeunes lancent une nouvelle offensive," *[Québec] Le Soleil* (15 March 2001) at A-12.

36   Frédéric Lapointe, "Table ronde: Quelles sont les conditions de réussite d'une réforme des lois du travail? Compte-rendu des interventions," in Jean Bernier et al., eds., *L'incessante évolution des formes d'emploi et la redoutable stagnation des lois du travail*, Département des relations industrielles de l'Université Laval (Sainte-Foy, Presses de l'Université Laval, 2001) at 153.

37   Information obtained in telephone conversations with Sophie Auger-Giroux, president of the AJFP, Patrick Lavallée, president of the GAPES, and Frédéric Lapointe, former secretary general of the ADJEQ and treasurer of the Force jeunesse group, an organization of young workers and professionals struggling to improve the conditions of employment and employment prospects of the younger generation (for more information, consult the following website: <http://www.forcejeunesse.qc.ca>.

38   Incidentally, a dispute pitting technicians employed by Northern Telecom Canada (Nortel) in Montreal against their union leaders was recently featured on the Internet when a group of technicians designed a secret site at which complaints could be received anonymously from employees critical of the Canadian Union of Communication Workers. René Lewandowski, "Les techniciens sont en rogne contre leur syndicat," *[Montréal] Le Devoir* (2 August 2001) at B-1.

39 National Assembly, *Journal des débats de la Commission permanente de l'économie et du travail*, Consultation générale sur le projet de loi n° 67: Loi modifiant la Loi sur les normes du travail en matière de disparités de traitement (3), 23 September 1999, No. 34, at 9 *et seq.*

40 Note that the dispute involving the members of the ADJEQ has still not been decided because both the employer and the union have challenged the jurisdiction *ratione materiae* of the Tribunal des droits de la personne in the Quebec Court of Appeal: *Commission des droits de la personne et des droits de la jeunesse* v. *Québec (Procureur général)*, [2002] R.J.D.T. 55 (C.A.) (application for leave to appeal to the Supreme Court of Canada granted: S.C.C. no. 29188).

41 In *Carrier* v. *Rochon* (14 September 2000), Montreal 500-09-007616-998, J.E. 2000-1807 (C.A.) (application for leave to appeal to the Supreme Court of Canada dismissed: [2001] 2 R.C.S. vii), the Quebec Court of Appeal stated in *obiter* that a measure that had a more severe impact on a group of persons who "were usually among young people" could constitute "discrimination on the basis of age" contrary to section 10 of the *Charter of Human Rights and Freedoms*, R.S.Q., c. C-12 (*per* Gendreau J., para. 29 [translation]).

42 Martin H. Malin, "The Supreme Court and the Duty of Fair Representation" (1992) 27 Harv. C.R.-C.L. L. Rev. 127 at 171; McUsic and Selmi, *supra* note 23 at 1343; Mancur Olson, *Logique de l'action collective* (Paris: Presses universitaires de France, 1978) at 117-18; W. Craig Riddell, "Labour Relations in Canada: A General Overview," in W. Craig Riddell, ed., *Labour Relations in Canada* (Ottawa: Royal Commission on the Economic Union and Canada's Development Prospects, Supply and Services Canada, 1986), 87.

43 Diane Veilleux, "Proposition d'une conception organiciste de la représentation syndicale" (1993) 34 C. de D. 899 at 913.

44 Karim Benyekhlef, "Démocratie et libertés: quelques propos sur le contrôle de constitutionnalité et l'hétéronomie du droit" (1993) 38 McGill L.J. 91 at 109-10.

45 The observation that "labour law in Canada" disregards "disparate views between groups of workers within a bargaining unit" has been made by high authority: *Lavigne* v. *Ontario Public Service Employees Union*, [1991] 2 S.C.R. 211 at 325 (*per* LaForest J.).

46 Marie-France Bich, "Petit manuel de guerilla patronale-syndicale: effets de la *Charte canadienne des droits et libertés* sur le Code du travail" (1987) 47 R. du B. 1097 at 1121.

47 *Syndicat catholique des employés de magasins de Québec Inc.* v. *Compagnie Paquet Ltée*, [1959] S.C.R. 206 at 212 (*per* Judson J.); *McGavin Toastmaster Ltd* v. *Ainscough*, [1976] 1 S.C.R. 718 at 724-25 (*per* Laskin J.); *Hémond* v. *Coopérative fédérée du Québec*, [1989] 2 S.C.R. 962 at 975 (*per* Gonthier J.); *Noël* v. *Société d'énergie de la Baie James* [2001] 2 R.C.S. 207 at 229 (*per* LeBel J., para. 43 and 44) [hereinafter *Noël*].

48 Robert P. Gagnon, Louis Lebel, and Pierre Verge, *Droit du travail*, 2nd edition (Québec: Presses de l'Université Laval, 1991) at 355 [translation].

49 René LaPerrière, "États-Unis d'Amérique," in Antoine Lyon-Caen and Antoine Jeammaud, eds., *Droit du travail, démocratie et crise en Europe occidentale et en Amérique* (Paris: Actes Sud, 1986), 189 at 195 [translation]. See also Sharon Rabin Margalioth, "The Significance of Worker Attitudes: Individualism as a Cause for Labor's Decline" (1998) 16 Hofstra Lab. L.J. 133 at 151: "Once a union secures bargaining authority, its position is legally secured, offering dissatisfied employees few exit options."

50 *Steele* v. *Louisville and Nashville Railroad*, 323 U.S. 192 (1944). Note that the principle laid down in this US case has been repeated in most labour codes now in force in Canada: *Canadian Merchant Service Guild* v. *Gagnon*, [1984] 1 S.C.R. 509 at 516 (*per* Chouinard J.); Karen J. Bentham, *The Duty of Fair Representation in the Negotiation of Collective Agreements*, School of Industrial Relations Research Essay Series, no. 38 (Kingston: Industrial Relations Centre, Queen's University, 1991) 4, n. 13.

51 At the stage of bargaining for the collective agreement, the union even has "complete latitude": *Centre hospitalier Régina Ltée* v. *Labour Court*, [1990] 1 S.C.R. 1330 at 1351 (*per* L'Heureux-Dubé J.).

52 *Noël, supra* note 45 at 232: "The analysis therefore focuses on the *reasons* for the union's action" (*per* LeBel J., para. 52).

53  Incidentally, in the United States, an allegation of a breach of the duty of fair representation was likened earlier to an allegation of direction discrimination (*disparate treatment*) requiring evidence of a discriminatory intent. Connye Y. Harper, "Origin and Nature of the Duty of Fair Representation" (1996) 12 Lab. L.J. 183 at 187.

54  Christian Brunelle, *Discrimination et obligation d'accommodement en milieu de travail syndiqué* (Cowansville, QC: Les Éditions Yvon Blais, 2001) at 93-96 and 134-41.

55  *Ford Motor Co.* v. *Huffman*, 345 U.S. 330 (1953) at 338: "A wide range of reasonableness must be allowed a statutory bargaining representative in serving the unit it represents, subject always to *complete good faith* and *honesty of purpose* in the exercise of its discretion" (*per* Burton J.) [emphasis added]. More recently, the US Supreme Court has asserted: "The doctrine of fair representation is an important check on the arbitrary exercise of union power, but it is a *purposefully limited check.*" *United Steelworkers of America, AFL-CIO-CLC* v. *Rawson*, 495 U.S. 362 (1990) at 374 (*per* White J.) [emphasis added].

56  Jean Rivero, "Les droits de l'Homme: droits individuels ou droits collectifs?," in Annales de la Faculté de droit et des sciences politiques et de l'Institut de recherches juridiques, politiques et sociales de Strasbourg, *Les droits de l'Homme: droits collectifs ou droits individuels*, tome XXXII (Paris: Librairie Générale de Droit et de Jurisprudence, 1980), 20 [translation].

57  This is what Marion Crain and Ken Matheny, "Labor's Divided Ranks: Privilege and the United Front Ideology" (1999) 84 Cornell L. Rev. 1542, *passim,* describe as a "*united front ideology.*"

58  Elizabeth M. Iglesias, "Structures of Subordination: Women of Color at the Intersection of Title VII and the NLRA Not!" (1993) 28 Harv. C.R.-C.L. L. Rev. 395 at 408.

59  Rabin Margalioth, *supra* note 47 at 160.

60  McUsic and Selmi, *supra* note 23 at 1342 and 1344.

61  Rabin Margalioth, *supra* note 47. Lévesque, Murray, and Lequeux, *supra* note 10 at 132, describe the end of an era as follows: "The predominance of the 'we' over the 'I'... What characterizes social change at the present time is the radicalization of the differentiation in the social relations underlying the union communities that predominated in the past" [translation].

62  Solange Lefebvre, "Le bouleversement des valeurs dans la société québécoise" (1996) 15 Revue Options CEQ 45 at 46-47.

63  Abraham, *supra* note 5 at 1293 and 1334; Rabin Margalioth, *supra* note 47 at 160.

64  John G. Kelly, *Human Resource Management and the Human Rights Process*, Vol. 1, 2nd edition (Don Mills, ON: CCH Canadian, 1991) at 204, para. 1105.

65  *Dickason* v. *University of Alberta*, [1992] 2 S.C.R. 1103 at 1131 (*per* Cory J.); Crain and Matheny, *supra* note 55 at 1559-60; Katherine Swinton, "Accommodating Equality in the Unionized Workplace" (1996) 33 Osgoode Hall L.J. 703 at 730.

66  Murray and Verge, *supra* note 9 at 111: "Unions must also ensure that there is a significant relationship of proximity between the member and the union institution, especially in light of the growing influence in society of other organizations that appeal ... to the identity-based interests of the employees" [translation].

67  Murray and Verge, *supra* note 9 at 130-31 [translation]. See also: H.W. Arthurs, "Labour Law without the State" (1996) 46 U.T.L.J. 1 at 15; Gregor Murray and Pierre Verge, "La représentation syndicale au-delà de l'entreprise" (1994) 35 C. de D. 419 at 429.

68  Gerald Hunt and David Rayside, "Labor Union Response to Diversity in Canada and the United States" (2000) 39 Relations industrielles/Industrial Relations 401 at 435: "Unions learn and change as a result of activism *inside* the union movement and not outside, perhaps more in the United States than in Canada. There is a respect given to 'sisters' and 'brothers' *within* labor that is not easily accorded to others, in particular because social movement activists outside labor are often seen as insensitive to working-class interests" [emphasis added].

69  Gisèle Bourret, "C'est toujours une question de droits" (1998) 11(1) Recherches féministes 231 at 231-32; Marion Crain, "Women, Labor Unions, and Hostile Work Environment Sexual Harassment: The Untold Story" (1995) 4 Tex. J. Women and L. 9 at 69 *et seq.*; Peggy Nash and Lewis Gottheil, "Employment Equity: A Union Perspective" (1994) 2 Canadian Labour Law Journal 49 at 51-52.

70 Meg Luxton, "Feminism as a Class Act: Working-Class Feminism and the Women's Movement in Canada (2001) 48 Labour/Le Travail 63 at 71-72.

71 Jean Bernier and André C. Côté, "Les accords d'entreprise au Canada," in Irena Boruta and Henryk Lewandowski, eds., *Les accords d'entreprise*, Acta Universitatis Lodziensis, Folia Iuridica 46, Chair of Labour Law and Social Security at the University of Lodz (Poland: University of Lodz, 1991), 12; Morin and Brière, *supra* note 11 at 132, para. II-4

72 Donald D. Cartier, "The Duty to Accommodate: Its Growing Impact on the Grievance Arbitration Process" (1997) 52 (1) Relations industrielles/Industrial Relations 185 at 186.

73 Laperrière, *supra* note 47 at 203.

74 *Syndicat des fonctionnaires provinciaux du Québec Inc.* v. *Bastien*, [1993] R.J.Q. 702 at 707 (C.A.): "[The collective agreement] derives its binding force not from the wishes of the parties and even less from free acceptance by the employees, but from the law" (*per* Rousseau-Houle J.) [translation].

75 *Vriend* v. *Alberta*, [1998] 1 S.C.R. 493 at 543 (*per* Cory J., para. 83) [hereinafter *Vriend*]. See also *Corbiere* v. *Canada (Minister of Indian Affairs and Northern Development)*, [1999] 2 S.C.R. 203 at 274 (*per* L'Heureux-Dubé J., para. 98) [hereinafter *Corbiere*]; *Winko* v. *British Columbia (Forensic Psychiatric Institute)*, [1999] 2 S.C.R. 625 at 678-79 (*per* McLachlin J., para. 83-84); *British Columbia (Public Service Employee Relations Commission)* v. *BCGSEU*, [1999] 3 S.C.R. 3 at 26 (*per* McLachlin J., para. 41).

76 *Weatherall* v. *Canada*, [1993] 2 S.C.R. 872 at 877 (*per* LaForest J.). See also *R.* v. *Big M Drug Mart Ltd*, [1985] 1 S.C.R. 295 at 347 (*per* Dickson J.); *Andrews* v. *Law Society of British Columbia*, [1989] 1 S.C.R. 143 at 169 (*per* McIntyre J.); *Forget* v. *Quebec (Attorney General)*, [1988] 2 S.C.R. 90 at 102 (*per* Lamer J.); *Eldridge* v. *British Columbia (Attorney General)*, [1997] 3 S.C.R. 624 at 671 (*per* LaForest J., para. 61); *Law* v. *Canada (Minister of Employment and Immigration)*, [1999] 1 S.C.R. 497 at 517 (*per* Iacobucci J., para. 25).

77 Jean-Michel Servais, "Égalité dans l'emploi ou droit à la différence? Un point de vue international" (1992) 33 C. de D. 515 at 519 [translation]. In *Commission scolaire St-Jean-sur-Richelieu* v. *Commission des droits de la personne du Québec*, [1994] R.J.Q. 1227 (C.A.), The Quebec Court of Appeal stated: "The equality recognized by section 10 [of the Quebec Charter] is also an equality *of fact*, a *concrete* equality" (*per* Rousseau-Houle J. at 1245) [translation] [emphasis added].

78 Daniel Proulx, "L'égalité en droit comparé et en droit canadien depuis l'arrêt *Andrews*," in Gérald-A. Beaudoin, ed., *Vues canadiennes et européennes des droits et libertés*, Actes des journées strasbourgeoises 1988 (Cowansville, QC: Les Éditions Yvon Blais, 1989), 151.

79 Michael Walzer, "Individus et communautés: les deux pluralismes" (1995) 212 Esprit 103 at 104-5.

80 Lise Noël, *L'intolérance: Une problématique générale*, Vol. 30 (Montréal: Boréal/compact, 1991) at 223 [translation].

81 Charles Fried, "Individual and Collective Rights in Work Relations: Reflections on the Current State of Labor Law and Its Prospects" (1984) 51 U. Chi. L. Rev. 1012 at 1035.

82 Crain and Matheny, *supra* note 57 at 1596-97.

83 Kim W. Jones, "Cultural Diversity Education: What Is Being Done?" (1993) 18(2) Labour Studies Journal 39; McUsic and Selmi, *supra* note 23 at 1357.

84 Crain and Matheny, *supra* note 57 at 1601: "Rather than pretending unity, the labor movement must recognize and confront the barriers that racial, gender, heterosexual, and class privilege pose to solidarity."

85 Lévesque, Murray, and Lequeux, *supra* note 10 at 151; Murray and Verge, *supra* note 9 at 109.

86 Anne Donnellon and Deborah M. Kolb, "Constructive for Whom? The Fate of Diversity Disputes in Organizations" (1994) 50 Journal of Social Issues 139 at 140-41.

87 Plato, *The Republic*, Cambridge Texts in the History of Political Thought, G.R.F. Ferrari, ed. (New York, Cambridge University Press, 2000), at 105 (para. 412), 160-161 (para. 462), and 164-164 (para. 464).

88 Swinton, *supra* note 63 at 704: "[collective bargaining agreements] tend to reflect the interests of the majority in the bargaining unit and, thus, may not always be sensitive to the needs of groups which are less well represented in the workplace."

89  Bentham, *supra* note 48 at 1-2; Crain and Matheny, *supra* note 55 at 1620-21; Pascal Noblet, "Égalité et discrimination positive: le cas de la France et des États-Unis" (1998) 52(4) Revue française des affaires sociales 131, at 132: "The union movement, which could have positioned itself as the harbinger of an alternative model of equality based on equality of conditions has, for its part, often appeared on the ground as the worst obstacle to the consideration of demands expressed by the movement for civic rights and the women's movement" [translation].

90  *Vriend supra* note 74 at 566 and 577 (*per* Iacobucci J., para. 140 and 176). See also: *Corbiere supra* note 74 at 284 (*per* L'Heureux-Dubé J., para. 116); *Reference re Secession of Quebec*, [1998] 2 S.C.R. 217 at 256, para. 67, and 292, para. 149; Benyekhlef, *supra* note 42, *passim*.

91  Christopher R. Schenk, "Union Renewal: New Directions" (2000) 3 (2) Workplace Gazette 96 at 101 [translation].

92  Bernard Adell, "Le droit et la régulation des relations du travail: l'équilibre difficile entre les droits collectifs et les droits individuels," in Gregor Murray, Marie-Laure Morin, and Isabel da Costa, eds., *L'état des relations professionnelles: traditions et perspectives de recherche* (Québec: Presses de l'Université Laval, 1996), 461 [translation].

93  Stephen Schecter, "De la limite et de la richesse dans la société québécoise contemporaine," in Bogumil Jewsiewicki and Jocelyn Létourneau, eds., *Identités en mutation, socialités en germination* (Sillery: Éd. Septentrion, 1998), 187 at 191, even speaks of an "explosion" that threatens democracy in that it would usher in "a society under the rule of law that was different in that it would be ... close to ungovernable" [translation].

94  Gagnon, *supra* note 12 at 73.

95  Murray and Verge, *supra* note 9 at 17: "Groupings emerge that are established on the basis of new identities: feminism, ecology, assertion of ethnicity, etc. Both in their existence and in the role that they aspire to play, these groupings challenge the exclusive nature of the union's role of functional representation of the citizen employee" [translation]. See, to the same effect, Fernand Morin, "La négociation collective selon le modèle de 1944 est-elle périmée?," in Colette Bernier et al., eds., *La négociation collective du travail: adaptation ou disparition?* (Sainte-Foy: Presses de l'Université Laval, 1993), 19-20.

96  Centrale de L'Enseignement du Québec, "Perspectives pour la prochaine ronde de négociation," *Nouvelles CEQ*, vol. 21, no 3 (mai/juin 2000) at 15 [translation].

97  McUsic and Selmi, *supra* note 23 at 1370.

98  Paul Steven Miller, "Disability Civil Rights and a New Paradigm for the Twenty-First Century: The Expansion of Civil Rights beyond Race, Gender, and Age" (1998) 1 U. Pa. J. Lab. and Emp. Law 511 at 523: "As the workforce becomes more multicultural, responding to worker differences, complaints, and predicaments will become more complex."

99  Brunelle, *supra* note 52, *passim*.

100 Susan Genge, "Lesbians and Gays in the Union Movement," in Linda Briskin and Lynda Yanz, eds., *Union Sisters: Women in the Labour Movement* (Toronto: Women's Educational Press, 1983), 162; Canadian Labour Congress, *Make Human Rights a Priority*, Policy Statement on Human Rights, 19th Statutory Assembly, 8-12 June 1992, para. 36; Canadian Auto Workers Canada, Statement of Principle: Human Rights – Workers' Rights: The Same Struggle, 11 November 1996: "Dissent ... on questions relating to human rights threaten the solidarity of the whole organization and impede our ability to make progress."

## Bibliography

### Jurisprudence
*Andrews* v. *Law Society of British Colombia*, [1989] 1 S.C.R. 143.
*Carrier* v. *Rochon* (14 September 2000), Montreal 500-09-007616-998, J.E. 2000-1807 (C.A.).
*Centre hospitalier Régina Ltée* v. *Labour Court*, [1990] 1 S.C.R. 1330.
*British Columbia (Public Service Employee Relations Commission)* v. *BCGSEU*, [1999] 3 S.C.R. 3.
*Commission des droits de la personne et des droits de la jeunesse* v. *Québec (Procureur général)*, [2002] R.J.D.T. 55 (C.A.).
*Commission scolaire St-Jean-sur-Richelieu* v. *Commission des droits de la personne du Québec*, [1994] R.J.Q. 1227 (C.A.).

*Corbiere* v. *Canada (Minister of Indian Affairs and Northern Development)*, [1999] 2 S.C.R. 203.
*Dickason* v. *University of Alberta*, [1992] 2 S.C.R. 1103.
*Eldridge* v. *British Columbia (Attorney General)*, [1997] 3 S.C.R. 624.
*Ford Motor Co.* v. *Huffman*, 345 U.S. 330 (1953).
*Forget* v. *Quebec (Attorney General)*, [1988] 2 S.C.R. 90.
*Marine Services Guild of Canada* v. *Gagnon*, [1984] 1 S.C.R. 509.
*Hémond* v. *Coopérative fédérée du Québec*, [1989] 2 S.C.R. 962.
*Lavigne* v. *Ontario Public Service Employees Union*, [1991] 2 S.C.R. 211.
*Law* v. *Canada (Minister of Employment and Immigration)*, [1999] 1 S.C.R. 497.
*McGavin Toastmaster Ltd* v. *Ainscough*, [1976] 1 S.C.R. 718.
*Noël* v. *Société d'énergie de la Baie James* [2001]2 R.C.S. 207.
*R.* v. *Big M Drug Mart Ltd*, [1985] 1 S.C.R. 295.
*Reference re Secession of Quebec*, [1998] 2 S.C.R. 217.
*Steele* v. *Louisville and Nashville Railroad*, 323 U.S. 192 (1944).
*Syndicat catholique des employés de magasins de Québec Inc.* v. *Compagnie Paquet Ltée*, [1959] S.C.R. 206.
*Syndicat des fonctionnaires provinciaux du Québec Inc.* v. *Bastien*, [1993] R.J.Q. 702 (C.A.).
*United Steelworkers of America, AFL-CIO-CLC* v. *Rawson*, 495 U.S. 362 (1990).
*Vriend* v. *Alberta*, [1998] 1 S.C.R. 493.
*Weatherall* v. *Canada*, [1993] 2 S.C.R. 872.
*Winko* v. *British Columbia (Forensic Psychiatric Institute)*, [1999] 2 S.C.R. 625.

**Books and Articles**

Abraham, David, "Individual Economy and Collective Empowerment in Labor Law: Union Membership Resignations and Strikebreaking in the New Economy" (1988) 63 N.Y.U. L. Rev. 1268.

Adell, Bernard, "Le droit et la régulation des relations du travail: l'équilibre difficile entre les droits collectifs et les droits individuels," in Gregor Murray, Marie-Laure Morin, and Isabel da Costa, eds., *L'état des relations professionnelles: traditions et perspectives de recherche* (Québec: Presses de l'Université Laval, 1996).

Akyeampong, Ernest B., "Aperçu statistique du mouvement syndical ouvrier" (1997) 9(4) L'emploi et le revenu en perspective.

—, "Le point sur la syndicalisation" (2000) Special Issue for Labour Day, L'emploi et le revenu en perspective.

Arthurs, Harry W., "Labour Law without the State" (1996) 46 U.T.L.J. 1.

—, and Robert Kreklewich, "Law, Legal Institutions, and the Legal Profession in the New Economy" (1996) 34 Osgoode Hall L.J. 1.

Auger-Giroux, Sophie, "Une relève en ruine" (2001) 25(1) Proforma: Bulletin de liaison des avocates et avocats de la section de Québec, Jeune Barreau de Québec 3.

Bédard, Éric, *Le pont entre les générations* (Montréal: Les éditions des intouchables, 1998).

Bellemare, Diane, Lise Poulin-Simon, and Diane-Gabrielle Tremblay, *Le paradoxe de l'âgisme dans une société vieillissante: enjeux politiques et défis de gestion* (Montréal: Éd. Saint-Martin, 1998).

Bentham, Karen J., *The Duty of Fair Representation in the Negotiation of Collective Agreements*, School of Industrial Relations Research Essay Series no. 38 (Kingston: Industrial Relations Centre, Queen's University, 1991).

Benyekhlef, Karim, "Démocratie et libertés: quelques propos sur le contrôle de constitutionnalité et l'hétéronomie du droit" (1993) 38 McGill L.J. 91.

Bernier, Jean and André C. Côté, "Les accords d'entreprise au Canada," in Irena Boruta and Henryk Lewandowski, eds., *Les accords d'entreprise*, Acta Universitatis Lodziensis, Folia Iuridica 46 (Lodz, Poland: Chair of Labour Law and Social Security, University of Lodz, 1991).

Bich, Marie-France, "Petit manuel de guérilla patronale-syndicale: effets de la *Charte canadienne des droits et libertés* sur le Code du travail" (1987) 47 R. du B. 1097.

Bourhis, Anne and Thierry Wils, "L'éclatement de l'emploi traditionnel: les défis posés par la diversité des emplois typiques et atypiques" (2001) 56 (1) Relations industrielles/ Industrial Relations 66.

Bourret, Gisèle, "C'est toujours une question de droits" (1998) 11(1) Recherches féministes 231.

Brunelle, Christian, *Discrimination et obligation d'accommodement en milieu de travail syndiqué* (Cowansville, QC: Les Éditions Yvon Blais, 2001).

Canadian Auto Workers, *Statement of Principle: Human Rights – Workers' Rights: The Same Struggle*, 11 November 1996.

Canadian Labour Congress, *Make Human Rights a Priority*, Policy Statement on Human Rights, 19th Statutory Assembly, 8-12 June 1992.

Carter, Donald D., "The Duty to Accommodate: Its Growing Impact on the Grievance Arbitration Process" (1997) 52 (1) Relations industrielles/Industrial Relations 185.

Centrale de l'enseignement du Québec, "Perspectives pour la prochaine ronde de négociation," *Nouvelles CEQ* (May/June 2000).

Charest, Jean, "Le mouvement syndical," in Robert Boily, ed., *L'Année politique au Québec 1997-1998* (Montréal: Presses de l'Université de Montréal, 1999).

Commission des Droits de la personne et des Droits de la jeunesse, *L'équité entre générations et les clauses "orphelins": des droits à défendre*, Actes du Forum droits et libertés (Montréal: Commission des Droits de la personne et des Droits de la jeunesse, 1999).

Coutu, Michel, "Les clauses dites 'orphelins' et la notion de discrimination dans la *Charte des droits et libertés de la personne*" (2000) 55 (2) Relations industrielles/Industrial Relations 308.

Crain, Marion, "Women, Labor Unions, and Hostile Work Environment Sexual Harassment: The Untold Story" (1995) 4 Tex. J. Women and L. 9.

—, and Ken Matheny, "Labor's Divided Ranks: Privilege and the United Front Ideology" (1999) 84 Cornell L. Rev. 1542.

Creese, Gillian, "Gendering Collective Bargaining: From Men's Rights to Women's Issues" (1996) 33 Canadian Review of Sociology and Anthropology/Revue canadienne de sociologie et d'anthropologie 437.

Crever, Charles B., *Can Unions Survive?: The Rejuvenation of the American Labor Movement* (New York: New York University Press, 1993).

Dagenais, Lucie France, *Travail éclaté: protection sociale et égalité*, coll. Études et documents de recherche sur les droits et libertés, Vol. 7 (Cowansville, QC: Les Éditions Yvon Blais, 1998).

Donnellon, Anne and Deborah M. Kolb, "Constructive for Whom? The Fate of Diversity Disputes in Organizations" (1994) 50 Journal of Social Issues 139.

Fried, Charles, "Individual and Collective Rights in Work Relations: Reflections on the Current State of Labor Law and Its Prospects" (1984) 51 U. Chi. L. Rev. 1012.

Fudge, Judy and Harry Glasbeek, "The Legacy of PC 1003" (1995) 3 C.L.E.L.J. 357.

—, "Rights on the Labour Law Ladder: Using Gender to Challenge Hierarchy" (1996) 60 Sask. L. Rev. 237.

Gagnon, Mona-Josée, *Le syndicalisme: état des lieux et enjeux*, coll. Diagnostic, Vol. 17 (Québec: Institut québécois de recherche sur la culture, 1994).

Gagnon, Robert P., Louis Lebel, and Pierre Verge, *Droit du travail*, 2nd edition (Québec: Presses de l'Université Laval, 1991).

Geman, Rachel, "Safeguarding Employee Rights in a Post-Union World: A New Conception of Employee Communities" (1997) 30 Colum. J.L. and Soc. Probs. 369.

Genge, Susan, "Lesbians and Gays in the Union Movement," in Linda Briskin and Lynda Yanz, eds., *Union Sisters: Women in the Labour Movement* (Toronto: Women's Educational Press, 1983).

Government of Quebec, *La présence syndicale au Québec* (Québec: Ministère du Travail, Service des études économiques, de l'exploitation des systèmes et de l'aide à la clientèle, 2001).

Harper, Connye Y., "Origin and Nature of the Duty of Fair Representation" (1996) 12 Lab. Law. 183.

Harvey, Edward B. and John H. Blakely, *Information Systems for Managing Workplace Diversity* (North York, ON: CCH Canadian, 1996).

Hunt, Gerald and David Rayside, "Labor Union Response to Diversity in Canada and the United States" (2000) 39 Relations industrielles/Industrial Relations 401.

Iglesias, Elizabeth M., "Structures of Subordination: Women of Color at the Intersection of Title VII and the NLRA. Not!" (1993) 28 Harv. C.R.-C.L. L. Rev. 395.

Jones, Kim W., "Cultural Diversity Education: What Is Being Done?" (1993) 18(2) Labour Studies Journal 39.

Kalbach, Warren E., "The Demographic Transformation of Canada's Work Force," in Audrey Wipper, ed., *Work: The Sociology of Work in Canada* (Ottawa: Carleton University Press, 1994).

Kelly, John G., *Human Resource Management and the Human Rights Process*, Vol. 1, 2nd ed. (Don Mills, ON: CCH Canadian, 1991).

Kumar, Pradeep, Gregor Murray, and Sylvain Schetagne, "Adjustment to Change: Union Priorities in the 1990s," in Government of Canada, Department of Human Resources Development, Workplace Information Directorate, *Directory of Labour Organizations in Canada 1998* (Ottawa, Canada Comunication Group – Publishing, 1998).

Laperrière, René, "États-Unis d'Amérique," in Antoine Lyon-Caen and Antoine Jeammaud, eds., *Droit du travail, démocratie et crise en Europe occidentale et en Amérique* (Paris: Actes Sud, 1986).

Laplante, Laurent, *La personne immédiate*, coll. La ligne du risque (Montréal: L'Hexagone, 1998).

Lapointe, Frédéric, "Table ronde: Quelles sont les conditions de réussite d'une réforme des lois du travail? Compte-rendu des interventions," in Jean Bernier et al., eds., *L'incessante évolution des formes d'emploi et la redoutable stagnation des lois du travail*, Département des relations industrielles de l'Université Laval (Sainte-Foy, Presses de l'Université Laval, 2001), 153

Lavallée, Patrick et al., "Les jeunes policiers de la CUM dénoncent leur syndicat," *[Montréal] Le Devoir* (3 November 2000) at A-7.

Leduc, Gilbert, "Les groupes de jeunes lancent une nouvelle offensive," *[Québec] Le Soleil* (15 March 2001) at A-12.

—, "Les jeunes profs sévères pour la CEQ," *[Québec] Le Soleil* (11 June 1998) at A-12.

Lefebvre, Solange, "Le bouleversement des valeurs dans la société québécoise" (1996) 15 Revue Options CEQ 45.

Lester, Gillian, "Toward the Feminisation of Collective Bargaining Law" (1991) 36 McGill L.J. 1181.

Lévesque, Christian, Gregor Murray, and Stéphane Lequeux, "Transformations sociales et identités syndicales: l'institution syndicale à l'épreuve de la différenciation sociale contemporaine" (1998) 30(2) Sociologie et sociétés 131.

Lewandowski, René, "Les techniciens sont en rogne contre leur syndicat," *[Montréal] Le Devoir* (2 August 2001) at B-1.

Lipsig-Mumme, Carla, "Unions Struggle with New Work Order" (1995) 16(8) Political Options 1.

Luxton, Meg, "Feminism as a Class Act: Working-Class Feminism and the Women's Movement in Canada (2001) 48 Labour/Le Travail 63.

Malin, Martin H., "The Supreme Court and the Duty of Fair Representation" (1992) 27 Harv. C.R.-C.L. L. Rev. 127.

McUsic, Molly S. and Michael Selmi, "Postmodern Unions: Identity Politics in the Workplace" (1997) 82 Iowa L. Rev. 1339.

Miller, Paul Steven, "Disability Civil Rights and a New Paradigm for the Twenty-First Century: The Expansion of Civil Rights Beyond Race, Gender, and Age" (1998) 1 U. Pa. J. Lab. and Emp. Law 511.

Morin, Fernand, "La négociation collective selon le modèle de 1944 est-elle périmée?" in Colette Bernier et al., eds., *La négociation collective du travail: adaptation ou disparition?* (Sainte-Foy: Presses de l'Université Laval, 1993).

—, and Jean-Yves Brière, *Le droit de l'emploi au Québec* (Montréal: Wilson and Lafleur, 1998).

Morin, Normand, "Quand le 'Nous syndical' est plus important qu'un droit fondamental," *[Québec] Le Soleil* (6 August 1998) at B-7.

Murray, Gregor, "Les transformations de la représentation collective au Québec," in Jean Bernier et al., eds., *L'incessante évolution des formes d'emploi et la redoutable stagnation des lois du travail* (Québec: Presses de l'Université Laval, 2001), 57.

—, and Pierre Verge, "La représentation syndicale au-delà de l'entreprise" (1994) 35 C. de D. 419.

—, and Pierre Verge, *La représentation syndicale: visage juridique actuel et futur* (Québec: Presses de l'Université Laval, 1999).

Nash, Peggy and Lewis Gottheil, "Employment Equity: A Union Perspective" (1994) 2 Canadian Labour Law Journal 49.

National Assembly, *Journal des débats de la Commission permanente de l'économie et du travail*, Consultation générale sur le projet de loi no 67 – Loi modifiant la Loi sur les normes du travail en matière de disparités de traitement (3), 23 September 1999, No. 34.

Noblet, Pascal, "Égalité et discrimination positive: le cas de la France et des États-Unis" (1998) 52(4) Revue française des affaires sociales 131.

Noël, Lise, *L'intolérance: Une problématique générale*, Vol. 30 (Montréal: Boréal/compact, 1991).

Olson, Mancur, *Logique de l'action collective* (Paris: Presses universitaires de France, 1978).

Paquet, Pierre, "Déclin et mutation des relations de travail fordiennes" (1993) 17(1) Possibles 85.

Plato, *The Republic*, Cambridge Texts in the History of Political Thought, G.R.F. Ferrari, ed. (New York: Cambridge University Press, 2000).

Proulx, Daniel, "L'égalité en droit comparé et en droit canadien depuis l'arrêt *Andrews*," in Gérald-A. Beaudoin, ed., *Vues canadiennes et européennes des droits et libertés*, Actes des journées strasbourgeoises 1988 (Cowansville, QC: Les Éditions Yvon Blais, 1989).

Rabin Margalioth, Sharon, "The Significance of Worker Attitudes: Individualism as a Cause for Labor's Decline" (1998) 16 Hofstra Lab. L.J. 133.

Riddell, W. Craig, "Labour Relations in Canada: A General Overview," in W. Craig Riddell, ed., *Labour Relations in Canada* (Ottawa: Royal Commission on the Economic Union and Canada's Economic Prospects, Supply and Services Canada, 1986).

Rivero, Jean, "Les droits de l'Homme: droits individuels ou droits collectifs?," in Annales de la Faculté de droit et des sciences politiques et de l'Institut de recherches juridiques, politiques et sociales de Strasbourg, *Les droits de l'Homme: droits collectifs ou droits individuels*, tome XXXII (Paris: Librairie Générale de Droit et de Jurisprudence, 1980).

Schecter, Stephen, "De la limite et de la richesse dans la société québécoise contemporaine," in Bogumil Jewsiewicki and Jocelyn Létourneau, eds., *Identités en mutation, socialités en germination* (Sillery: Éd. Septentrion, 1998).

Schenk, Christopher R., " Union Renewal: New Directions" (2000) 3 (2) Workplace Gazette 96.

Servais, Jean-Michel, "Égalité dans l'emploi ou droit à la différence? Un point de vue international" (1992) 33 C. de D. 515.

Swinton, Katherine, "Accommodating Equality in the Unionized Workplace" (1996) 33 Osgoode Hall L.J. 703.

Termote, Marc, "Les défis démographiques du Québec" (1998) 22(3 and 4) Possibles 35.

Vallée, Guylaine, "Pluralité des statuts de travail et protection des droits de la personne: quel rôle pour le droit du travail?" (1999) 54 (2) Relations industrielles/Industrial Relations 277.

Veilleux, Diane, "Proposition d'une conception organiciste de la représentation syndicale" (1993) 34 C. de D. 899.

Walzer, Michael, "Individus et communautés: les deux pluralismes" (1995) 212 Esprit 103.

Zeytinoglu, Isik U., and Jacinta K. Muteshi, "Gender, Race and Class Dimensions of Nonstandard Work" (2000) 55 (1) *Relations industrielles/Industrial Relations* 133.

# Contributors

**Darin Barney** is Assistant Professor of Communication at the University of Ottawa.

**Nicholas K. Blomley** is a Professor in the Department of Geography at Simon Fraser University.

**Nathan Brett** is Chair of the Department of Philosophy at Dalhousie University, where he teaches philosophy of law and political theory.

**Christian Brunelle** is an Assistant Professor in the Faculty of Law, Université Laval, where he teaches human rights and labour law.

**Damian C.A. Collins** is a doctoral candidate in the Department of Geography at Simon Fraser University.

**Natalie Des Rosiers** is President of the Law Commission of Canada and a Professor in the Faculty of Law, University of Ottawa.

**Lisa Philipps** is an Associate Professor, Osgoode Hall Law School of York University.

**Stepan Wood** is an Assistant Professor at Osgoode Hall Law School, where he teaches environmental, international, and property law.

# Index

ADJEQ. *See* Association de défense des jeunes enseignants du Québec (ADJEQ)
Age discrimination: in collective agreements, 170, 179n41
Agreement on Technical Barriers to Trade, 129, 131, 154n42
AJFP. *See* Association des jeunes de la fonction publique du Québec (AJFP)
Alberta: Leaders Environmental Approval Document (LEAD), 133, 135, 150, 155n52
"Anti-free ride" principle, 4, 9-10, 11-16, 31; family-run businesses, 25-8. *See also* Caregiving: law reform and
Anticommons, 91n31
Arendt, Hannah: views on mass society, 110; views on public sphere, 95-101, 107; views on technology, 112; views on work, 110, 112
Association de défense des jeunes enseignants du Québec (ADJEQ), 168-9, 170, 179n40
Association des jeunes de la fonction publique du Québec (AJFP), 169, 170
Associations: industry associations, 157n68; parallel to unions, 168-70, 173. *See also* Unions
Athens. *See* Greece

Begging: effect on retail businesses, 52-3; as a form of expression, 41; as a monetary transaction, 41, 42, 45-7. *See also* Panhandling regulation
Biological patents, 68-9, 79-80; as control of research tools, 84-5; cost/benefits of, 82-5, 86-9, 91n31; as form of privatization, xii-xiii, 84-5, 87-9; gene patents, 85-7, 92n46; life forms as inventions, 81-4

Biotechnology industry, 92n50. *See also* Biological patents
British Columbia: forest management programs, 151n18
Business law: reform, 3-4, 20-8
Businesses: absorption of caregiving costs, 3, 4, 9-10; family-run, 25-8; incorporated, 21, 26-7, 35n78; partnerships, 26-7. *See also* Business law; Corporations; Environmental management systems (EMSs); Self-employment

Calgary: city centre, 51; panhandling regulation, 60
Canada: Internet usage, 114
Canadian Patent Office, 68
Canadian Standards Association (CSA), 129, 153n22, 157n67
Canadian Union of Communication Workers, 178n38
Caregiving: as an economic activity, 3-4, 5-11; commodification of, 13-14; ethical dimensions of, 13-14; family values and, 11-13; law reform and, 3-4, 16-31; paid domestic workers, 8, 17
*Carrier v. Rochon*, 179n41
CEPA. *See* Environment Canada: *Compliance and Enforcement Policy for the Canadian Environmental Protection Act, 1999* (CEPA)
CESD. *See* Commissioner of the environment and sustainable development (CESD)
Citizens: as clients to the state, 106, 114, 146
City centres: economic vitality, 51-5; social polarization within, 53, 54-5
Commissioner of the environment and sustainable development (CESD), 130

Corporations, 21, 26-7, 35n78; valuing of caregiving, 21, 26-7, 35n78
CSA. *See* Canadian Standards Association (CSA)

**D**emocracy: concept of "majority rule" and, 170-6; role of digital technologies, xi-xii, 94-5, 107-17; role of "publicity," 103-4
Digital technologies: defined, 109; impact on democratic citizenship, xi-xii, 94-5, 107-17; role in individuation, 111-12
Domestic workers, 8, 17. *See also* Caregiving
Downtowns. *See* City centres
Due diligence: EMSs and, 136, 158n73, 158n74
DuPont: Onco mouse patent applications, 68, 69, 80-4, 89n1

**E**cological modernization, 147
Economics: city centres, 51-5; effects of public–private dichotomy, xii-xiv; European bourgeoisie, 102; meanings associated with money, 45-51; as part of private sphere, xii, 96, 99-101; role of unpaid caregiving in the economy, x, 4, 5-11
Edmonton: city centre, 51-2, 54; pan-handling regulation, 60
Employers: absorption of caregiving costs, 3, 4, 9-10
Employment: length of work weeks, 8, 19; part-time and non-standard, 8, 17-20. *See also* Employment standards; Labour market trends; Self-employment; Unpaid work
Employment standards: coverage limita-tions, 17-20; *Employment Standards Act (ESA)* (Ontario), 18-19; law reform, 3-4, 16-20
EMSs. *See* Environmental management systems (EMSs)
Environment Canada, 130; *Compliance and Enforcement Policy for the Canadian Environmental Protection Act, 1999* (CEPA), 155n55, 155n56, 155n60
Environmental management systems (EMSs), xii; benchmarking, 135-6, 157n71; defined, 123-4; mandatory implementation, 134-5; rewards for implementation, 133-4; role in depoliti-cization of issues, 140-4, 145-8, 149-50; role of public authorities, 125-38, 147-8, 149, 152n20, 153n25, 155n55, 156n58, 156n60, 156n63; standards, 123, 124-5. *See also* ISO 14000 series

*ESA* (Ontario). *See* Ontario: *Employment Standards Act (ESA)*
Expertise: depoliticization role, 140-1, 142-4, 158n89; role in governmentality, 139-40

**F**amily law: reform, 3-4, 29-31
Family-run businesses, 25-8
Fédération des syndicats de l'enseign-ment, 169
Financial institutions: discrimination against businesswomen, 21-2, 25
Forest management programs, 150n4, 151n18
Forest Stewardship Council, 150n4
Fraternité des policiers et policières de la Communauté urbaine de Montréal, 169
Fredericton: panhandling regulation, 60

**G**APES. *See* Groupe d'action pour l'équité et l'égalité salariale du Service de police de la Communauté urbaine de Montréal (GAPES)
Gas pipeline industry, 132, 135, 157n64
Gendered inequalities of work, 3-4, 8, 14-15, 17-18, 21, 33n33
Genes: patenting of, 68, 85-7, 92n46. *See also* Biological patents
Geron Corporation, 68
Governance, xiv-xv, 160n107; shifting characterization of, 137-40, 144-8, 160n107. *See also* Government opera-tions; Public authorities
Government operations: implementation of EMSs, 130-1, 154n37
Governmentality: defined, 139-40
Greece: ancient *polis*, 95-101, 107
Groupe d'action pour l'équité et l'égalité salariale du Service de police de la Communauté urbaine de Montréal (GAPES), 168-9, 170

**H**abermas, Jürgen: views on public sphere, 55, 58-9, 101-8, 118n42
Hamilton: panhandling regulation, 60
*Harvard College* v. *Canada (Commissioner of Patents)*, xi, 68, 69, 80-4, 89n1
Homeless people. *See* Poor people
Human embryos: patenting of, 68

**I**ncome Tax Act (Canada): caregiver credit, 29, 36n104; child-care expenses, 24, 35n92, 36n95; effects on small busi-nesses, 23-4, 35n90, 35n91; income-splitting, 27-8; marital credit, 28-9, 36n103

Printed and bound in Canada by Friesens

Set in Stone by Artegraphica Design Co.

Copy editor: Stacy Belden

Proofreader: Cathy Owen

Indexer: Christine Jacobs